RACE AND PUBLIC POLICY

Research in Ethnic Relations Series

The Politics of Community
The Bangladeshi Community in East London
John Eade

Race and Borough Politics
Frank Reeves

Ethnic Minority Housing:
Explanations and Policies
Philip Sarre, Deborah Phillips
and Richard Skellington

Reluctant Hosts: Europe and its Refugees
Danièle Joly and Robin Cohen

Democracy and the Nation State
Tomas Hammar

Antiracist Strategies
Alrick X. Cambridge and Stephan Feuchtwang

Ethnic Minorities and the Criminal Justice System
Robert Waters

Pacific Migrant Labour, Class and Racism in New Zealand
Fresh off the Boat
Terrence Loomis

Migration, Socialism and the International Division of Labour
The Yugoslavian Experience
Carl-Ulrik Schierup

Race and Public Policy

A study of local politics and government

SHAMIT SAGGAR
Lecturer in Politics
Queen Mary and Westfield College
University of London

Avebury

Aldershot · Brookfield USA · Hong Kong · Singapore · Sydney

Published by
Avebury
Gower Publishing Company Limited
Gower House
Croft Road
Aldershot
Hants GU11 3HR
England

Gower Publishing Company
Old Post Road
Brookfield
Vermont 05036
USA

ISBN 1 85628 097 7

Printed in Great Britain by
Billing & Sons Ltd, Worcester

Contents

List of tables and figures

Tables

Figures

Glossary of abbreviations used in the text

BACA	Barnet African Caribbean Association
BCRC	Barnet Community Relations Council
BEAG	Barnet Elderly Asians Group
BHAS	Barnet Housing Aid Service
BHTS	Barnet Home Tutor Scheme
BIB	British Indians Board
BNP	British National Party
BPCC	Barnet Police Consultative Committee
BPMG	Barnet Police Monitoring Group
BPLG	Barnet Police Liaison Group
CARD	Campaign Against Racial Discrimination
CIAC	Commonwealth Immigrants Advisory Council
CPRS	Central Policy Review Staff
CRC	Community Relations Council
ECRC	Ealing Community Relations Council
EFRA	Ealing Federation of Ratepayers Associations
EIFC	Ealing International Friendship Committee
EMG	Ethnic Minority Group
GGCRC	Golders Green Community Relations Committee
GLC	Greater London Council
HCS	Hindu Cultural Society
IANL	Islamic Association of North London
INA	Indian National Association
IVS	Institute for Voluntary Service
IWA	Indian Workers Association
LBB	London Borough of Barnet
LBE	London Borough of Ealing
MCC	Middlesex County Council
NCCI	National Committee for Commonwealth Immigrants

NCCL	National Council for Civil Liberties
NF	National Front
NCWP	New Commonwealth and Pakistan
PEP	Political and Economic Planning
PWA	Pakistan Welfare Association
RPE	Race Policy Environment
RRB	Race Relations Board
S.11	Section 11, Local Government Act 1966
S.71	Section 71, Race Relations Act 1976
SAAG	Suburban Asian Action Group
SAAW	Sangam Association of Asian Women
SBC	Southall Borough Council
SDEE	Southall Divisional Education Executive
SIFC	Southall International Friendship Committee
SRA	Southall Residents Association
SYM	Southall Youth Movement
UCA	Unified Community Action
UM	Union Movement
UNA	United Nations Association
UP	Urban Programme
URB	Ugandan Resettlement Board
VLC	Voluntary Liaison Committee

Preface and acknowledgements

The origins of this study lie in the spring of 1984 when, as an undergraduate, I first became convinced of the need for further research on the role of ethnic minorities in the political process. I was particularly drawn to the under-researched area of race issues in urban politics as well as to longer-standing debates concerning community power. As I go on to observe later in this study, political scientists (in Britain at least) have rather shied away from the analysis of conflicts of race and ethnicity in the context of urban politics. The stuff of 'Black, Brown and Green Votes' (as one psephologist has put it) has been the subject of more than adequate research time, funds and effort over the years. But matters to do with policy-making in our multi-racial cities has curiously remained at the fringes of an otherwise highly developed and sophisticated literature on urban political analysis. Of course generalisations can never be enitirely watertight and the work of Ken Young (and colleagues) has been an important exception. His co-authored PSI report, *Policy and Practice in the Multi-racial City*, provided a timely and important contribution to the literature. In addition, his co-edited volume, *Ethnic Pluralism and Public Policy*, added weight to the view that students of the British policy process had a lot of ground to make up compared with their colleagues across the Atlantic. Both publications - together with several journal articles - served to establish a framework for research and debate on the very topics that I felt had been neglected by the discipline.

An allied academic debate that my research was also shaped by was that concerning the evaluation of of the liberal race relations reforms of the 1960s pioneered by Roy Jenkins and others. Here a number of stimulating perspectives have emerged in recent years including Michael Banton's *Promoting Racial Harmony*. This short book initially inspired me to broaden out my study of local politics and government and to address myself to the debate on the successes and failures of Britain's multi-racial society. In a sense it is not sufficient to say that I disagree with his views (which I do), since much of the theoretical side of my work seeks to offer additional, supplementary explanations for the apparent poor record of the so-called race relations industry. I would like to think that my views provide a fresh and critical perspective to this debate.

To that end, the broad thrust of this study seeks to build upon the foundations previously laid by these two writers. Even though I disagree with their respective views (for very different reasons), I hope that this study will precipitate further debate on these topics. I wish to thank them for their influential work. Having already met and worked alongside the former, I hope to meet the latter one day.

Turning to specific acknowledgements, it is often the case that writers are faced with terrible dilemmas over who should and should not receive special mention for their help. Many individuals have assisted me in my studies but inevitably space precludes me from mentioning all but a handful of them. I would like to thank all my teachers and colleagues in the Department of Government at the University of Essex where I spent six memorable years as undergraduate, postgraduate and teacher. I am particularly grateful for the help and advice received from two members of staff. Firstly, I would like to thank Ivor Crewe who kept a watchful eye on the project for almost four years. Secondly, the study was greatly aided by the timely, though unplanned, arrival of Rod Rhodes, who acted as my supervisor during its early stages and stayed close to its progress afterwards. His advice over reading material - not least the chapter by Bachrach and Baratz handed me a compass at a moment when my literature review had lost direction - and his endless witticisms about by written work, served to encourage my studies. In many ways, Rod's fresh input made the difference.

Financial support for the project was provided by the Economic and Social Research Council (award number: A00428424236) and I am most grateful for their assistance.

Truly immeasurable thanks are due to Rita Alfred. Her painstaking corrections and improvements of my work proved to be a valuable help to me throughout the months and years of my research. Added to this, her "insider information" on the strange workings of the "Macintosh" got me out of a tight corner on more than one occasion. Married life with her is always fun, though I wonder whether she can say the same of a husband who has yet to master basic grammar!

My gratitude also goes to Neelam Thapar for her timely assistance with the job of compiling the index.

Special mention has to be made of the inspiration I derived from my uncle, Devinder. His own achievements in the world of social research in the United States almost fifteen years ago, served as a crucial role model in my formative years. His doctoral thesis - forever on my desk - acted as a permanent reminder of the fruits of hard work and critical thought.

Finally, it is unlikely that this study would ever have been undertaken or completed without the encouragement provided by my father. Through his unmistakable confidence, any and all self-doubts were overcome. My work will always be inspired by him and the treasured memory of my mother.

Credit having been duly apportioned, the remaining errors are, as they say in the trade, mine alone.

Shamit Saggar
London
June 1990

To the memory of my uncle,
Braham Dev Saggar,
whose patience and attention to detail served as a
perfect example to me in my education and career

1 Introduction

Opening remarks

In 1985 Professor Michael Banton published a short book entitled *Promoting Racial Harmony* in which he surveyed some of the most common explanations for past disappointments with race relations policies. His book was one more example of recent reappraisal in academic and political circles of the record of race policy in Britain. Politicians, governments, parties, the press, and others, have become increasingly concerned with the supposed shortcomings of public policy in this field. This study aims to place these shortcomings into the context of a policy framework which has been largely redundant for more than a decade.

Nowhere has disappointment with race policy been felt more deeply than in the world of local politics and government. Local race-related public policy has come in for heavy scrutiny, and the present picture reveals a sharp dissensus of opinion between relevant policy actors as to the way forward. Today, radical Labour Party politicians in many London boroughs persistently attack the "racism" of town hall bureaucracies; meanwhile, paternalistically-minded Conservatives denounce the "race obsession" and "reverse discrimination" of their opponents. Both perspectives clearly have their points, not least in terms of political rhetoric. A central argument of this study is that the behaviour of local authorities dealing with race issues has become ineffective and random, in the absence of a clear, orienting framework for race policy.

A common explanation for this situation has been to blame race relations policies, said to be inadequate to the scale of the problem. Alternatively, local political systems have been labelled as being racially discriminatory towards their black[1] citizens. Another view has been to castigate black people and black groups for placing unrealistic demands on local public services. All of these views however miss the main point: that conflict over race policy has been a surrogate for conflict about the nature of the underlying framework of such policy. The common spectale of conflict between politicians of the Left and Right over race policy is often a mask for contrasting perceptions of the suitability of the policy framework.

1

An historical appreciation of the constraints placed on public policy by the policy framework laid down almost a quarter-century ago, is conspicuous by its absence in the literature on the politics of race in Britain. This study proposes to fill this important void in the literature.

The liberal settlement revisited

There is a widespread view in Britain which suggests that the performance of the so-called "race industry" has been poor and unremarkable at best and intentionally harmful to race relations at worst.[2] This view stems from many sources and generally goes unchallenged, sometimes even by members of the industry itself. Attacks on the achievements of both the industry's personnel as well as its policy-making machinery have become commonplace. Neither these attacks, nor their rebuttals, have been placed in the context of a guiding framework within which the industry has grappled with race policy. Although criticism has commonly been directed at the "race industry" and its accompanying race policies, the goals, instruments and frameworks of public policy are rarely considered, let alone evaluated. This study presents an account of what has gone on - and may have gone "wrong" - in the local politics of race policy. It argues that to merely identify what constitutes race policy can itself prove to be a tough challenge. We can empirically describe it and move towards its theoretical definition, without necessarily being able to anticipate or explain its conceptual setting from one issue or locality to another. The study presents a typology suggesting that it can be one of four things, and possibly more. The animal has not one face but many, making its positive identification - let alone understanding - complex and fraught with misconceptions.

Almost a quarter-century ago, a chain of events was set in motion amounting to 'the nearest we have come to "a decent race relations policy"' (Bonham-Carter, 1987: 6).[3] A bold and far-reaching liberal settlement was arrived at during that era, which placed a heavy emphasis on trying to defuse simmering racial tension. Local authorities were placed in the front-line of handling and responding to the public policy demands created by a multi-racial society. Very little additional policy machinery or policy instruments were contained in the settlement. The prime goal of policy was the maintenance of racial harmony. The settlement signalled the way ahead for race policy in the years to come. An important conceptualisation of public policy on race-related matters was forged through the liberal settlement, one which has remained with policy-makers, on and off, ever since.

The result has been that, a generation later, policy-makers are confronted with a series of sharp and dramatic choices in British race relations. From Whitehall and Westminster to local government town halls, many of the aims and values of the original liberal settlement are under question, and, in many cases, have been for some while. Everything, as they say, is "up for grabs". Such a perspective may not be an over-exaggeration since the evidence from local politics in many London boroughs suggests that few of the old certainties about race relations still hold true. It is not just in the Brents and Lambeths that "things have changed", but so too in the Ealings and, to some extent, in the more conservatively-inclined boroughs of outer London such as Barnet and Harrow.

This study suggests that there has been an underlying shift of emphasis away from the traditional liberal policy framework for local race relations. Alternative conceptual frameworks have arisen in its place, with the radical Left paradigm being the best known (see for example Lansley et al, 1989). However, this study also argues that these alternative routes for race policy are, in a number of ways, the consequence of the local application of the original liberal policy framework.

The local borough context

Banton (1987) discusses three rival conceptual frameworks - the liberal, conservative and radical perspectives - in relation to three important studies of the politics of race and

2

immigration policy since 1962.[4] Sadly, he does not explore the impact of any of these frameworks when applied to the conflicts and tensions of local political systems. Such an exploration, this study suggests, would find considerable resonance with the language and substance of the dominant liberal framework in the ebb and flow of conflict over local race-related public policy.

This study attempts to classify the experience of local race policy via a detailed examination of race and local politics and policy-making in two London boroughs. Local race policy is not one thing, but many. It can be characterised at different moments and circumstances, ranging from "diffusion" and "paternalism", through to "frustration" leading to "radicalism". These different outcomes are, in essence, the product of the application of the traditional liberal framework in local political systems. The evidence suggests that these characterisations of local race policy have followed a rough chronological sequence, though they are not by any means mutually exclusive nor at similar stages among even virtually neighbouring boroughs. In the case of one of the boroughs studied (Ealing), the process appears to have run full course from being diffused and paternalistic in the 1960s, to frustrated in the late-1970s and early-1980s, and eventually wholeheartedly radicalised by the mid-1980s. The picture painted of the second borough (Barnet) suggests the continuing survival of highly diffused, paternalistic aims and values amongst a large cross-section of participants. The reality of local race policy could not be very much more contrasting from one place to another.

These results - currently shaping the different race relations options facing policy-makers - are the product of the liberal settlement. To imagine a very different picture of race relations in Britain would certainly require a very different conceptual starting point. To that end, many of the critics of the so-called "race industry" are indeed pointing to some of the underlying features - and sometimes weaknesses - of the broader policy framework, of which the industry itself forms only the most visible part.

A climate of change

In 1988 the London Borough of Ealing published an illuminating report examining aspects of the recruitment of ethnic minority teachers by the authority. The report presented the findings of an independent commission of inquiry, following a 'politically and racially disasterous' recruitment drive in the wake of the election of a new Labour administration in May 1986 (LBE, 1988: 1). Even the most casual review of this weighty document cannot escape the impression that characterisations of the relationship between race and public policy as being 'attitudinally determined' (and therefore largely beyond the control of policy-makers and processes) are not to be found between its covers. Indeed, at the outset of the report, the authors are at pains to state their alternative, and somewhat more penetrating, conception of race in the policy process:

> If...one conceives of the problem in terms of objective structures and processes that obstruct racial equality in employment and service provision, then the focus is bound to be on their replacement by alternative, equality-oriented structures and processes. (LBE, 1988: 10)

The report's findings were wholeheartedly embraced by the incumbent Labour administration. A new and radically different conception of race in the policy process had seemingly become the new orthodoxy.

One does not have to travel very far back to contrast this radical conception with another more paternalistic approach. As recently as the early-1980s, a somewhat illiberal Conservative administration in Ealing operated within a clearly stated set of beliefs which systematically refused to acknowledge the so-called "race dimension" in its own policies and practices. "Colourblindness", insisted the authority, was the only way to go about the business of mass public service delivery. The mid-1960s provide us with evidence of an earlier, more consensus-oriented age in the politics of race policy. For example, in 1966, the inspirational head of the liberal reform movement, Roy Jenkins, mapped out a rather different policy goal for policy practitioners centred on the largely "colourblind" theme of "racial harmony" (Jenkins, 1966). British race relations - and local race-related public policy-making in particular - have continued to function and evolve within the policy framework established under Jenkins' stewardship. Liberal aims, values, assumptions, and conceptions of race and public policy have dominated much of what has followed during the 1970s and 1980s. This study aims to examine the nature and implications of the liberal framework for race policy at the local borough level.

Placing the study in context

This study has four main aims. Firstly, the basic aim of this study is to highlight the influence of the narrow conceptualisation of race inherent in the framework for local race-related public policy. The study argues that a full understanding of race and public policy in local politics and government needs to be placed in the context of that policy framework.

Secondly, the study aims to provide a description of local experience. The impact of race on British politics has often been greatest at the local level. Many of the tensions and conflicts thrown up by racial divisions have been to do with aspects of local public services, education and housing being prime examples. If we are to learn more about the political aspects of these conflicts, we must refer to empirical case studies of local political systems. This study incorporates such a strategy and examines in detail the evidence from two London boroughs.

Thirdly, the study aims to shed light on the 'culture of inexplicitness' (Young, 1985b: 286) that has shrouded the policy agenda of race. Race-related public policy in Britain has been described as an exercise in avoiding specifics. For example, Young (1983: 288) writes: 'There is an entrenched resistance to any specific discussion of ethnicity within the British policy debate'. However, this view does not go much beyond merely stating this pertinent feature of race policy. It begs the question: why is there such resistance and what are its origins? Moreover, not all local policy debate is devoid of direct recognition of an "ethnic dimension". Young's perspective, whilst acknowledging a recent 'rediscovery of race' (1985b: 294), fails to appreciate the nature and underlying causes of the rising spectacle of race-specific policy debate. That is to say, the picture painted in the existing literature remains depressingly over-generalised. The experience of local race policy, despite its steadfast emphasis on the avoidance of overt race-specific conflicts, nonetheless contains a number of interesting and significant variations. This study identifies and accounts for these variations.

Finally, this study aims to identify the processes by which race issues are absorbed and "disappear" into the policy process. It is widely accepted that the impact of race has been heavily determined by the 1960s' bi-partisan consensus to "de-politicise" race issues. For example, Messina (1984: 56) defines this process as: '[when] certain political issues or citizen concerns are deflected or removed from the agenda of political parties and/or government'. However, Messina (1984, 1985a and 1989) concentrates on providing a framework of *party competition*, and thus neglects the consequences of the consensus on the policy process beyond the behaviour of political parties. It is precisely the question of how the *policy process* has handled and sought to deflect race issues (including the behaviour of political parties) that concerns this study and distinguishes it from others.

In fact, race issues have been better absorbed into the existing policy processes of some local authorities than others. Furthermore, effective "routinisation" has tended to occur in relation to certain types of race-related issues more than others. Some local authorities have proven particularly adept at side-stepping many fundamental race-related public policy issues. They have done so by a variety of tactics. The most significant has been to question the legitimacy or right of other policy actors to seek to reform the way in which local race policy is organised and debated. Moreover, race has simultaneously been conceptualised in very narrow terms as a consequence of the influence of the policy framework. This conceptualisation has served certain local authorities extremely well in their attempts to rebuff the introduction of broader conceptualisations into local race policy debate. By examining the behaviour of two local authorities, this study will investigate the similarities and contrasts between different local attempts to "routinise" or absorb race issues. A small and interesting literature exists on the "routinisation" of difficult or threatening demands by local authorities (Dearlove, 1973; Saunders, 1975). However, the relevance of aspects of this material to the case of local race policy has yet to be explored; this study will include such an exploration.

Themes and hypotheses

The themes that will be addressed in this piece of research are four-fold. Firstly, the nature of the *liberal policy framework* developed during the 1960s will be investigated. This policy framework clearly played an important role in shaping the choices for local race policy. The study asks: what was the basis of the influence of the policy framework, and how has it promoted certain choices over others?

Secondly, the local arena for policy debate on race issues (or *race policy environment*) will be examined. The policy environment will be described in the context of two local political systems over a twenty-one year period (the London boroughs of Ealing and Barnet between 1965-86). This description will illustrate a major argument embodied in the study, namely, local experience of the relationship between race and public policy has varied enormously. Building upon this description of local variation, the study will identify the major characteristics of the policy environment, and outline a brief typology. Local race policy appears to be different things in different local political systems. Moreover, once placed in historical context, it can be characterised in different ways at different moments during the twenty-one year period examined. A generation ago, local race policy debate was rather diffuse and easily dominated by paternalistically-oriented Conservative *and* Labour local authorities. At some point during the mid-1970s, mounting frustrations over the relevance and capacity of the policy debate to deal with grassroots problems led to a number of dramatic developments. The result has been a radical shake-up of what is permissible and possible on the policy agenda, with a new emphasis being placed on the recognition of the "ethnic dimension" of public policy.

Thirdly, the study will look at how local authorities have tried to absorb race into the policy process and assess the efficacy of their attempts. Town halls have occupied a unique position in the local politics of race since the 1960s. Their role and responsibilities have grown in the period since, reaching a pinnacle in the third Race Relations Act (1976).[5] In recent years some policy analysis-oriented research has appeared evaluating local authorities' performance, but it has not been placed within the context of - let alone analyse - the liberal policy framework (Young and Connelly, 1981; Young, 1982 and 1985a). On the basis of an empirical survey of developments in two London boroughs, the study will discuss local authorities' organisational and political suitability to the requirements of race issues and conflicts. An obvious area of investigation must be the apparent mismatch between the functional demarcation lines of local authorities' service delivery responsibilities on the one hand, and the cross-cutting, multi-functional nature of race issues on the other.

Finally, there is a long-standing need to explore some of the consequences of the race-related public policy debates documented in this study. The notion of "colourblindness" in public policy has become an accepted feature of the policy terrain (FitzGerald, 1986a). There is a peculiar lack of a consensus either to "do something" about the problems facing black Britons, or to permit blacks to become the principal subjects of public policy programmes (Young, 1983). He reports that: 'there is a notable lack of agreement on the legitimacy of using [specific programmes] to the *specific* benefit of black populations' (1983: 288 - emphasis in original). It has been argued that black people and black interests have effectively been rendered "invisible" on the British political map (Messina, 1984). To be sure, a similar lack of visibility characterises the public policy process in general and the local "management" of race issues in particular. "Colourblind" orientations towards the place of race and ethnicity on the public policy agenda have had important implications for the policy environment and policy framework. The resiliance and durability of the former has been stretched on a number of occasions during the past two or more decades, including a period of sustained crisis during the late-1970s and early-1980s. This study characterises these crises and discusses their long-term consequences for the survival of the liberal policy framework. It argues that, despite a number of tactical retreats, the liberal paradigm continues to shape both race policy as well as wider debates concerning what is, and is not, "legitimate" and "acceptable" as public policy options.

In brief, the basic hypotheses explored in this study are three-fold. Firstly, much of the developments in race and public policy at local borough level in this period, are traceable to the race policy framework established during the 1960s' era of reform. Secondly, the immediate political conflicts documented in the empirical chapters are frequently about wider issues to do with the way in which the policy framework defines areas of legitimate and non-legitimate jurisdiction for the race policy environment. Finally, recent "progressive" developments in certain boroughs (notably Ealing, between 1986-90) are explained as the result of a reactive and partially successful challenge to the traditional, paternalistically-oriented policy environment.

A note on contents

The main body of the study is composed of seven further chapters. The following two chapters serve to set the scene of our enquiry, both in terms of the surrounding literature and the theoretical framework of the study. Chapter 2 is devoted to carrying out a critical review of the relevant literature, and examines what research to date has to say about ethnic minorities in local political systems. Chapter 3 outlines the major developments in British race relations during the 1960s. These developments became known as the "liberal hour" and mark the most intensive period of reform and laying of "ground-rules" for race policy. The chapter also maps the nature of the policy framework established at that time. This framework is labelled as the liberal settlement in Chapter 3, and Chapter 7 later in the study compares this framework with the actual experience of race-related public policy.

Chapters 4, 5 and 6 are empirical in nature and focus on developments in two outer London boroughs over a twenty-one year period between 1965-86. Chapter 4 reviews developments in race and local politics in Ealing Borough, from local government reorganisation in 1965 to the local elections of May 1986. Chapter 6 reviews developments in Barnet Borough. In between, Chapter 5 is devoted to a case study of the origins and evolution of educational dispersal policy - also known as "bussing" - as practiced by the education authority in Ealing from the mid-1960s until the early-1980s.

The next two chapters return to more theoretical themes. Chapter 7 contains a theoretical discussion of the relationship between the policy framework and the policy environment. It classifies local race policy environments - and their inherent "rules-of-the-game" - within four significant categories, illustrating their chronological inter-relationship to, and conceptual basis within, the liberal policy framework. Chapter 8 presents an overview of the previous empirical material, placing it in the context of the expectations and organisational resources of local government. Finally, Chapter 9 ends the study with a short discussion relating the findings and conclusions of the study to debates on the politics of race policy in Britain.

Notes

1. The term "black" is used interchangeably throughout the study with "ethnic minority" and occasionally with "immigrant". These terms refer to persons residing in Britain of either African, Caribbean or South Asian origin. No particular significance is attached to the use of three terms in

any given context and, it follows, that no particular political or sociological inference should be drawn from their use at various points in the study. Additionally, the terms "Asian" and "Afro-Caribbean" are sometimes deployed; these terms, however, are usually used in relation to specific references to these fairly discrete ethnic groups.

2. For a considered review of five hypotheses for the disappointment with the outcomes of British race relations policies since 1965, see Banton, 1985, especially pp.vii-x and pp.121-31.

3. Mark Bonham-Carter, the first chairman of the Race Relations Board, was in fact quoting the words of Deakin, 1970.

4. These three characterisations were loosely based on three recent publications: Banton, 1985; Miles and Phizacklea, 1984; and Layton-Henry, 1984. It should be noted that, as Banton accepts, there is a lack of a clearly defined volume outlining or advocating a conservative perspective. Banton's own title and that of Miles and Phizacklea are nominated as liberal and radical perspectives respectively, with Layton-Henry's falling somewhere between the two.

5. The role of local authorities is spelt out in Section 71 of the legislation. A duty is placed on local authorities to provide conditions for: (a) equality of opportunity, and (b) good relations between people of different races. For a discussion of the implications for local authorities and a brief evaluation of their role see CRE, 1983.

2 Race and politics: a review of the literature

Introduction

Recent years have witnessed a growing volume of literature concerned with the politics of race in Britain (Layton-Henry, 1984; Layton-Henry and Rich, 1986; Solomos, 1989). The bulk of this literature has been concerned with examining the position of ethnic minorities in the mainstream political process, with a strong emphasis placed upon non-white electoral behaviour (CRC, 1975; CRE, 1980 and 1984; Studlar and McAllister, 1984; Saggar, 1984; Layton-Henry, 1978 and 1988). Research has also focused on a number of other areas including *inter alia* the relationship between race and class, the politics of urban unrest, and the impact of race on specific policy areas (Gilroy, 1987; Benyon, 1984; Glazer and Young, 1983). As a result, the academic literature on the relationship between race and politics is made up of many different theoretical and empirical approaches. It is not surprising then that the researcher wishing to conduct a comprehensive survey of the material is faced with a mammoth task.

The researcher's task is further burdened by the highly differentiated and heterogeneous nature of Britain's ethnic minority populations. Writers all-too-frequently talk about "the black community" or some other over-arching term. This, however, ignores the great internal diversity within Britain's black population, between, among others, Asians and Afro-Caribbeans, Indian sub-continental and East African Asians, different religious and linguistic groups, and so on. Moreover, the patterns of political activism adopted by different ethnic minority communities vary enormously, both in terms of the forms of group mobilisation, and in terms of the points of access to the political process such groups attempt to penetrate. Sadly, the bulk of the literature on race and politics in Britain does not seriously attempt to recognise these important distinctions.

Nonetheless, any review of this material must try to draw together some tentative generalisations about how the topic has been approached by different writers and the conclusions they have drawn. For instance, as Jacobs (1986: 2) suggests, the

9

researcher could begin by identifying the 'important commonly exhibited characteristics of black organisations in different cities'. This strategy would help to give some insight into differing - and possibly contrasting - styles of ethnic minority group (hereafter EMG) organisation and mobilisation. In addition, the strategy may be instructive in identifying the public policy debates that urban-based EMGs have been most keen to get involved in, as well as help to guage the fruits of their efforts.

The researcher could also draw up an inventory of the activity - and inactivity - of various central and local government agencies in the field of race. For example, a full history of local authorities' involvement in so-called "race policy" could provide an insight into the traditional "colourblind" approach of public agencies. Indeed, this tradition has been fraught with ambiguous, indecisive - and occasionally contradictory - policy goals. Another starting point could lie in exploring the socio-political relationships that serve to structure patterns of ethnic minority political activism. This approach could also be expected to explain the sociological and political position of ethnic minorities in British society, as well as the causes of the discrimination and disadvantage experienced by these communities. This approach however, has been plagued by academic dissension and controversy (Banton, 1987). Indeed, political-sociologists have generally been unable to agree on questions to do with the position of ethnic minorities in British society, let alone their relationship with the major institutions of government.

A much longer standing approach used by researchers interested in race and politics has been the familiar local area study. The shelves of publications from the 1960s and early-1970s are littered with an assortment of such studies of inner-city areas with strong immigrant concentrations. Within this category, writers have tended to limit their attention to how the social and political fabric of these communities has been affected by the non-white influx. Local "race relations" or "community relations", in short, soon became the exclusive focus of their attention. Such writers were clearly interested in the dynamics of black-white interaction at the grass-roots, community level. Moreover, they rarely widened their focus to the relationship between black and white social and political institutions, let alone to questions about the approach of local public agencies towards the issue of race in local policy-making. This literature features strongly in our survey since it provides us with important clues as to how community relations *actually* - as opposed to might or could have - fared in the Handsworths, Southalls and St Pauls of Britain during the past thirty years. Moreover, as this study contains its own area studies (of two outer London boroughs), this literature helps to highlight the contrasts between the experiences of these different areas.

Finally, the researcher may elect to concentrate on the patterns of relationships that have evolved both within local government agencies and between such agencies and external community groups. Indeed, these complex and under-reported links between government agencies and community groups have recently begun to feature in local and central government policy-making. These links or relationships have not been fully explored by researchers who have all-too-often concentrated on other, more visible, dimensions of the race-politics nexus. Within political science more generally, the literature on the mechanics of public policy-making and the shaping of the policies that eventually emerge through group-government relations, has received renewed attention in recent years (see for example Rhodes, 1988). This literature helps to assess a number of questions to do with how different public agencies have tackled race-related public policy issues, and, just as important, how such agencies have frequently failed or refused to tackle these issues.

I shall review and comment on *two* broad schools of literature in this chapter. For convenience, I have grouped the literature under the following headings: firstly, the broad and scattered themes of behavioural and institutional approaches to race and politics; and secondly, the narrower and more tightly organised area of race and urban politics. Following that, I shall devote some space to assessing the overall contribution of the existing academic literature on the race-politics nexus, and highlight what I think are its most significant shortfalls. These criticisms are crucial to any modern political analysis of the relationship between race and public policy in British local government.

10

Behavioural and institutional approaches

The political science and sociological literature on race and ethnicity is voluminous. Fortunately, the bulk of it is of marginal relevance to the thematic concerns of this study. However, it is necessary to identify that which is relevant. Five main themes usefully summarise this large and diverse literature.

Black immigrant communities

Firstly, there is a well established sociological tradition dealing with the socio-political impact of black immigrant settlement in Britain. Many of these studies have been focused on the local community level (Bagley, 1970; Jenkins, 1971; Morrison, 1976). Detailed accounts of black-white social relations during the early years of such settlement in Sparkbrook (Birmingham), Nottingham and Handsworth (Birmingham) are provided by Rex and Moore (1967), Lawrence (1974) and Rex and Tomlinson (1979) respectively.

One of the problems with this material has been its excessive preoccupation with the close examination of the lives and social experiences of black people within the researchers' respective geographical areas of study. Consequently, it has tended to ignore the impact on these communities of wider socio-political structures and processes. Indeed, the contrasting experiences of black settlement in different areas can be accounted for, at least in part, by their different social and political contexts. A curious feature of many of these studies has been their *failure* to include such factors within the broader mapping of local race relations. Naturally, limited exceptions to this general pattern can naturally be found, but these are few in number and comparatively recent (Ben-Tovim *et al.*, 1986; Jacobs, 1986). The impact of this form of myopia can be far reaching. For example, Rose's (1969) seminal survey of race relations in the Britain of the late-1960s established the existence of widespread anti-immigrant sentiment and racial discrimination. However, he put forward somewhat incomplete explanations for this state of affairs which focused attention on the "alien" or "stranger" nature of these new communities. The heavy concentration of black people in deprived inner city areas, he implied, was the cause of the problem, and a policy for their dispersal was advocated. Zubaida (1970) strongly attacked Rose's position since it side-stepped explanations to do with *inter alia* the racially antagonistic nature of local public and private institutions, the discriminatory nature of local public service delivery, and the racially hostile outlook of local white populations.

Mainstream political participation

Secondly, a great deal of research has been conducted on aspects of the relationship between black people and black groups on one hand and the mainstream political process on the other. This party- and psephologically-oriented literature has often appeared to dominate the research on black politics, eclipsing other equally important and interesting areas of research.

The electoral studies of black people - both as voters and candidates - have reported high and consistent levels of participation as well as skewed support for the Labour Party (CRC, 1975; Crewe, 1983; CRE, 1984; Saggar, 1984; Layton-Henry and Studlar, 1984; Layton-Henry, 1988). The explanations offered for skewed partisanship and voting are complex. A tentative consensus has begun to emerge which argues that the black electorate has internalised negative anti-Conservative beliefs. These beliefs have revolved around a sense of latent racism in the Conservative Party (Saggar, 1984). A few writers have predicted a swelling undercurrent of Asian support for the Conservative Party - especially among the self-employed - but the data here is far too thin to support such generalisations (Layton-Henry, 1978).

Other studies have highlighted the massive under-representation of black people at all levels of the representative system, and concluded that most potential constitutional and institutional reforms are unlikely to yield significant improvements (Crewe, 1979 and

1983). Further research has shown the extent of blocking mechanisms - such as the voting system and parties' candidate selection systems - which serve to undermine the representation of black people and black interests (Deakin, 1965; FitzGerald, 1983 and 1984; Le Lohé, 1983). Studies of black participation in the major parties have noted the difficulties faced in trying to promote black interests and candidates in mainstream party politics (Layton-Henry, 1980; Behrens and Edmonds, 1981). Finally, writer such as Miles and Phizacklea (1984) have questioned the relevance of studying the formal relationship between black politics and mainstream party politics, suggesting instead that black people and black political interests should be seen as a "racialised fraction" of the working class movement.

Local area studies

Thirdly, a considerable amount of research has been carried out under the loose heading of local area studies. The local area study has commonly been used to assess the validity of writers' theoretical arguments about race relations (Rex and Moore, 1967; Rex and Tomlinson, 1979). Despite the inadequacies of much of this research in explaining race conflicts within prevailing social and political relations, the preoccupation of writers with all-things-local has mushroomed in recent years. For example, focusing on the cities of Liverpool and Wolverhampton, Ben-Tovim *et al.* (1986) provide a lively account of the local politics of community relations and local Labour Party initiatives.[1] The authors describe in detail how barriers to the limited introduction of race-related policy issues onto the political agendas of both cities were erected, challenged, and finally overcome.

FitzGerald's (1986a) case study of Ealing Borough pinpoints a number of pertinent features of race issues and conflicts in local government. However, the case study is sadly lacking in its appreciation of key developments in a thirty year history of race in the local politics of Ealing Borough and its predecessors. Somewhat in contrast, Messina's (1984 and 1989) study of the same borough does make a serious attempt to trace these historical developments. The result is a much fuller understanding of how local black people and their political interests were able to 'slip between the cracks of a competitive, two-party representational system' (Messina, 1985a: 1). His main concern is the response of the mainstream party system to non-white interests, drawing the following generalisation from the case of Ealing Borough:

> Competitive two-partyism does not automatically ensure that the interests of even sizeable minorities will be represented politically; even under seemingly favourable circumstances, the concerns of minorities in a two-party system might be "aggregated" but not necessarily "articulated". (Messina, 1987: 24)

Within this literature there are very few examples of local area studies that have systematically attempted to place black political activity within the context of a broader framework of local politics and policy-making. One of the notable exceptions is Katznelson's now-dated (1970 and1973) comparative study of the politics of race and migration in Britain and the United States. The British case is characterised by Katznelson as the politics of racial "buffering" and deals with Nottingham during the 1950s and 1960s. "Racial buffering" refers to the effective integration and/or co-option of some sections of the local black political élite into the mainstream institutions of local politics in the city, including local parties, the council, community relations bodies, etc. The result was to place local black interests in a hostile local political environment, forcing activists to operate at the margin of local politics through "buffer" bodies such as the local community relations council (hereafter CRC).

However, not all local area studies have been willing or geared to research the historical background of local social and political development. This obvious weakness has meant that numerous snapshot accounts of local race relations litter the shelves of the library (Richmond, 1973; Ratcliffe, 1981; Wallman, 1982; Bhachu, 1985). Taken as a whole, these studies contribute little to our understanding of the impact and handling of race at the level of local politics because of the failure to place current practices in historical context. Herein lies a major void in the literature which this study aims to fill.

The community relations movement

Notwithstanding this criticism, Katznelson (1973) ackowledges the potential bridge-building contribution of the community relations movement. He argues that this approach, firmly rooted in the 1960s' "liberal hour" of reform, offered the best hope of blunting extremism within black and white communities. The analytical recipe outlined by writers such as Katznelson embodies the approach to local race relations that have been so prominent in Britain since the late-1950s. However, many commentators have since argued that these voluntary community relations initiatives, far from promoting the sorts of goals so strongly endorsed by Katznelson and other liberal writers, have only served to produce the opposite result. For one thing, radical commentators such as Ben-Tovim and Gabriel (1982), Sivanandan (1982) and Dummet and Dummet (1982) have seen as its price the effective emasculation of an independent black civil rights movement.

In defence of Katznelson's position, his own argument favoured a community relations-type strategic approach to race conflicts in British society. This strategic approach was footnoted with an appeal for the Community Relations Commission (1968-77) and its local committees to 'become far more outspoken and active in seeking an equitable allocation of jobs, housing and schooling for their...constituency' (Katznelson, 1973: 187). In other words, as long ago as the early-1970s, Katznelson had come to recognise one of the major weak links in the liberal settlement. This same weakness re-emerged more forcibly a decade or so later as Young's (1985b: 286-7) description of a 'culture of inexplicitness' in British race policy. Race issues have commonly been conceptualised by policy-makers and others in terms that are racially inexplicit, and Katznelson's remarks merely represented an early call to recognise - and remedy! - this "culture". However, crucial questions remain unanswered: where did this "culture" come from, and what have been its main consequences for local politics and government? The aim of this study is to provide answers to these central questions.

The outlook of writers and policy-makers alike during the 1960s and early-1970s was one which held that a new and manageable strategy for race relations could be formulated and executed within a bi-partisan, de-politicised consensus. Messina (1984 and 1985a) in particular has documented this outlook and the reasons behind it. He argues that, by the mid-1960s, governments increasingly faced the likelihood of race relations becoming unmanageable. Desperate searching for joint cross-party support on strategic questions eventually resulted in agreement to pursue a broad, though ill-defined, policy goal of racial harmony (see also Chapter 3 below). A philosophy of "community relationsism" was to be the cornerstone of this strategy. Although little significance was attached to the precise definition and possible consequences of such a policy goal, the essential point of the approach was to signal the "liberal hour" in British race relations thinking. Banton (1985) sees the philosophy of "community relationsism" as something of an interim social and political plan of action based on a distinct understanding of racial harmony as a "public good". He writes of the legal and institutional reforms of the 1960s that:

> These were non-party measures passed because discrimination was seen as contrary to the British people's conception of themselves and their society... [This] reflected the ascendancy of liberal over conservative assumptions about race relations. (Banton, 1985: 126 and abstract)

Modern-day CRCs are rooted in the community relations movement of the late-1950s and 1960s. Although many of these voluntary liaison committees (hereafter VLCs), "committees for inter-racial friendship" and other such bodies were already in operation by the time the first Race Relations Act was enacted in 1965, this date clearly marks a watershed in their development. The development of a quasi-institutional CRC identity from the mid-1960s onwards is given considerable emphasis by Banton (1985 and 1987). It was during this early stage in the "liberal hour" that the philosophical concept of racial harmony first began to dominate the approach of the main policy actors. Given the central role played by CRCs in both promoting and later developing this policy goal, it is necessary to inspect some of the research that has been carried out on the role of CRCs in local politics and policy-making.

More often than not, CRCs feature within wider research on, typically, race relations local area studies. For example, Katznelson's (1970 and 1973) study of Nottingham and Rex's (1967 and 1979) co-authored studies of two different areas of Birmingham, treat CRCs somewhat separately from local politics. CRCs, at best, feature at the margin of many other local area profiles (Jenkins, 1971; Richmond, 1973; Morrison, 1976). On the other hand, CRC-centred research often has a soffocatingly narrow focus. Hill and Issacharoff (1971)[2] and Lawrence (1974) in fact warn against a framework that puts CRCs at the heart of the analysis of local race relations. Morever, such a framework would imply that there are no other relevant factors - such as the local authority, the local education executive, local political parties, etc. - serving to shape local race relations and race-related policy-making.

It is implausible to look at CRCs without reference to their local social and political environment. Barker (1975) exemplifies this weakness. He tries to draw comparisons between a handful of CRCs operating within very diverse settings: inner city, suburban, town and rural. Whilst noting their diverse geographical location, Barker's qualifications to his generalisations go no further, and certainly not as far as any serious attempt to control for variances in, *inter alia*, local political make-ups, historical immigration legacies, socio-political characteristics of black communities, etc. The work, performance and profile of CRCs are not viewed as being related to, or a function of, local political systems. The typology produced by Barker therefore, whilst interesting, does not help to explain why CRCs may differ in type and outlook. Barker has uncovered very little to explain *why* (what he labels as) a "platform-type" CRC in an inner city London borough behaves as it does, nor *why* a "bridge-type" CRC in a West Midlands industrial town should be characterised as such.[3] The preoccupation with classification continues to permeate research on CRCs. The problem with this approach goes beyond placing different labels on what appear to be superficially different and contrasting CRC-types. The weakness stems from providing simple functional description, without fully explaining the factors leading to these descriptions and differences.

At least two analytical gaps must be filled in order to utilise a typology such as Barker's, not to mention provide answers to the above questions. Firstly, sufficient account needs to be taken of different local political environments. That is, we need to explore the hypothesis that, for example, additional independent factors peculiar to a borough's local political system may serve to explain the evolution of the "platform-type" CRC approach to local race relations. For instance, there may be parallel local issues that have tended to nurture platform or campaigning styles of participation by local community pressure groups. Additionally, local government budgetary constraints - especially in London and other metropolitan areas - may also indirectly structure local debates on the role of CRCs. Certainly, the fiscal restraint placed upon urban local authorities in recent years has encouraged competitive, campaigning political strategies by a whole host of community organisations, keen to keep their respective "issue-interests" high on the agendas of town hall decision-makers. Consequently, the demands of these groups have been articulated in the context of a more aggressive defence of minority group rights, particularly in the distribution of local public services, grant-aid, etc. CRCs, it should be remembered, have been a part of this wider process.

Secondly, we need to consider various social and community explanations for contrasting CRC types. Having reported the ethnic composition of the different CRC case study areas, Barker says nothing further about "ethnicity" as a potential

14

explanatory factor. The assumption is that the plethora of social, community and political organisations catering for and run by black groups in these areas had nothing to do with the "strategies and styles" of the various CRCs. This view is extremely myopic since, if nothing else, all of these CRCs were undoubtedly heavily reliant on the support and participation of local EMGs. Thus, there is an urgent need for explanations of CRCs' activities to recognise the full range of relevant factors. CRCs neither operate within a political vacuum untouched by local politics, nor within a social-community vacuum beyond the influence of their main client group, EMGs.

The liberal policy framework

Finally, a closely related body of literature has developed which has been broadly concerned with evaluating the content and the outcome of the liberal-oriented framework for public policy on race issues. However, it should be said that the handful of writers interested in this field have, in the main, only examined single and rather isolated aspects of the liberal policy framework (Young, 1985a). Others have produced essays reflecting - often superficially - upon the overall strengths and weaknesses of the liberal settlement of the 1960s (Banton, 1987; Bonham-Carter, 1987). Few have attempted to theoretically explore the impact of the liberal settlement upon the framework for and content of public policy.

Both Hill and Issacharoff (1971) and Lawrence (1974) point out that researchers have often falsely confused the absence of overt racial conflict with a state of racial harmony, when the two are, in fact, conceptually different. A sense of local racial harmony might have something to do with a local CRC, but equally, it might not. It may be the result of an unusual degree of mutual tolerance among local black and white communities. Alternatively, as Lawrence (1974) believes, the explanation may have something to do with the modest and undemanding way in which black immigrants - in Nottingham in this case - defined their social, economic, political and cultural position in British society. Further, he strongly questions the basis on which earlier studies, notably Katznelson's (1970 and 1973), concluded that Nottingham enjoyed unusually "good" race relations. Lawrence's attitudinal survey data suggested that the views of local race relations held by CRC activists were missing the mark: in fact local race relations were poor and under further threat of deterioration, yet those claiming responsibility appeared to think and claim otherwise.

On the specific question of CRCs' role within local race relations, Hill and Issacharoff (1971: 284) have argued that 'community relations practical work is compounded by its lack of theoretical founding'. The present study argues that the philosophy of "community relationsism" has been one of the main policy instruments created by the liberal settlement and its accompanying policy framework. As such, it has systematically failed to address certain basic questions pertaining to the broader policy framework for race relations. One of the most important of these questions relates to the ambiguous conceptions of racial harmony and equality held by a number of key policy actors:

> If one really does want to see the rights of Commonwealth citizens protected and community "harmony" maintained, one cannot escape from the fact that these goals may be incompatible and that one may need to be subordinated to the other. *The particularly important point to be made about 'harmony' is that this may appear to exist...even in a racialist society.* Harmony itself does not indicate the existence of equality. (Hill and Issacharoff, 1971: 284 - emphasis added)

Race and urban politics

The review of this literature ought to begin with a qualifying remark: the literature is composed in essence of two related bodies. A first group is concerned with the 'urban context affecting city-based pressure groups and communities' (Jacobs, 1986: 4). In recent years a growing number of writers have begun to examine the policy issues and processes that have developed from this context (Newton, 1976; Cockburn, 1977; Saunders, 1979; Dunleavy, 1980). This field of research has become an established specialist area within political science and policy analysis. A second group, starting from the context of urban political analysis, has sought to examine the position of urban-based black groups organising, mobilising and competing for public resources in the context of limited resources for the major cities (Young and Connelly, 1981; Jacobs, 1986).

Urban politics involves a number of things. For instance: competition for scarce economic and other resources; sociological differentiation within and between different groups; understanding of organisational patterns of public agencies such as local authorities; race-related, inter-group competition and conflict; and so on. Consequently, the scope of urban political research has tended to be very wide indeed and "localism" has tended to prevail. As Dunleavy (1980: 1) reports, urban politics has often been guided by 'the orientation of many political scientists and political sociologists towards the study of local political institutions'. That said, the argument behind the view that contemporary British black politics should be interpreted in an urban political setting centres on empirical evidence which shows that most activity has taken place within urban environments (Runnymede Trust/NCVO, 1980; Stewart and Whiting, 1982; Jacobs, 1986; Saggar, 1987a). Further, it has been apparent for some time that much of this activism has *not* been played out at the level of national politics. Instead, in the absence of a single national black or ethnic minority pressure group, the bulk of black political activism has been an essentially local and urban phenomenon (Heinemann, 1972; FitzGerald, 1984: 62).

The literature therefore deals with the urban political analysis of the interaction between the full spectrum of urban-based community pressure groups on one hand and public agencies on the other, as well as the analysis of specifically black urban groups operating in a similar context. Inevitably, there will be some degree of overlap. If urban political research is to provide us with a helpful framework, it will be by demonstrating firstly how black groups operate alongside non-black groups in local politics, and secondly how black and non-black groups have precipitated a variety of different policy responses from different local authorities (Young and Connelly, 1981; Young, 1985a; FitzGerald, 1986a).

Access to the policy process

Political science has long been concerned with the study of pressure groups' difficulties - and successes - in gaining and retaining access to the political and policy-making system (Richardson and Jordan, 1979; Jordan and Richardson, 1987). Similar theoretical questions have been posed by studies at the local level, often involving detailed analyses of the policy responses and non-responses of local borough or city councils. Bachrach and Baratz's (1970) seminal study of Baltimore, Dearlove's (1973) study of Kensington and Chelsea, and Newton's (1976) study of Birmingham stand out particularly.

The main point of reference for most urban political research has been the question of *access* - both implicit and explicit - to the political system in general, and the policy-making process in particular. Writers have evaluated the impact of access, first on the policy outputs of local government, and second on the degree, if any, to which groups compromise their independence. On this latter question, Richardson and Jordan (1979: 41) have adapted and deployed a cost-benefit analysis based on Olsen (1976), concluding that where access is relatively "open", the costs to the group of participation will tend to diminish in importance. Notwithstanding this relationship, both relatively "open" and "closed" local government institutions will always involve costs to groups on the "outside" interacting with policy-makers on the "inside". 'Groups entering into a relationship with government' writes Jacobs (1986: 25), '*will compromise their full independence* to some degree by the very nature of mutual co-operation' (emphasis in original).

Another dimension of the group-government nexus involves the question of how much influence, if any, participating groups are able to wield over policy. According to Olsen's (1976) analysis, we would naturally expect more limited points of access to government to make it more difficult for groups to have direct influence. However, even with relatively limited access, groups are often attracted towards participating on the basis of promises of influence over local representatives and officials. Thus, the potential for influence acts as a powerful incentive to participate. Jacobs (1986: 75-77) has argued that, on both counts, black groups are faced with extremely few points of access and opportunities for influence at the national level. The local urban political stage, however, is more likely to offer local EMGs 'access enabling influence' (Jacobs, 1986: 77).[4] Richardson and Jordan (1979), however, warn that "open" systems or styles of government are not likely to be so "open" about decisions affecting the substance of policy outputs. "Openness", they argue, is more likely to be about the character of group-government relations. Actual policies cannot be expected to reflect directly any "openness" there may be between groups and government, ie. groups will not get what they want. Furthermore, it is likely that access will become easier when the broad, substantive policy priorities of groups and government converge (Dearlove, 1973; Saunders, 1975). The concepts of "access" and "influence" used by urban political research will be selectively utilised in this study and related to characterisations of group-town hall relations in local race-related public policy-making.

Black urban competition

There is no single, coherent body of literature on urban politics. Thus, it is not easy to place our discussion of black people and black groups living and operating in an urban setting within this literature. Dunleavy (1980: 21) in particular criticises the generalistic, umbrella nature of the term "urban", suggesting that some writers have incorrectly used it interchangeably with the study of local politics. Indeed, by defining urban politics in terms of the 'politics of collective consumption', he rejects previous geographical or institutional definitions and approaches to the "urban" topics in political science (1980: 163). Urban politics in this study returns to an analysis of competition by and between groups, politicians, officials and others, over the distribution of public resources - education and grant-aid being prime examples.

Such a definition is certainly compatible with, and conducive to, the study of black politics in an urban setting. However, it remains insufficient in at least two important senses. Firstly, whilst black people - like their white counterparts - will be engaged in competition for these collective consumption-type resources, some, and possibly many, will find themselves excluded from access to discussions on the distribution of these resources. That is to say, the ways in which some public agencies (such as local education or housing authorities) have handled their responsibilities for the provision of public education and housing for urban collective consumers in general, may reveal little as to how service delivery has been shaped by the presence of local black populations. The definition is unlikely to uncover much about how race has served to structure the whole question of local government service delivery to black communities.

Secondly, the casual observer of patterns of black political activism in urban Britian will soon realise that the concerns and priorities of black people and black groups have often extended well beyond mainstream areas of public service delivery. In other words, whilst black people - in common with their white counterparts - need and expect to be housed and educated, it would be myopic to see black collective consumption patterns as being the same as those of white people and groups, but writ small. A cursory glance at the nature of black politics in the inner cities shows a mammoth escalation in demands by radical - as well as not so radical! - black groups for specialist, ethnically-related, forms of service delivery. These demands have not just been in housing and education service delivery. Such demands have also been responsible for the creation of what has been termed as a "new *black* political agenda". This new agenda has involved aspects of ethnic minority culture, lifestyle, heritage, consciousness, etc. reflected in new policies being pursued by certain radical local authorities (Ben-Tovim, *et al.*, 1986; Rex, 1986; Jacobs, 1986; Saggar, 1987b).

Some urban political research has sought to suggest a connection between urban politics and social class as an explanation for urban social movements (Clarke and Ginsburg, 1977). Of course this may simply be an attempt to introduce "urbanism" into wider political debates about social and political conflict. However, Jacobs (1986) contends that many groups are actively engaged in the pursuit of demands reflecting their interests both as distinctive class groups as well as distinctive urban groups. Urban politics has consequently come to embody an important measure of traditional class politics.

Therefore, it is perhaps useful to think in terms of *three* discrete issue areas that reflect the urbanised spatial location of much of the black populace. Firstly, black people may have interests in urban issues to do with the politics of collective consumption in the context of competing demands for the resources of local authorities. Secondly, black people may have traditional class interests that are coherently and effectively articulated - more than they would otherwise be - as a consequence of their disproportional urban setting. Finally, black people are likely to have a stake in specifically race-related aspects of local public policy-making. It is this last - and perhaps increasingly common - facet of black urban politics that we are mainly concerned with in this study.

Local pressure group studies

A study of urban politics could also begin by drawing on earlier material looking at the nature of the relationship between local community organisations and local authorities. Dearlove's study (1973) of this relationship in the Royal Borough of Kensington and Chelsea drew a sharp distinction between the process of policy-*making* on the one hand and the process of policy-*maintenance* on the other. Public policy is analysed in terms of both the decision-making processes establishing particular patterns of resource commitments, *and* the processes requiring decision-makers to engage in the routine defence of such resource commitments. He adds that government (including local government) will always tend towards seeing policy in terms of the maintenance or continuity of previous resource commitments (1973: 4).

This orientation has an impact on the operations and fortunes of black groups in local politics. For instance, if a group is concentrating its energies solely at the level of race-related policy demands, then, given the relative "newness" - or even "novelty" - of such demands, questions of resource re-allocation will be hard to avoid. For local politicians or officials to take an active interest in these policy issues would inevitably involve policy-making as opposed to policy-maintenance. If they are to go this far, the question then becomes: which groups will they be willing to deal with, under what terms, and in respect of which legitimate policy issues?

In answer to the above question (but especially its first component), Dearlove (1973: 157) has argued that local pressure or community groups can essentially be viewed as one of two types: "helpful" versus "unhelpful". The basis for this classification has to do with government wishing to embark on some measure of revised resource commitment, ie. policy-making. Government is actively involved in the process of searching for useful allies to help it in its tasks. Thus, the "helpfulness" of a given group is seen as a partial function of the strength of government commitment to policy change. It is not sufficient for a particular group to merely appear to be more "helpful" to government under these conditions. Instead, the emphasis is on government actively searching out potentially "helpful" groups if and when policy change is pushed further up the agenda of a particular policy sector. "Unhelpful" groups, in contrast, will feature especially when policy change is far from government's agenda or when the group's reputation, demands, and communication methods are viewed as threatening to the broad priorities of government. He argues that "unhelpful" groups 'either do not make claims on the council, or else make claims that conflict with the coucillors' own views as to the proper course of council activity' (1973: 168).

This analysis provides a useful approach to questions of EMG-local government relations. However, it rather begs the question whether there may have been, and still are, alternative reasons for casting certain EMGs as "unhelpful". Dearlove's conception of "helpfulness" is, by its own terms of reference, "de-racialised". That is, it ignores, because it does not begin to conceive of, situations where black groups present local government with unwanted race-specific demands involving policy change. In addition, such policy changes may be resisted not purely because local government is resistant to all or most forms of policy change. Resistance to policy change - ie. policy-maintenance - may frequently be explained in terms of local government's cautious (at best) or hostile (at worst) disposition to forces trying to introduce "the race dimension" into local political debate. In other words, we must take great care not to confuse Dearlove's generalised notion of "unhelpfulness" with deep-rooted institutional resistance to race-related issues emerging onto the political agendas of local authorities.

Mobilising bias in urban politics

Aspects of the North American urban politics literature are instructive and complement British writing, most notably the analysis of the mobilisation of bias in the decision-making processes of urban institutions such as city government. Bachrach and Baratz (1970: 43) define the mobilisation of bias as:

> [A] set of predominant values, beliefs, rituals and institutional procedures ("rules of the game") that operate systematically and consistently to the benefit of certain persons and groups at the expense of others. Those that benefit are placed in a preferred position to defend and promote their vested interests.

Selective use of this material may help us to plug the gaps which Dearlove's (1973) conception of "helpfulness" appears unable to resolve in relation to black groups and black political activity. Bachrach and Baratz (1970: 44-46) describe at least five ways in which dominant political actors can defend and promote their position - each relevant to the case of EMGs operating in urban political settings. Furthermore, they warn the researcher against over-enthusiasm in attempting to identify the "non-decisions" of policy-maintainers. The development of a scheme to identify "non-decisions" has relevance for black urban politics where claims - not to mention evidence! - of the systematic exclusion of black interests from the policy-making process are common. Attention, they advise, should be centred on "important" or "key" decisions of dominant policy actors. "Key" decisions in the case of black urban politics operate at three levels: a "black political agenda"; EMGs' demands for access to the policy process; and EMGs' policy preferencs. All three must:

> involve a genuine challenge to the resources of power or authority of those who currently dominate the process by which policy outputs in the system are determined. (Bachrach and Baratz, 1970: 47-8)

Not all challenges offered by black groups interacting with local government's dominant position are as they appear. Such challenges have featured heavily in black urban politics. However, local authorities have all-too-often resisted these challenges by indicating that any form of policy change or policy-making is not on their agenda for discussion. Many town halls have ensured that considerations of the potential "helpfulness" - or otherwise - of certain groups simply never arise, thereby pre-empting such EMG challenges.

Radical perspectives

Some commentators have attempted to place the race-related issue demands of black groups within an overall class analysis - an approach which extends not only to the analysis of black urban politics but to the politics of race in Britain in general. Miles and Phizacklea for example (1982 and 1984) have emphasised the importance of race as a new factor serving to divide the working class, both generally as well as in urban political conflicts in particular. Their analysis cites survey evidence showing that white working class respondents (in Harlesden in north London in this case) had confusing and often conflicting beliefs about the reasons for local urban decline. These cohorts voiced both class-related and race-related explanations for the social and economic deprivation of their own urban communities. The authors assert that, to a large extent, the "urban crisis" of the inner cities, was highlighted and underscored by the settlement of large numbers of black people in these communities. Another commentator, Sivanandan (1976: 350), echoes this point:

> The forced concentration of immigrants in the deprived and decaying areas of the big cities highlighted (and reinforced) existing social deprivation; racism *defined* them as its cause. (Emphasis added)

The radical perspective concludes therefore that *racism*, not *race*, constitutes the crucial element of the urban "crisis". That is, the experience of black groups in relation to, and in competition with, white groups and a predominantly white local political system, lies at the heart of black urban political analysis. Through an understanding of this relationship we can begin to explain the discriminatory policies and practices that many black communities have endured. Discrimination at the hands of public policy-makers and implementers, radicals argue, has little to do with narrow sociological explanations such as racial stereo-typing or cultural handicaps.

Comparative policy-oriented research

A recent feature of the literature on race and politics has been the growth of *comparative* policy-oriented research (Jacobs, 1982; Young, 1983; Glazer and Young, 1983; Banton, 1984). Attention has focused on the style and substance of actual policies pursued by government in respect of urban-based black minority populations on both sides of the Atlantic. The outcome of much of this work has been to highlight the many important contrasts that exist between Britain and the United States, both in conceptual approaches to such areas of policy innovation and in substantive policy direction. Jacobs (1986: 6-7) characterises this contrast as follows:

> These studies have revealed...both the potential for black representation and political influence (USA) and the relative under-development of black politics in representative and representational terms (Britain).

Young (1983 and 1985b) notes two major conceptual characteristics of the approach of British policy-makers to race-related public policy. Firstly, he suggests that the main policy tools in this area have been peculiarly caught up in the related, yet separate, policy debate on urban economic decline. The comparatively recent political debate as to what should or could be done about black urban deprivation amounts to 'little more than a rediscovery of race within the longer standing concern for urban deprivation' (Young, 1985b: 290). Moreover, potential policy initiatives to arrest racial disadvantage are effectively still-born, owing to the marginal and ambiguous status of the handful of policy instruments that can be deployed - eg. the Urban Programme (hereafter UP) and Section 11 of the Local Government Act 1966 (hereafter S.11). Secondly, a whole series of "psycho-cultural" factors appear to bear heavily on the outlook of virtually all participants in the race-related decision-making process. These factors are especially pronounced when the British case is contrasted with others such as the USA. According to Prashar and Nicholas (1986: 122), there is an 'ambivalence about the explicit identification of ethnicity or reluctance to shed established notions of ethnic assimilation'. Further, Young and Connelly (1981: 159) complain that in the specific case of British local government:

Local authorities cannot be asked to play a leading role in promoting racial equality until there is a far better understanding among them of the basic premises of a multi-racial society; nor can they develop policies to achieve it without grasping the need to be explicit about issues of race.

Young (1983) argues that the essential difference between British and American practice has been not so much pragmatic as conceptual in nature. Despite this distinction, he points to some limited evidence of change taking place in Britain. Although there has not been any significant reform of the major tools of policy (eg. UP and S.11), there has been more recently (mainly post-1982) signs of some radical local authorities attempting to challenge the inexplicitness that has dogged race-related public policy for so long (Young, 1985b; Saggar, 1987b and 1991). Later chapters in this study will be concerned with characterising race policy inexplicitness in local politics and government (Chapters 4, 5 and 6), and linking this phenomenon with the broader approach of the policy process to issues of race and ethnicity (Chapters 3, 7 and 8).

According to the literature, racial inexplicitness or "colourblindness" has tended to dominate the discussion of race and ethnicity, both at the level of substantive public policy as well as the guiding conceptual framework of policy. The focus of the literature however has fallen mainly on "colourblind" race policy without fully examining the historical and ideological factors responsible for the contextual setting of such policy. It has yet to be seen whether future public policy will continue to be so shrouded in the sort of "colourblindness" that we have seen for so long. Policy-makers in local and central government are increasingly in a dilemma. Pressure - political as well as bureaucratic - has steadily built up and begun to challenge the legitimacy of existing conceptual notions of race and ethnicity in the policy process. However, the full impact of replacing established norms has barely begun to be thought through, let alone reflected openly in policy discussion. Meanwhile, confusion and ambiguity prevail across many aspects of the policy debate on race. If racially explicit interventionism is to be the strategic approach of the future, this will depend upon:

> the prior recognition of the need to make explicit provision, and devise procedures, for a society which is characterised by the pluralisms of ethnicity, faith, language and culture. (Young, 1985b: 301)

Race and inner cities policy research

A number of policy analysts have turned their attention to central government policy initiatives and central-local relations in the field of race relations and inner cities policy. According to Young (1983 and 1985b) these initiatives really amount to the consideration of three main items of public policy: the three Race Relations Acts (1965, 1968 and 1976); the UP (both traditional, 1968 onwards, and reformulated, 1977 onwards); and the S.11 programme. The result, he argues, is that Britain in fact boasts very little that could be specifically described as "race policy". The latter policy items constitute the major spending programmes devised by government for policy-makers keen to foster an ethnically-plural society (see Chapter 3 below for further details of the origins of this vision in the 1960s). Additionally, particular areas of public policy such as the inner cities' strategies of successive governments have been investigated in detail by researchers (Edwards and Batley, 1978; McKay and Cox, 1979).

However, weak targetting and a sense of ambiguity over policy goals, has meant that even these handful of policy instruments have missed the *essential* point of bringing race onto the public policy agenda - both at central and local levels. Race and racial groups have only featured as a by-product of these particular sets of policies because:

> The stumbling block to the realisation of this potential is to be found in another of the...established norms of British social policy: compensatory programmes are more acceptably aimed at *areas* than at *groups*. (Young, 1983: 228 - emphasis in original)

21

An additional area of interest has been the analysis of the equal opportunities policies of local government (Young and Connelly, 1981; Ouseley, 1981 and 1984; Young, 1982 and 1985a; FitzGerald, 1986a; Prashar and Nicholas, 1986; Saggar, 1987b). The policies and practices of other public bodies such as public corporations, the civil service, the health services, the armed forces, and so on, have also been the subject of research (Little and Robbins, 1983; RIPA, 1983). This literature has highlighted and assessed the tremendous pace of innovation that has taken place in recent years in the policies and practices of certain local authorities and other public agencies. Research has also thrown light on exactly what types of equal opportunities policies have been adopted and with what results. One important conclusion has been that these developments in local government have generally been quite modest in scale, though not always in ambition (Young, 1984; Profitt, 1986; Saggar, 1987b). In many ways they have only touched the surface of local authorities' service delivery programmes, and often consist of little more than the formal adoption of statements of intent. Budgets for policy innovation and developmental work have been restricted in an environment whereby race equality commitments have had to compete against local government's broader financial difficulties. Consequently, ambitious race equality strategies have often become piecemeal and frustrated in their application to local authorities' own employment practices, let alone mass public service delivery programmes.

This study will address itself to questions of why these developments - and the strategic forces behind them - were so long in appearing in local race-related public policy. In short, what has changed to account for these recent developments - either at the level of the framework of policy or elsewhere - and why? These specific questions will be returned to in Chapters 3, 7 and 8 below.

Conclusion

There is no single school of thought in which this study can, or indeed ought to, be placed. This chapter has presented an overview of the contribution of a wide body of literature dealing with the relationship between race and politics and public policy. Each of the two main groups of literature have approached this relationship from different theoretical and methodological perspectives. We must therefore draw upon the strengths of each and through this study attempt to resolve some of the weaknesses.

For instance, the behavioural and institutional approaches to the study of race and politics have been mainly concerned with trying to locate the position of black immigrants and their children in a white, racially discriminatory society. Inevitably, there is a subtle tendency to fuse together a whole range of black political interests into a manageable conception of a single homogeneous black political interest. Writers within this school have been concerned with providing snap-shot pictures and overarching explanations of complex political and social tensions between black and white communities. Unfortunately, their interest in the public policy issues through which these tensions have arisen and been fought over - particularly at the local level - has been minimal.

Such a perspective remains a major weakness of this group of literature. In short, the broad brush approach to these tensions and conflicts has eclipsed both the subtleties of such divisions as well as their impact within local political systems. A degree of "fine tuning" of overgeneralised, aggregate research data is therefore required.

Turning to the literature on race and urban politics, some useful conceptual approaches can be identified to complement the behavioural and institutional material. There appear to be two main tributaries flowing into the analysis of black groups in urban politics. Firstly, there is the analysis of new and challenging social movements operating in urban contexts (Jacobs, 1986; Ben-Tovim *et al.*, 1986). The social, community and political activism of various black communities has been immense during the past thirty years. New and multifarious black organisations have emerged in recent years and have begun to turn their attentions towards local politics and policy-making with increasing intensity. Nationally, organisations such as the Indian Workers Association of Great Britain are probably the best known of these groups. Locally, a plethora of smaller organisations are to be found, seeking to represent all types of black communities, based around religious, linguistic, nationalist, cultural and various other group identities. (A cross-section of these local - and occasionally national - groups feature in the case studies of two London boroughs in Chapters 4, 5 and 6.) Secondly, there is the longer established analysis of group-government relations in urban politics. This has been a more tradititional concern of political scientists, especially those interested in the growth of pressure group politics. However, comparatively little work has been done to examine this relationship in the case of black groups that are in competition both with one another and with existing groups for the distribution of scarce public resources.

This study, therefore, falls into something of a grey area in the literature. It uses a theoretical framework based on the analysis of ideological values and historical development in shaping public policy. Local policy debates, conflicts and outcomes can be seen as the most immediate setting or environment for race policy. However, this study contends that the explanation of these factors requires them to be placed in the context of a policy framework. The following chapter maps out the origins and features of such a framework for race-related public policy in Britain. Subsequent chapters chart the influence of the policy framework by describing and explaining the impact of race issues on local politics and public policy in two London boroughs.

Notes

1. Interestingly, Ben-Tovim *et al.*, 1986: 7-11 are at pains to set out their arguments defending their research from the long standing charge of investigation amounting to "surveillance" work. At the outset of their study they explain why they chose to adopt what they describe as an "action research" methodological approach to their investigation of race and local politics in Liverpool and Wolverhampton. It has yet to be seen the extent to which their approach truly satisfied black community activists' fears about the purpose and potential use of their study.

2. The eight CRCs studied by Hill and Issacharoff, 1971 were in the following areas: Hackney and Tower Hamlets (inner-city boroughs); Ealing (outer-suburban borough); Birmingham, Bradford, Huddersfield and Sheffield (large, heavy industrial county boroughs); and High Wycombe (small, light industrial county borough).

3. Barker, 1975: 51 argues that the CRCs surveyed across a range of towns and boroughs in England could be classified under three headings. Firstly, the "shelter-type" CRC that 'assists immigrants with their problems as an interpreter, guide, information channel and advisor on rights.' Secondly, the "bridge-type" CRC that 'provides a meeting place for community organisations from minority ethnic groups and acts as a stimulator.' Finally, the "platform-type" CRC that 'sees its role as a campaigning organisation, drawing public attention to the problems of racial discrimination and inner city deprivation.'

4. Jacobs, 1986: 77 discusses the 'access enabling strategies' adopted by a number of radical Left local authorities in recent years. He is particularly concerned with the activities of the well-publicised Ethnic Minorities Unit of the now defunct Greater London Council (hereafter GLC). He argues that the types of black groups that "did business" with the Unit commonly shared a set of broad policy commitments with Labour, rather than Conservative or other, GLC councillors. Access to the GLC was necessarily made easier as a result of the sharing of outlooks between the Labour GLC councillors and these groups. Thus, the "openness" of the system centred more around character than substance.

3 The liberal settlement: setting the agenda for race and public policy

Introduction

In this chapter I chart the major developments during the 1960s in terms of the framework in which race-related public policy was to be forged and implemented during the 1970s and 1980s. Using evidence from this period, I show how questions about the overall framework and certain goals of policy were first brought into public discussion, largely through the efforts of the then Labour Home Secretary, Roy Jenkins. Further, although the efforts of Jenkins and others have come to be known as the "liberal hour" in British race relations, the major developments of this era in fact owe much more to the emergent consensus on race between the two main parties. Although the central features of the "liberal hour" were to come under attack and eventually collapse before the end of the decade, both the consensual position of race in British politics and the broader framework of race-related public policy were to endure beyond the era of Jenkins. Elements of both the consensus and the framework stretched well into the 1970s and, to a lesser degree, into the 1980s.

The chapter is concerned with mapping the essential terms of the policy framework created and legitimised through the efforts of the reforming Home Secretary and other influential "liberal hour" enthusiasts. The over-riding policy goal inherent in this early framework was the promotion of racial harmony. Herein lie a number of important clues regarding the impact race was to have - and indeed was already having in the 1960s - on local political systems. In due course the promotion of racial harmony would also prove to be a major reason for the apparent splintering of race policy strategies into a number of different and contrasting approaches and experiences. Evidence for these differences can be seen in near-neighbouring London boroughs and is described in Chapters 4-6 below.

The first part of the chapter is mainly devoted to an examination of the putative "liberal hour" in the politics of British race relations; this is an historical analysis of developments in *national* politics during the mid- and late-1960s. The second part is devoted to a discussion of some theoretical and conceptual questions. These questions are concerned with trying to characterise the "model" of race relations upon which the 1960s' policy framework was built. This framework set the agenda for the legitimate goals of public policy and the parameters of race relations activity that would endure in *local* politics during the following two decades.

The rise and fall of the "liberal hour", 1962-70

The duration of the "liberal hour" in British race relations can be seen in terms of four separate phases - a series of quarter-hour episodes, as it were. Firstly, the period between the passage of "RAB" Butler's 1962 Commonwealth Immigrants Act and Labour's arrival in office in October 1964, represents the emergence of a quasi-liberal consensus geared towards removing race from the arena of party competition. Secondly, the fourteen month tenure of Labour's first Home Secretary, Sir Frank Soskice, lasting until December 1965, in which the main foundations were laid on which his successor, Jenkins, was to later forge ahead. Thirdly, the period of Jenkins' Home Secretaryship, ending with his Wilsonian swap with the Chancellor in November 1967, amounted to the core of the "liberal hour", both in terms of reform and the prospect of reform. Finally, the period following Jenkins' departure until the 1970 General Election when James Callaghan reigned at the Home Office, was characterised by the casting of a number of lethal shots at the liberal race consensus, most notably through the Kenyan-Asian crisis and the rise of Powellism.

1962-64: emergence

In a number of important ways the 1962 Commonwealth Immigrants Act marked the close of the era of *laissez-faire* control of black immigration. The policy prior to the legislation had been, in essence, not to have a policy. No meaningful control or regulation was exercised. Any immigration-related public fears were largely addressed with calls for bi-lateral agreements between Britain, the "Mother Country", and Commonwealth sending countries.[1] Elsewhere, serious consideration of a policy aimed at assisting the black immigrant population already taking root in British cities was not yet on the agenda. Lord Gardiner, the Lord Chancellor in the incoming Labour administration, later described the period up to 1965 in the following terms:

> Just as until 1962 we had no real national plan about immigration, so we had no national plan as to how those who were here were to be integrated or assimilated into the population. (H.L. Deb. 264, 10 March 1965, Col.166)

After 1962 issues of race and "colour" began to permeate inter-party debate to a much greater extent than before the Act. In particular, the Labour Opposition, largely at the call of its Fabian-style leadership, and notably its leader Hugh Gaitskell, contested the need for controls, especially through such draconian legislation. But, the parties' failure to achieve a full consensus on the issue continued until the 1964 General Election, with Labour opposing the renewal of the Act's provisions every autumn after its 1962 enactment.

This early period is particularly significant because it highlights the way in which race and integration issues were, and remained, closely aligned with those of black immigration. This *dualism*, connecting race with immigration, is a thread that runs strongly throughout the "liberal hour" of the 1960s, and indeed served to structure events and public discussion in the 1970s and 1980s. Miles and Phizacklea (1984) identify this process and argue that its roots lay in the late-1950s with the construction of a "race-immigration problem". Whatever its origins, it is apparent that the direction and substance of the progressive "liberal hour" environment was highly conditional upon the maintenance of a favourable immigration climate. An important consequence was the way in which early ideas concerning public policy for the promotion of integretion - alongside the goal of assimilation - were discussed. The 1960s were littered with periodic short-term crises over immigration, and it is as well to remember that this was the backdrop to the genesis of race-related public policy-making in British central and local government.[2]

In his first speech as Labour leader in early-1963, Harold Wilson accentuated the contrasting positions of the two parties on race by firmly committing his party to the introduction of a Bill outlawing selected forms of racial discrimination.[3] Clearly Labour's initial response was one of underlining and reinforcing its own philosophical stand on race, based as it was on its attachment to the ideals of the Commonwealth, anti-colonialism and equality. One interpretation of Labour's stance might focus on aspects of liberal values and general progressive forces - notably socialist internationalism - within the party (Deakin, 1970). Another interpretation might, more cynically, highlight the fact that in the period immediately following the 1962 Act, the issue of black immigration had largely ceased to be salient, thereby allowing "race-liberals" a period of ascendancy in the party.[4]

The favourable political climate on the race issue - for Labour at least - changed during the course of the 1964 General Election. This turnaround was largely the result of events in the West Midlands constituency of Smethwick.[5] The new party of government learnt dramatically of the potentially disastrous impact of the race issue, both in terms of the political climate in general, and its own immediate electoral fortunes in particular. The 'cloud no bigger than a man's hand' described by Deakin (1970: 104) was nonetheless one that had cast a very large and uncomfortable shadow over the direction of policy open to the new Labour administration. Moreover, the shadow cast by this cloud was to fundamentally alter perceptions of how far governments could successfully resist populist pressure putatively hostile to non-white immigration. Both the Labour Government and the Conservative Opposition were put on the defensive on the issue. The Smethwick episode, writes Deakin (1970: 104), was:

> generally seen at the time as a clear expression of popular resentment, frustrated too long by neglect, and acted as an immediate stimulus to action...it intensified pressure on the Government to devise some form of policy which could be put into early effect.

Narrow questions of immigration control and proposals for legislation against discrimination aside, there existed very few points of dispute between the parties. Even on immigration, the Labour Party's opposition to the annual renewal of the 1962 Act was in due course tempered, such that by the 1964 General Election, the Labour Party's manifesto had all but conceded the principle of the "need" for control.[6] Earlier, the party's new leader, Wilson, had suggested a shift in Labour's position when he stated to the House of Commons in November 1963: '[On] the general issue about the control of immigration...we do not contest the need for control of immigration into this country' (H.C. Deb.702, 27 November 1963, Col.1254; quoted in Foot, 1965: 176). All that remained was the question-mark over the form of control, with the party's frontbenchers apparently undecided over the need for legislation, preferring instead the idea of bilateral negotiations with the main sending countries (Foot, 1965: 161-94).

Katznelson (1973) describes the period 1962-64 as one in which the politics of race became "structured" or were made "coherent". The primary purpose behind this structuring, he contends, was the agreement among both parties to build a consensus on this potentially volatile issue 'which, it was hoped, would be capable of relegating race from the political plateau to the valley below' (Katznelson, 1973: 139). This guiding aim can be seen in the words of Roy Hattersley - then a junior Home Office minister - in March 1965, by which time the structuring of the consensus had begun to mature:

> We are all in favour of some sort of limitation. We all wholeheartedly oppose any sort of discrimination. We all wholeheartedly agree that there should be assimiliation or adjustment, whatever word one prefers to use. Those three points of view characterise the views and principles of both major parties. (H.C. Deb. 709, 23 March 1965, Cols. 378-79)

Through these well-chosen words we can clearly see the premise upon which the bi-partisan consensus had been, and was continuing to be, built. The emerging consensus was one on which the reforming initiatives of the new Labour administration would be based and extended. The race consensus triad - based on control, anti-discrimination and integration - had been forged, thereby forming the infrastructure of the liberal reforms and initiatives that were to follow. The Conservatives, whilst in agreement with Labour on the three components highlighted by Hattersley, were largely content to leave the running to liberally-inclined reformers among Labour's ranks. "Race-liberals" nonetheless remained pragmatic and responsive to the potentially damaging consequences of a perceived "loose" immigration policy. The Conservative's over-riding aim, shared with Labour, was the reduction of the saliency of race. Their strategy for the achievement of this aim, however, differed in that it concentrated solely on the 1962 restrictive legislation. As Butler later recalled, the Conservatives 'mistook the effort of 1962 for a solution. We were too complacent'.[7]

The only "integrative" measure in the 1962 legislation, addressing Hattersley's (albeit later stated) third criteria, was the creation of the Commonwealth Immigrants Advisory Council (hereafter CIAC). CIAC was a committee of experts advising the Home Secretary on matters 'affecting the welfare of Commonwealth immigrants in this country and their integration into the community' (Cmnd. 2266: 2), especially in the areas of education, health and housing. According to Katznelson (1973: 146):

> Macmillan's government were convinced that immigration controls and the appointment of an advisory council would adequately de-politicise race and provide for harmonious race relations.

However, as Miles and Phizacklea (1984) have argued, the internal contradictions of this dual strategy, if anything, only increased the likelihood of further complicating and undermining the policy goal of racial harmony. They argue that the strategy amounted to an immigration policy that practised discrimination precisely at the point of entry into British society. Thus, the public claims of the parties, ranging from the repudiation of discrimination to the pronouncement of formal equality, were themselves undermined by this central contradiction. This criticism applied as much to Labour's post-1964 strategy as to that of the Conservatives between 1962-64. To be sure, the philosophical paucity of the two parties' approach to, and execution of, race-related public policy at this time is something that has gone on to plague official strategies on race for over a quarter century. Moreover, it lies deeply embedded in the *liberal framework* for public policy established during this early and influential period.

The remit given to CIAC included examination of the arrangements made by, and powers of, local authorities to assess the sufficiency of welfare programmes for immigrants. The Committee was also supposed to recommend whether 'any further action [could] usefully be taken by the Government to stimulate action by local authorities' (Cmnd. 2266: 2). It was given an important function in terms of laying down the direction and goals of, firstly, local authorities' responsibilities, and secondly, the role of central government in getting town halls to recognise these responsibilities. At this time (1962-64) the precise areas of responsibility of local government in relation to Commonwealth immigrants was undefined. CIAC was supposed to inject a degree of precision and coherence into this new and vacant policy sphere. It both highlighted the Government's early "integration" measures and complemented the remaining, dominant side of its overall strategy, ie. effective controls. CIAC's first report (Cmnd. 2119), published in July 1963, dealt with issues of housing. The second (Cmnd. 2266, February 1964), dealt with education themes, including English language provision, giving tacit support for early dispersal experiments (see also Chapter 5 below). The third (Cmnd. 2458, September 1964), was concerned with the problems of immigrant school-leavers. Through its first three submissions, the only official body responsible for the promotion of racial harmony had already begun to grapple with, and dispense cautious advice on, a number of key areas of local government responsibility. Moreover, all these initiatives took place prior to the change in government in October 1964. The result was that the new Labour administration did not begin its re-assessment of local problems and possible solutions in a complete policy vacuum.

The new Labour administration had the advantage of the early experience of CIAC's investigations and recommendations. CIAC's first three reports had begun to map out the future - as well as current - areas of local conflict in the wake of black immigration. It was becoming increasingly clear that most of the damaging conflicts over race were occurring at the local level.[8] In all three policy spheres examined - housing, education and employment - the issues revolved around competition between black and white community interests for scarce public resources. In the case of the former two policy areas - in which local authorities were forced to play some role due to their statutory obligations as mass providers of these public services - this competition had yielded a very real and immediate sense of crisis. This crisis had emerged both in terms of local authorities' management of the terms of reference of such competition (eg. succumbing to populist anti-immigrant sentiment), and in terms of the rules and procedures they deployed for the effective resolution of such competition (eg. educational and housing dispersal policies).[9] (Chapters 4-6 below explore examples of these local crises in greater detail.)

1964-65: foundations

The second phase of the "liberal hour" ran through the term of Labour's first Home Secretary, Sir Frank Soskice. This period is noted mainly for Labour's change of heart on its immigration policies, especially on the need for formal controls, as well as its steady acceleration of new integration-building measures. I shall briefly consider each of these aspects of Labour's strategy and discuss the extent to which developments in the former tended to influence, if not constrain, developments in the latter.

As Deakin (1965 and 1970) notes, Labour's revised policy on Commonwealth immigration was largely due to the loss of its Shadow Foreign Secretary, Patrick Gordon-Walker, at the hands of the Smethwick electorate in autumn 1964. The party embarked upon a *volte-face* in response. Firstly, the 1962 Act was renewed as an interim measure whilst the Government awaited the outcome of Lord Mountbatten's mission to a number of key Commonwealth capitals. His remit was to seek support for Labour's original preference for bilateral controls.[10] Secondly, Labour was determined not to remain on the defensive on the immigration issue. Thus, the frontbench, and the Prime Minister in particular, launched a combative attack on the Smethwick victor, labelling him a 'Parliamentary leper' for his open use of racist sentiment at the hustings (quoted in Foot, 1965: 66).

This critique of the populist Right was designed to prepare the way for the progressive, liberal measures aimed at promoting racial harmony that were to follow. Nonetheless, Miles and Phizacklea's (1984) critique remains most pertinent at this juncture since the Labour frontbench, by agreeing to renew the 1962 Act, had effectively made themselves hostages to fortune should public anxieties over immigration become salient once more. Labour had begun to lay the foundations of a strategy that was to eventually cost both itself and the bi-partisan concept of racial harmony dearly.

Labour's own race relations strategy was gradually unfolding during this early period in office. In essence little changed. A premium was placed on defusing the explosiveness of the race issue. Where the strategy did appear to be new, this was mainly in terms of its concentration on firstly, building the machinery of conciliation (in its attack on discrimination) and secondly, building the machinery of community relations (in its promotion of racial harmony at the local level). On these initiatives Labour received greater support than opposition from the Conservative frontbench.[11] Thus, the contrast with the previous period of Conservative rule was less than it appeared. The emphasis, as before, was on maintaining the consensus to remove race from party political debate.

The themes of the strategy were essentially threefold. Firstly, in March 1965 the

Prime Minister appointed Maurice Foley, the Labour Member for West Bromwich, as the new minister for immigrants and race relations. Foley's responsibilities would be to examine the general policy instrument of local government in the attempt to build harmonious grassroots community relations. According to the parliamentary statement on his appointment, the new minister would take charge of:

> the co-ordination of effective government action with, and through, local authorities and voluntary bodies to see that speedier action is taken on integration, in the widest sense of the word, in terms of housing, health, education, and everything that needs to be done. (H.C. Deb.708, 9 March 1965, Cols. 248-50)

In fact this was more of a confidence-building exercise by the Prime Minister and Home Secretary, both keen to be seen to be "doing something" to promote goodwill on a sensitive issue. The initiative addressed the integration criteria raised by Hattersley,[12] and other aspects of the strategy included the sponsoring of local community relations efforts. Foley's activities were mainly concerned with carrying out special fact-finding missions to various "troubled" areas on behalf of his ministerial colleagues.[13] The growing body of race and community relations agencies could not claim to have *their* man in government, but it was now reasonable to claim that they had *a* man in government.

Secondly, in April 1965 Labour announced the decision to implement its mainfesto pledge to 'legislate against racial discrimination and incitement in public places' (quoted in Hindell, 1965: 390). The new legislation had been a long time in preparation. The Race Relations Bill was based in part on Fenner Brockway's unsuccessful Bill (introduced annually since 1956) and, more practically, on the drafting efforts of the Martin Committee[14] and the Campaign Against Racial Discrimination (hereafter CARD). The Bill was essentially built around the principle of conciliation. As a result, it soon won a powerful ally in the new Conservative Home Affairs spokesman, Peter Thorneycroft, who was able to persuade the Shadow Cabinet not to oppose the Bill outright. Eventually, all of the Bill's contentious criminal sanctions clauses were thrown out during the committee stage, largely because of Soskice's wish to maintain a bi-partisan front in this sensitive area (H.C. Standing Committee B, 24 June 1965, Cols. 318-44). The Act that finally emerged was a greatly watered-down affair, centred on a 'haphazard, secretive and inefficient process' of conciliation (Hindell, 1965: 405). But, as Deakin (1970: 105) has remarked, 'at least it had provided the initial basis for future measures in this field by establishing an administrative agency in the shape of the Race Relations Board'.

The Act itself concentrated on setting up a machinery for conciliation in cases of alleged discrimination.[15] The conciliation function was carried out by the new Race Relations Board (hereafter RRB), which acted as a "watchdog" and co-ordinating body. Its powers to investigate complaints, however, ran the risk of turning into a sham since, among other weaknesses, it was not empowered through law to compel attendance of witnesses.[16] This weakness, coupled with the fact that the Act did not apply to the employment and housing markets, meant that the cumulative impact of the legislation was marginal. Calvocoressi (1968: 51), writing at about the same time as the Bill was being presented to Parliament, has criticised the Act on these grounds:

> The present Act [1965] goes a very long way indeed in separating conciliation from compulsion. Too far. In my view Parliament failed to distinguish between two kinds of compulsion. There is a difference between compelling a man to desist from discrimination and compelling a man to attend and answer questions in relation to a complaint that has been made about him.

Thirdly, in August 1965 the Government published its long awaited White Paper entitled *Immigration from the Commonwealth* (Cmnd. 2739). As a document spelling out the themes and goals of future public policy, the White Paper was possibly the

30

single most revealing development during this period. Its significance is not just, as its title suggests, in relation to the question of *immigration*, but also in terms of how the even more thorny question of *integration* was to be approached. The White Paper, like the 1962 Act that had gone before it, embodied a *dualism* unique to race relations that sought to combine a strategy on immigration with a strategy on integration. Its rationale was based on strict immigration control being a necessary prior condition of successful integration. It also recognised in a reasonably explicit way that severe social tensions had arisen through black immigration. The White Paper argued that public policy was required to address this reality (Cmnd. 2739: 10):

> At the present time it must be recognised that the presence in this country of nearly one million immigrants from the Commonwealth with different social and cultural backgrounds raises a number of problems and creates various social tensions in those areas where they have concentrated. If we are to avoid the evil of racial strife and if harmonious relations between the races who now form our community are to develop, these problems and tensions must be resolved and removed.

The strategy for the resolution of racial tension involved further restriction on new immigration on one hand, and on the other the creation and expansion of local voluntary efforts aimed at building harmonious race relations. The real thread of the new, publicly-stated official policy was encapsulated by Hattersley, speaking a few months before publication of the White Paper: 'Without integration, limitation is inexcusable; without limitation, integration is impossible'.[17]

The White Paper proposed the reconstitution of the National Committee for Commonwealth Immigrants (hereafter NCCI) as the main measure to bolster integration at the grassroots. NCCI had orginally been set up on the advice of CIAC in February 1964.[18] The White Paper formally laid down the role of the infant NCCI. NCCI was endowed with an expanded budget to enable it to move away from purely national consultative work, and towards building an effective network of local voluntary bodies originally known as Voluntary Liaison Committees (hereafter VLCs).[19] Once again, however, a major actor or institution of public policy on race appeared to be trying to square the circle. That is to say, although NCCI's superficial role of acting as an umbrella body for local VLCs was clear enough, the same could not be said about the precise policy goal NCCI was set to serve. Such a goal was defined in the loosest possible way as the general promotion of harmonious race relations. In short, racial harmony was dubbed the name of the integration game.

The creation and activities of NCCI - and indeed VLCs at the local level - begged the question: how was racial harmony to be promoted and hopefully attained? As Calvocoressi (1968: 53) notes, many of these local bodies were too rigidly locked into traditional, paternalistic conceptions of racial harmony 'radiating goodwill with the benignest of countenances but not being very stern about racial discrimination when they came across it'. Similarly, the ambiguous role of NCCI merely underlined - rather than answered - the above question.[20] Putting the question another way, were they supposed to promote the welfare of immigrants in response to discrimination practiced by society at large, or to play a harmonising tune that sought to alleviate tensions by getting immigrants to blend more effectively into (white) British society? Critics of NCCI, such as Calvocoressi (1968: 53), retorted that the answer was less than clear. They argued that progress could only be made through a clear endorsement of the former interpretation over the latter:

> [This] discrepancy points to a dilemma which lies at the heart of NCCI itself as well as in local groups. NCCI is both a national group concerned with the national weal and a watchdog concerned with the plight of the Commonwealth immigrant minority. Is it meant to soothe the social fabric of the community as a whole or to attack specific abuses in it? Was it meant to do both, and if so, is this possible? It has now...garnered enough experience - and

criticism - to turn back to its *terms of reference* and ponder whether they are the right ones. (Emphasis added)

Other, even sterner, critics saw NCCI as part of a wider exercise to marginalise black immigrants and their potential political demands through "buffer" institutions, ie. VLCs (and later CRCs).[21] It was relatively easy to view NCCI as part and parcel of the long-running bi-partisan agreement to try to de-politicise the race issue. In doing so, the political participation and interests of black immigrants also underwent a process of de-politicisation. The attempt to remove race from politics has been criticised by Hiro (1971: 282) as an ultimately flawed strategy:

> In spite of the continued efforts of the hierarchy of the NCCI to isolate the welfare of the coloured citizens from "politics", this subject remains, in the final analysis, political...The welfare of coloured citizens depends on the *political* decisions of the City Fathers. It is for political reasons that...local councils have been unenthusiastic about liaison committees and community relations councils. (Emphasis in original)

The disbelievers were not restricted to commentators and activists outside the NCCI-VLC infrastructure. The possibility of NCCI following potentially contradictory paths was not lost on members of the Committee itself. A sense of ambiguity existed as to the proper function of NCCI and VLCs. Moreover, these doubts extended to the philosophical conceptualisation of key terms of the emerging liberal policy framework, such as "liaison" and "integration", and so on. Questions remained unanswered as to the purpose of liaising between the black and white communities, as well as over the definition of "integration" that these bodies were supposed to be working towards. As the Committee later commented just before its supersession in late-1968:

> The National Committee and the Voluntary Liaison Committees have to steer the most difficult course of all. The concept [of] "liaison" indicates the tightrope on which they must walk. Success depends on retaining the confidence of the authorities in order that one's views will be heeded when it comes to policy-making. No less important is the confidence of the immigrants. (NCCI, 1968: 14)

By the close of the highly active year of 1965, an embryonic Race Relations Act was on the statute book and an important White Paper had been published. In addition, by renewing the 1962 Immigration Act, the Labour Government had effectively adopted a restrictionist line on black immigration.[22] A great deal of activity had already taken place and yet it was still early days in the era of reform. The biggest single instigator of liberal reform had yet to make his mark. In December 1965 Roy Jenkins was appointed as the new Home Secretary. Arguably, liberally-inclined race and community relations activists now looked to Jenkins as *their* man in government. Judging by the pace and scope of the new Home Secretary's early initiatives - in tone as well as content - they were not to be disappointed. The "liberal hour" in British race relations had fully dawned.

1965-68: maturity

In many ways it is difficult to present an account of this era in race relations without acknowledging the weighty contribution of Roy Jenkins, both in terms of his fresh political approach, and in terms of his own personality.[23] An early manifestation of Jenkins' liberal approach was in his choice of Mark Bonham-Carter as the first chairman of the newly created Race Relations Board. Bonham-Carter, for his part, stipulated that his appointment was conditional upon being able to submit a detailed evaluation of both the Board and the 1965 Act to the Home Secretary after an initial year in the job.[24] Jenkins' willingness to take a bolder, higher profile in his new job meant that an on-going evaluation of legislation was clearly placed high on the agenda from an early point. The principal reason behind this evaluation, of course, was Jenkins' careful tactical preparation of the ground for an extension of the 1965 Act at the earliest suitable moment.

The shift towards a more liberal climate however, was soon tempered by the Government's decision in late-1965 to renew (again) the provisions of the 1962 Act. It was becoming increasingly clear that an intellectual and practical gap in the overall direction of race relations policy had to be filled. The Government could either continue on its present course and manage the race issue in a reactive, *ad hoc* fashion or, as Jenkins was to attempt, address itself to overall strategic policy aims as well as solutions. The opportunity came in Jenkins' address to an audience of members and officers of VLCs organised by NCCI in May 1966. The Home Secretary turned his attention to the concept of an 'integrated multi-racial society', defining this broad policy goal in terms of the key concept of 'equal opportunity' (Jenkins, 1966: 215). Jenkins' speech signalled a clear vision of the strategic direction he intended for the various items of liberal reform, both current and planned. Furthermore, the pluralist emphasis placed on a notion of "tolerance" undoubtedly set the tone - both in rhetoric and practice - of the broader liberal settlement that was to remain the lasting feature of race relations beyond this period. Jenkins and his supporters were now set on an intellectual and practical experiment in social policy that contrasted sharply with the tone of the earlier debate on race. The achievements under Soskice had in fact been the evolutionary next step of the post-1962 race consensus. The initiatives that were about to take place under Jenkins, although born of that same consensus, nonetheless sought to attain a series of somewhat different and more challenging goals.

The important thing to remember about this era, of course, was Jenkins' success in being able to carry the triad of his governing party, the Opposition, and a sufficiently large section of élite opinion with him. This success was doubly significant since Jenkins proposed to address reform issues - for example, the extension of anti-discrimination legislation into employment and housing markets - that had previously not been a part of the cautious bi-partisan consensus. Both liberalisation and de-politicisation were well under way during 1966-67, and Jenkins' main contribution lay in giving these processes a significant boost. Jenkins was both diverging from the implicit consensus and, ironically, attempting to reinforce its essential character.

Possibly the most significant long-term legislative change to take place under Jenkins was his successful inclusion of a special clause in an otherwise unrelated piece of legislation. Section 11 of the Local Government Act 1966 (hereafter S.11) sanctioned a 75 per cent central government subsidy to local authorities in respect of immigrant-related public services, and fulfilled a long-standing commitment by Labour to allocate new resources to town halls facing heavy demand for such forms of service delivery.[25] S.11's original purpose was to help fund special English language tuition for immigrant children but since the late-1960s its scope and scale has grown massively. Revised guidelines introduced in the early-1980s has enabled S.11 monies to be directed at ethnic minority-related service delivery in general and not, as the original "ten year rule" did, to "first generation" immigrants alone.[26] The S.11 reform can be seen in terms of a broader concern which tried to place the demands made by ethnic minorities on local public service delivery into a series of specially constructed and marginalised policy measures. The notion of discrete, race-related public policy programmes had clearly arrived by the mid-1960s with the passage of S.11. These programmes, Jenkins and his supporters hoped, would signal the way forward.

A similar picture emerges at this time through the general rise of the community relations movement, and the specific institutional reforms of the CRC organisational structure, eg. in 1965 and 1968. In the case of S.11, town halls were not just given special subsidies for their programmes, but, more significantly, Whitehall was keen to encourage a greater degree of responsibility for such programmes by local government. The CRC infrastructure was also reformed and reinforced at this time, with the emphasis clearly on encouraging voluntary effort (eg. the 1965 White Paper and the 1968 legislation). Moreover, CRCs were both supported directly by the centre and, equally importantly, encouraged to work alongside local authorities in their all-important voluntary, confidence-building initiatives. The prevailing ethos was one which tried to devolve responsibility downwards in the hope that the volatile character of the race issue would effectively disappear from the national political stage. In this process we can observe the genesis of a leading role for local government in race relations, one which was to be capped a decade later through the Race Relations Act 1976.[27]

In many ways the race relations "lobby" could not have been better led than by Jenkins. His reputation both for an astute sense of timing and the art of the possible in politics made for an engaging and inspiring leadership. He was quick to exploit the favourable political climate on the immigration issue in order to introduce various confidence-building measures to improve the climate further. The only criticism of his tactics was that he only aimed to exploit the window of opportunity on the immigration issue. Consequently, he allowed his entire liberal strategy to become a hostage to fortune on the issue - something which critics such as Hiro (1971) charge, may not necessarily have happened had he challenged the populist basis of the immigration debate itself. For example, although Jenkins had provisionally decided to proceed with a second round of anti-discrimination legislation soon after he took office, he had also correctly sensed that the impending second general election (and Labour's return) could not be risked by hasty action. A typically Jenkinsite rule-of-thumb prevailed: controversial legislation should come early, rather than later, in the life of a second (secure) parliament.

Jenkins spent the early part of his period as Home Secretary (from late-1965 to the second general election in spring 1966) preparing the way for the new Bill he was set on pursuing in the new parliament. Detailed preparation was needed in order to amass sufficient ammunition for the anticipated battle to secure its passage. The fruits of four examples of such behind-the-scenes work emerged during 1966-67, interspersed either side of the July 1967 announcement of new legislation. Firstly, the Street Report was published in October 1967, examining anti-discrimination practice in the United States and its relevance for British race relations (Street *et al.*, 1967).[28] This important document provided powerful evidence that an extensive framework of law could be effectively used even in sensitive areas such as race relations. Secondly, in April 1967 an independent research body, Political and Economic Planning (hereafter PEP), published an equally influential report on the extent of racial discrimination in British society (PEP, 1967).[29] According to Heinemann (1972: 136), the PEP Report 'demonstrated clearly that discrimination was not a defensive fantasy in the minds of interested parties...but a harsh reality scarring British life'. Thirdly, Jenkins' strategy clearly required the endorsement of a representative black "umbrella" body 'which could both speak for the victims and act as an informed critic of the status quo' (Deakin, 1970: 115). In the absence of any better alternatives, Jenkins called on his supporters among the CARD pressure group to perform this role, which many of its leading members did most effectively.[30] Finally, additional liberal allies were called upon to give support to the idea of extending the law. Thus, from late-1966 onwards a number of influential press leader-writers began to subtly endorse Jenkins' views on the need for a new Bill as the only effective redress against a major social evil.[31]

Inevitably, both in terms of substance as well as personnel, many of these liberal reformist pressures were inter-related and overlapping. Together, they made for a climate in which the onus was on Jenkins' conservative critics to publicly argue the case against extending the framework of law. Such a climate ensured that racial discrimination was labelled as a major social evil by a variety of related sources, whilst racial harmony was rapidly emerging as what Banton (1985: 69-98) describes as a 'public good'. Furthermore, the emerging policy on race was part and parcel of a wider vision in which 'Jenkins set out his criteria for a civilised bourgeois socialism' (Deakin, 1970: 108). The weight of rational argument and evidence was lined up on the side of arresting a social evil and promoting a public good. Meanwhile, the favourable immigration climate meant that conservative critics found themselves on the defensive on the race issue as a result of a combination of domestic liberal lobbies and external migration flows.

The movement of public opinion during 1967 was crucial to both the success of the Bill, and the future credibility of Jenkins and the whole liberal ethos of the debate on race. The concurrent events taking place in urban areas of the USA during the hot summer of 1967 proved to be another powerful force in the debate. A superficial sense of alarm was engendered by the nightly television broadcasts of a society in the grip of racial turmoil. Despite this ominous shadow, liberals were not prepared to be put on the defensive. In fact, many utilised the example as an argument in favour of recognising and tackling racial discrimination and disadvantage before it was "too late". Support for this line of argument was even found on the Opposition benches from the Conservative Member for Chelmsford, Norman St John-Stevas, who characteristically lectured the House on the merits of the enlightened liberal argument: 'Let us not be Bourbons' he said, 'and let us learn cheaply and vicariously from the experience of others' (H.C. Deb.735, 8 November 1966, Col. 1252).

However, by the autumn of 1967 it was apparent that dark clouds threatened the legitimacy of the "liberal hour" from all around. A subtle deterioration in the mood of the debate on race relations appeared to be coming about. A number of precipitating factors were behind this shift, although opinion is sharply divided on the relative importance of each.[32] It is worthwhile surveying a few of the most commonly cited developments, although it is less than clear whether these factors were symptoms or causes of the eventual demise of the "liberal hour".

The case of CARD is illustrative. By mid-1967 several serious and damaging internal political battles within the pressure group had begun to get out of hand, resulting in a series of public splits, coups, counter-coups, and the possibility of dissolution. Additionally, new internal alliances began to emerge which differed from earlier factionalism between radicals and moderates. Heinemann (1972: 161-211) notes that an Afro-Caribbean camp begun to line up against an Anglo-Asian camp, culminating in the venomous November 1967 national convention. CARD, a leading lobbying force within the liberal-reforming consensus, had begun to openly splinter and collapse - an ominous sign of what lay ahead for the "liberal hour" more generally. A "political obituary" in *The Guardian* (4 December 1967) commented:

> [This is] the silliest dispute of the decade. The change could not have come at a worse time. With the draft of the government's new anti-discrimination laws about to be published, there is an urgent need for effective lobbying to see that strong and practical legislation is passed this time. Only the opponents of racial equality in Britain can benefit from this split in CARD.

Potentially much more serious than the factional fighting within an élite pressure group, was the resurgence in late-1967 of the old immigration debate-cum-panic. The "Africanisation" policies of President Kenyatta of Kenya lay behind this latest immigration scare. The result was that the backdrop to the winter-spring debate on the Race Relations Bill, was the growing menace of reactionary, anti-immigrant sentiment at both mass and élite levels. This sentiment climaxed with Enoch Powell's own dramatic intervention on 20 April 1968 in which he likened his own vantage point over impending British racial conflict with that of the Roman centurion witnessing the bloody demise of an earlier empire. The crisis immediately provided the Conservative Right with powerful ammunition both to reinforce the dualism of the "race-immigration problem", as well as to challenge the basis of the liberal assumptions about race relations that had generally prevailed for the previous five years.

The sudden buoyancy of the Right in response to the Kenyan-Asian crisis illustrated the underlying weakness and fragility of the liberal consensus. In a related episode, the provocative public remarks of Duncan Sandys MP, a former Conservative frontbencher,[33] only served to demonstrate the impotence of existing legislation. The Sandys dispute sharply highlighted the obvious limitations of existing anti-discrimination legislation and gave added credence to both radical *and* conservative critics of the liberal consensus. The "liberal hour" was openly under attack from every direction.

For a brief spell the Government's nerve held in the face of the crisis. Jenkins signalled his perseverance to battle on, though in both tone and content his emphasis was on past, rather than future, achievements. The mid-November 1967 Commons debate on the renewal of the 1962 Immigration Act illustrated this attitude. Although he did not know it, the debate was Jenkins' last public contribution to race relations as Home Secretary (in the 1964-70 Wilson adminstration at least).[34] The substance of the debate was remarkable in many ways, most notably because it was one of the last occasions on which a genuine bi-partisan consensus on race existed (on the floor of the House of Commons at least). Lengthy and flattering compliments were traded between Jenkins and his opposite number, Quinton Hogg. The main speeches of the debate were largely constructive in that they focused on "integration" issues. However, the real clue lay in the debate's general concern for past integration measures, rather than on the much more difficult question of how such goals were to be pursued in the future under an altogether less favourable immigration climate. For Labour's part, the threatening immigration crisis was - at this stage - responded to with little more than the publicly-stated hope that it might resolve itself in time (H.C. Deb.754, 15 November 1967, Cols.453-73). The arguments of Government politicians in defence of the concept of a multi-racial, integrated society carried little more conviction than their line on the immigration crisis. Few believed that the ethos of the "liberal hour" would last much longer.

The third, and most important, phase of the race relations "liberal hour" finally came to a close in late-November 1967 when its figurehead and greatest public champion, Jenkins, was replaced as Home Secretary by James Callaghan. A new and ultimately final phase in the "liberal hour" had thus begun.

Post-1968: demise

In a sense, the final "quarter-hour" deals with the period following Jenkins' departure until the end of the Labour Government. It is not however necessary to concern ourselves with the entire period up to the 1970 General Election. Instead, the developments of 1968 are particularly important, most notably the Kenyan-Asian immigration crisis and rise of Powellism, and the passage of the second Race Relations Act. The nature of these events confirm the view that the "liberal hour" had effectively run out of steam by the autumn of 1968.

The most significant aspect of the Kenyan-Asian crisis was undoubtedly the long-awaited opportunity it gave to Enoch Powell[35] and his supporters. The most immediate outcome of his series of speeches beginning in early-1968 was a massive increase in the saliency of race and immigration. In a few short months much of what Jenkins and his supporters had spent years lobbying for appeared to be lost. Not only had the climate changed, but more seriously, the underlying values and assumptions about race relations were suddenly under concerted attack from a number of sources ranging from the conservative to the reactionary (Powell, 1969; Nairn, 1974). In the event, many specific policy initiatives - such as anti-discrimination legislation and special provision for areas of high immigrant settlement - emerged from the Powellite whirlwind, severely frayed at the edges and on the defensive in terms of public opinion.

Against this background, the Government introduced two further liberalising reforms, one expected and one not. The first was the successful passage of the second Race Relations Act, though not without a long and bitter parliamentary fight.[36] Apart from extending the scope of the 1965 Act into the employment, housing and insurance markets, its other main feature was wholesale reform of the local community relations infrastructure. Local race harmony-building initiatives had previously been an aspect of the 1965 Act, though not a very important one. The entire VLC structure and its relationship with a central, umbrella-cum-"watchdog" body was now overhauled. RRB and NCCI were both abolished and replaced by a single body, the Community Relations Commission. The Commission took over both the "watchdog", quasi-legal role of the former, and the grassroots VLC co-ordinating role of the latter. Moreover, its powers and relationships over these two areas of responsibility were also revised. For instance, the Commission was allocated a much larger budget to enable it to directly fund, and get more closely involved in, the work being discharged at local level by VLCs (now renamed community relations councils).[37]

The second major reform initiative of 1968, unlike the Race Relations Act, had not been on the cards for much more than a few months - perhaps weeks - prior to its announcement. The Prime Minister's May Day speech announced the launch of a major new item of social policy, the Urban Programme (hereafter UP), to be administered in conjunction with local government (Wilson, 1968). This new initiative was basically designed to fuse together a variety of central-local funding programmes that were based on a selection of special criteria, one of which was defined as a "substantial" local immigrant population. In fact, at first the Programme was a rather crude, half-baked instrument of social policy, both in its terms of reference and its overall policy goals. Its birth was largely due to the Government's - and essentially the Prime Minister's - determination not to be outflanked by the popular appeal of Powellism. Wilson publicly stated that the new policy proposed a funding arrangement that sought to offset some of the underlying tensions between racial groups in depressed inner city areas.[38]

Both of these Government initiatives resembled hangovers from the by-now fading "liberal hour". Each illustrated the extent to which liberal values and assumptions about race relations had come under attack by 1968. The turnaround in the fortunes of these values and assumptions had been dramatic. Beyond 1968 the energies and skills of race-liberals were deployed in battles against conservatives - as well as reactionaries - proposing rival conceptual frameworks based on alternative values and assumptions about race relations. The main focus of Jenkins' tenure had been the consolidation and extension of the liberal race policy experiment. The future now lay in the altogether more explosive arena of combatting conservative values and counter assumptions, whilst simultaneously keeping the lid on simmering racial tension. Quintin Hogg, the Conservative's moderate frontbench spokesman on race relations, remarked that the ascendancy of Powell's arguments was analogous to 'flicking ash in a roomful of gunpowder' (H.C. Deb.763, 23 April 1968, Cols.67-81). Politicians and their supporters who had previously identified with the tone and content of the "liberal hour" were, by mid-1968, pre-occupied with a more immediate task - namely, to ensure that no-one lit an unwelcome match, and if they did, to smother the flame before it led to unimaginable racial strife.

The "liberal hour" had come to a close on a disappointing note. Many of the high expectations of a few years earlier had been dashed. The mood of British race relations was not only moving sharply to the populist Right, but the underlying values and assumptions of the "liberal hour" were also under threat. This sea-change notwithstanding, the most important contribution of the "liberal hour" era lay in the broader conceptual framework for race-related public policy that had taken root in national and local politics. The period between the early- and late-1960s had been critical to the development of a *liberal policy framework* in Britain, a framework that would underpin subsequent debates on the future course of race-related public policy.

The "liberal hour" and the policy framework

This section will consider the nature of the local, race-related public policy framework that was both created and legitimised during the "liberal hour". This framework, in turn, went on to dominate local race initiatives for more than twenty years. The "liberal hour" demonstrated a number of the key dimensions around which race-related public policy would be organised and evolve over the following two decades. The main thrust of this study is to describe and explain the experience of local politics and government in the context of the liberal settlement (see also the discussion in Chapters 7 and 8 below). It aims to map out the theoretical and conceptual nature of the policy framework for race relations in general and local government race-related practice in particular.

There are four significant features of the liberal settlement that require further discussion. These features are the essential components of the arena of local political debate and conflict over race-related public policy, termed in this study as the *race policy environment* (hereafter RPE).

A multi-racial society

The central conceptual basis of the liberal settlement was that of a multi-racial society. Explanation of this concept is not necessarily to restate the terms and events of the "liberal hour" as done above. The 1960s' episode was an experiment in social policy. Beneath this experiment however, lay a larger picture of an emerging racially- and ethnically-plural Britain society. The basis of the initiatives of Jenkins and others was undoubtedly a quasi-intellectual vision of the nature of British society in the wake of large-scale black immigration. This vision was probably best illustrated by Jenkins' own description of a multi-racial society stated to NCCI in May 1966, the nub of which was a subtle rejection of the "melting pot" principle (Jenkins, 1966).[39]

The key achievements of the "liberal hour" - notably two instalments of anti-discrimination legislation - were doubly significant in that "liberal hour" enthusiasts appeared to win tactical victories *without* any significant strategic advances. That is to say, the advances secured in outlawing certain forms of discrimination, building a VLC/CRC network, and placing selected duties on local authorities, were really more to do with immediate political arguments in favour of redressing a newly-indentified social evil. The process only fleetingly touched on wider questions about the nature and shape of a multi-racial society, and even then with few lasting gains for supporters of Jenkins' multi-racial vision. In that sense, it should be noted that Jenkins' conception of race policy was, at the very least, rather different to that of others in his party, the Opposition and the press and public. The former's broad vision of race and ethnicity in the public policy process can be contrasted with the latter's more narrow vision.

In the longer term, the concept of a multi-racial society has not become any clearer in the minds of local and national policy-makers alike. The concept remains one of the great undefined terms of British social policy in recent years: a single conceptual term with a variety of confusing, and possibly contradictory, interpretations. To be sure, policy actors throughout local politics and government usually have little difficulty in immediately recognising the language and essence of the liberal settlement. And yet the bulk of local conflict over race policy continues to be centred on basic disagreements over what a multi-racial society should - or should not - look like (see also empirical evidence of such disagreements in Chapters 4, 5 and 6 below).

Racial harmony as a public good

Banton (1985: 69-98) argues that the most significant achievement of the "liberal hour" lay in establishing a conception of racial harmony as a public good. This concept, he suggests, is comparable with the public good of pollution-free air derived through the earlier ecological and environmental debate surrounding the 1956 Clean Air Act. However, the flip-side of this concept was a narrow, short-term understanding of racial harmony. This understanding was anti-discriminatory in tone and substance, but remarkably silent on issues relating to racial equality. The interest of politicians and their supporters lay in a social problem and its short-term solution through a policy instrument based largely on local voluntary effort. This short-term perspective did not extend either to the longer-term efficacy of that policy instrument, nor to the constraints for racial equality-oriented issues that would be encountered in local politics.

Equality and harmony were not fully recognised as concepts - let alone goals - that might involve public policy-makers in awkward choices. Moreover, where such choices could not be avoided, it was usually the larger, more universally familiar notion of racial harmony that triumphed. The events of the "liberal hour" in particular are littered with endorsements of the ideal of racial harmony, without any significant understanding of the existence of inequality and its potentially disharmonious consequences. The liberal settlement implicitly either confused these two goals or else superficially associated them with one another. The consequences were to be felt all too dramatically in local race policy conflict.

The systematic ambiguity of policy actors towards these two policy goals may help to answer the question raised by Banton (1985: vii-x): why has the output of the "race relations industry" been so disappointing in relation to its input over the past quarter century? He poses a number of possible answers, all touching on different aspects of the nature of the debate over race policy. This study argues that such disappointment is best understood when the terms or framework of race policy are set out and compared with the expectations or inputs of policy.

At a general level, there has been a failure to understand the conceptual nature of the goal of a harmonious multi-racial society that underpinned Jenkins' and others' initiatives during the "liberal hour". This failure has subsequently been reflected in the arguments of critics of the "liberal hour". Some of the most common of these criticisms are considered by Banton (1985: 121-31); they include *inter alia*: the aims and conduct of the personnel of the "race industry"; the anticipated speed of minority and majority adjustment; the decisiveness of central government action; the resistance of white citizens to limited government action; and finally, the problems involved in fitting a race policy into an established administrative system designed to serve an ethnically-homogeneous population (see also Chapter 7 below). All of these specific criticisms can be placed within wider critiques of the "liberal hour" consensus and policy framework. The framework, for instance, put forward a strategy that sought to attain a "social peace" using a blend of local voluntary initiatives and a devolved role for local government. Specific questions, such as those highlighted by Banton (1985: vii-x), remained unanswered. Instead, the emphasis fell on assigning readily-available policy instruments with the task of attaining racial harmony-oriented policy goals. Thus, the assorted agencies of "community relations", together with their (sometime) town hall sponsors, were effectively put into the frontline of creating and regulating a multi-racial society. Such a society was to be first-of-all in harmony, and only secondly, equal.

This assignment of tasks reflects what appears to have been at the very least a serious ambiguity about two distinct, yet related, overall goals of policy: between racial harmony on one hand and racial equality on the other. That is not to say one goal necessarily or consciously supplanted the other, but rather that there was a poor understanding of the distinction between them. Indeed, as the empirical chapters demonstrate, the ethos of VLC/CRC activists throughout the 1960s and 1970s has been the pursuit of the former as a means or route to the latter.

The philosophy of "community relationsism"

A key instrument of policy - as seen during the central debate led by Jenkins and others - was to be the encouragement and development of a local community relations movement.[40] Messina (1987) and other, more radical, commentators (Ben-Tovim *et al.*, 1986: 82-95; Hiro, 1971: 279-85; Katznelson, 1973: 175-88) have all convincingly argued that VLCs/CRCs should be viewed as an attempt to defuse or de-politicise race by its devolution into marginalised, "buffer" bodies. The community relations initiative was closely allied to the creation of harmony in local grassroots race relations. Both VLCs and later CRCs were supposed to fill a local vacuum for black political activism, thereby limiting the impact of race issues on local political systems.

An analogy can be drawn at the national level where NCCI and its successors (the Community Relations Commission, 1968-77, and the Commission for Racial Equality (hereafter CRE), post-1977) have often been described pejoratively as a "cover" for government inactivity on race (Ben-Tovim and Gabriel, 1982). According to the Runnymede Trust's evidence to the 1975 House of Commons Select Committee on Race and Immigration's investigation of the administration of race relations in Britain:

> The central failure has been not to define the nature of Government concern with race relations, not to clarify the objectives of policy and not to assess the

scope and potential Government failure...there has been *no driving force* at the centre. Everyone thought that because you had the Community Relations Commission you had a policy. (H.C. 448-III, 1975: 234-42 - emphasis added)

Hiro (1971), Hill and Issacharoff (1971) and Katznelson (1973) all point to the persistent failure to set out the goals and jurisdiction of VLCs/CRCs. For one thing, the leadership of many EMGs felt that they were participating in local VLCs/CRCs as a means towards redressing their communities' grievances over discrimination and subsequent cumulative disadvantage. However, Katznelson (1973: 177) is probably closest to the mark when he notes that the 1965 White Paper institutionalised the "buffer" relationship between Commonwealth immigrants and their white "hosts". Yet NCCI and VLCs/CRCs were still expected to perform the somewhat distinct task of speaking for the ethnic minorities. The dual role expected of these community relations bodies proved to be frustrating and impossible to reconcile. NCCI, for its part, saw its own role and that of the VLCs/CRCs in no uncertain terms:

> It should be emphasised that this is not a committee to serve the interests of one section of the community but a committee to promote racial harmony. It is therefore beneficial to all. (NCCI, 1967)

Meanwhile, radicals within CARD criticised the whole ethos of the NCCI-centred race relations strategy. Writing at the height of the CARD split, Nandy (1967b: 6) argued that '[NCCI] has generated an atmosphere of superficial liberalism and generalised goodwill. Its characteristic style is paralysis and non-statement'.

Therefore, serious ambiguities existed and have persisted in conceptions of "community relations" and its principal agencies. This ambiguity has been felt particularly sharply at the local level among the main policy actors involved in race issues such as local authorities, EMGs and, of course, VLCs/CRCs themselves. The failure to clearly designate roles and aims for the community relations movement has contributed to undermining the credibility of liberal conceptions of a multi-racial society. The loss of credibility has been registered most sharply amongst those who argued the case for a local machinery to tackle the symptoms - if not always the causes - of racial disharmony during the 1960s, ie. local VLC/CRC activists.

The philosophy of "community relationsism" became one of the key foundation stones upon which Jenkins and others built the early framework for public policy on race. It was also one of the major instruments of such public policy. However, in both conceptual and actual terms, it soon came to be seen as an excuse for policy. This view was felt most notably in many local communities, thereby accelerating the relegation of the philosophy of "community relationsism" to the periphery of the local politics of race during the late-1970s and 1980s.

De-politicising race

A distinctive feature of the 1960s' race consensus was the major political parties' desire to remove race from the national political platform. Thus, a series of processes were implemented to devolve responsibility as well as much of the debate over race to other bodies and policy settings. The rise of the community relations movement is an example of this process. Whitehall was equally keen to build a partnership with town halls on race (the 1965 White Paper and the 1965 Race Relations Act both confirmed this tendancy). In the first instance, this move towards "localism" involved trying to get greater awareness of, and support for, local VLCs/CRCs from local authorities. Later, this initiative was extended to establishing a formal funding relationship between the centre and periphery on race: eg. the S.11 programme. Later still, the second Race Relations Act directly encouraged town halls in their VLC/CRC-sponsorship role. Finally, this process was capped through the third Race Race Relations Act which formally laid down a number of general promotional duties for town halls.

Beneath this institutional devolvement of day-to-day responsibility, there were three concurrent processes taking place. Firstly, the centre (notably the governing party of the day) was keen to absolve itself of primary responsibility for the management of race relations at the grassroots. Secondly, there was a realisation that racial harmony was not a policy goal well suited to central management; at most an approximate, though loose, co-ordinating role could be assigned to a NCCI-type body. Thirdly, the institutions of local government and VLCs/CRCs were looked upon as potentially suitable bodies for the management of the difficult responsibility of ensuring racial harmony.

However, two caveats must be added to any impressions of coherence in the centre's early race relations strategy. Firstly, local government and local VLCs/CRCs effectively found themselves *pushed* into the frontline as a consequence of the centre's reluctance to allow race to become a legitimate national issue. Secondly, local government was *not* well-equipped for, nor welcoming of, its new-found prominence in the new local environment for race policy (this point will be returned to in Chapter 7 below).

A race policy environment

The shift of emphasis away from central policy-making processes and towards "localism", coupled with policy goal ambiguity, effectively gave rise to a new environment for race policy. This environment was local in nature and made up of many of the relevant policy actors found in local politics and government. Moreover, the race dimension meant that foremost among the community organisations active in the race policy environment (hereafter RPE) were VLCs/CRCs. Additionally, many EMGs came to play an increasingly prominent and conspicuous role (see also Chapters 4, 5 and 6 below).

The RPE therefore amounted to, and may be defined as, a locally-constructed race relations constellation of interests (Rhodes, 1985). This definition involves a number of things. To begin with, a RPE will emerge in those urban areas in which various interests either coalesce on certain issues or, as has been the case more routinely, compete for dominance in terms of shaping the areas of legitimate concern for local policy debate. Most commonly these RPE interests will include: CRC activists and officers; local authority race-related "policy-professionals" of one form or another (often housed within distinctive race bureaucracies of some kind); other local authority professionals who have been co-opted into race-related service delivery programmes (often in areas such as housing and education); the political party "bosses" or leaderships and party groups of local government (often representing sharply contrasting perspectives on areas of legitimate and non-legitimate concern for the RPE). Additionally, there are EMG interests of contrasting character and background that have also come to play an increasingly prominent role in CRCs and local government. The involvement of EMGs is a frequently overlooked aspect of the local RPE in the established literature (see also Chapter 2 above).

The important point to make about the RPE "constellation" is that its *organisational coherence* represents the central variable - both dependent and independent - utilised in this study (see also Chapter 8 below). It is through its various participants that contrasting conceptions of "harmony", "equality", "community relations", etc. are advanced. Debate and conflict over various race policy concepts will take place both across, as well as within, different groups or categories of RPE participants. That is to say, it is just as common to come across local politicians debating in favour of their different respective conceptual understandings of say, "community relations", as it is to locate similar debate between CRC officers and EMG leaders.

The RPE therefore allows us to explore not just narrow conflict between policy actors over policy processes and outcomes, but also broader conflict over what race-related public policy is and is not. The common theme is the degree and scope of rival, and occasionally contradictory, *conceptualisations* of race and public policy in general, and race and local government service delivery issues in particular. Many conflicts over race policy can often be explained in terms of how, and the extent to which, different

41

policy actors have conceptualised race. The RPE variable must therefore also allow for variance along this dimension (see also Chapter 8 below for further discussion of the conceptualisation of race in public policy).

Conclusion

This chapter has outlined the main conceptual and theoretical themes that will be explored in greater detail in the following chapters. The themes are discussed with reference to an empirical examination of two outer London boroughs over a twenty-one year period. My purpose is to chart the emergence of the local RPE in the mid-1960s, and to document and assess its development until the mid-1980s.

The basic argument of this chapter has been to highlight the influence of the developments of the "liberal hour" in creating a policy framework which has structured local race policy experience. That said, the relationship between race and public policy in recent years has been shifting to a new, as yet partially-defined, conceptual framework. The lessons of the public policy mould created during the "liberal hour", whilst *crucial* to any understanding of local race policy experience, are decreasingly relevant to local government race policy practice. The following chapters seek to document and explain the gradual movement of ideas and practice starting from the near-hegemony of the original liberal framework some twenty or thirty years ago, to a more heterogeneous state of competition between rival conceptual frameworks in recent years. The liberal policy framework remains the most relevant to the terms of this study. However, we are also concerned with the ebb and flow between the values and assumptions of the liberal settlement and those of "conservative" and "radical" policy frameworks. The relationship between the RPE and these various conceptual frameworks is returned to in the concluding chapter.

Notes

1. For an extended discussion of the 1962 Commonwealth Immigrants Bill, see Deakin, 1970. Deakin also places emphasis on the support for the idea of a multi-racial Commonwealth within Labour circles in the late-1950s and early-1960s. This support was coupled with a commitment to socialist internationalism popular on the Left of the party, and centred on the "link" with Nehru's India. This relationship is examined in a study of Labour MPs' positions on socialist foreign and international policy by Bartholomew *et al.*, 1961.

2. These periodic mini-crises (for the period 1948-65) are best documented by Foot, 1965: 124-94.

3. In fact the party had been formally committed to making discrimination illegal since 1958; see Labour Party, 1958. This became party policy endorsed by conference in 1962; see Labour Party, 1962.

4. The publications and activities of the Fabian Society stand out in particular as examples of pre-1962 liberal-inclined thinking in the Labour Party. In addition, revisionists in the party during this period were busy constructing a vision of growth-oriented socialism in which manpower shortages had to be planned for and negotiated through Commonwealth immigration; see Crosland, 1956 and Jenkins, 1959.

5. For a helpful and detailed case study of the electoral contest in Smethwick, see Deakin, 1965: 77-105.

6. A key proponent for modification of the party's policy on immigration was its Shadow Foreign Secretary, Patrick Gordon-Walker, who was later rebuffed by the Smethwick electorate in 1964. His own revisionist-pragmatic views on race and Commonwealth issues in general, and the need for bi-lateral controls in particular, were set out in Gordon-Walker, 1962: 390.

7. R.A. Butler interview with Katznelson, 1973: 146.

8. Local level tension was mostly experienced in service delivery areas such as education and housing. This tension was first recognised officially through the 1965 White Paper and a Department of Education and Science circular of the same year; see Cmnd. 2739 and DES, 1965.

9. Chapter 5 in particular examines local educational service delivery in general and the dispersal episode in particular in Ealing Borough from the late-1950s to early-1980s. For an alternative account of the bussing episode in Ealing, see Messina, 1984 (especially Chapter 4).

10. Mountbatten's mission to the Commonwealth capitals was conceived of shortly before the New Year, and was designed to seek support for bi-lateral controls on immigrant numbers in rough accordance with growth rates in the British economy. However, by June 1965 it was quite clear that the mission had failed to exact any firm promises or deals to restrict numbers in such a way. The White Paper of August 1965 contained the Government's response to the situation. The situation was becoming increasingly awkward to manage since not only had bi-lateralism been firmly ruled out, but Conservatives led by Selwyn Lloyd were looking for even more draconian controls; see Kaufman, 1965.

11. At least one of the explanations for the Conservative's conditional support for the strategy was because of the party's own attachment to the ideals of Commonwealth in the post-colonial era. This argument is put forward at length by Horowitz, 1970.

12. Hattersley had been speaking in a debate initiated by Thorneycroft for the Conservatives on general race and immigration themes. Soskice closed the debate by saying: 'there has been...a very great deal of unanimity on the broad aspects of the problem with which we are faced', H.C. Deb. 709, 23 March 1965, Col. 443.

13. Foley's first fact-finding visit in his new ministerial capacity was to Southall in the London Borough of Ealing (west London) in March 1965. Interestingly, Foley's appointment was as a Parliamentary Under-Secretary at the recently-established Department of Economic Affairs, a choice thought to be a reflection of George Brown's close interest in the area of immigration; see Katznelson, 1973: 148.

14. The Martin Committee was a Sub-Committee of the Society of Labour Lawyers dealing with racial discrimination matters. Its chairman was Professor Andrew Martin of Southampton University. Other members included four barristers and a second academic: Peter Benenson, Anthony Lester, F. Ashe Lincoln, Cedric Thornberry and Michael Zander.

15. The American experience of anti-discrimination laws played an important part in the evidence and proposals gathered by the Martin Committee. An additional influence was undoubtedly the seminal study of race in US society by Myrdal, 1944.

16. For a critical evaluation of the conciliation basis of the Act, see Calvocoressi, 1968: 49-52.

17. Quoted in Miles and Phizacklea, 1984: 57.

18. The rationale for the establishment of the reconstituted NCCI are briefly set out in Cmnd. 2266: 14.

19. These local bodies were known as Voluntary Liaison Committees (VLCs). By the time of the second Race Relations Act 1968, many had become known as, and/or formally changed their names to, Community Relations Councils (CRCs); see H.C. 448-III.

20. Calvocoressi's view is echoed by Hiro, 1971: 279-85; Nandy, 1967a: 35-40; and Hill and Issacharoff, 1971: 163-201.

21. This view is taken up and re-interpreted in a more contemporary setting in relation to the Commission for Racial Equality and local CRCs by Ben-Tovim and Gabriel, 1982: 152-60.

22. The closing of the "immigration door" is the central theme of Foot's 1965 study of the Labour and Conservative experiences of immigration policy between 1948-65. For a radical critique on this point see Alavi, 1965, who argues that the second and third parts of the 1965 White Paper were in contradiction to one another. This argument is also advanced by Deakin, 1970; Kramer, 1969; and Miles and Phizacklea, 1984. However, Katznelson, 1973: 150 takes a dissenting view: 'in *political* terms...the document and its policies are coherent; immigration controls and the local and national liaison committee structure were two sides of the same coin of depoliticisation' (emphasis in original).

23. Jenkins was always something of an implausible "prince" of the liberal hour, mainly because of his personality and *bourgeois* temperament to politics. These characteristics made him a strange figurehead for the race relations lobby. For CARD's perceptions of Jenkins, both as a politician and as their parliamentary champion, see Heinemann, 1972: 111-60.

24. Bonham-Carter's views of the efficacy of the strategy following two years in the job are set out in RRB, 1967.

25. The House of Commons was reminded by Hattersley of the need to alleviate heavy local demand and the tensions this demand was causing. In his speech he spoke both as a frontbencher as well as the Member for Birmingham, Sparkbrook, where, he reminded parliamentary colleagues, such problems were being encountered, H.C. Deb. 729, 14 April 1966, Cols. 1333-37.

26. The 1982-83 review of the S.11 programme carried out by the Home Office was responsible for this change. Other revisions included getting local authorities to carry out inventories of their establishment of S.11-funded officers, carrying out evaluation exercises of these posts, and conducting consultation exercises with local ethnic minority communities on local authorities' S.11 programmes. For further details see Connelly, 1985; Home Office, 1982 and 1983; and Young, 1985b.

27. In 1974-75 the House of Commons Select Committee on Race Relations and Immigration investigated the organisation and administration of race relations. Its 1975 published report discusses the role of local government in tackling racial inequality and promoting harmony at length with the extensive use of evidence from interested parties; see H.C. 448-III. Herein lies the genesis of S.71 of the Race Relations Act 1976.

28. Professor Harry Street of Manchester University was commissioned by NCCI and RRB to examine US experience of anti-discrimination laws, and report on their efficacy and applicability to the British case. The final report was co-authored with two of Street's colleagues on the panel of enquiry: Geoffrey Howe, Q.C. (a barrister) and Geoffrey Bindman (a solicitor).

29. The PEP Report was eventually published in an updated paperback form in 1968; see Daniel, 1968.

30. The response of leading "Fabian-style" CARD members to Jenkins' call to arms for support for his proposed legislation is described in considerable detail by Heinemann, 1972: 111-60.

31. For example *The Sunday Times* editions of 8 January 1967 and 23 January 1967 carried out an investigation into the need to extend the law into the field of employment. The investigation reported the deep-seated hostility of both the CBI and the TUC to such a move. In addition, *The Guardian* edition of 13 January 1967 described CARD's "Green Document" proposals for the first draft of the Bill as 'the most cogent case for extending the Race Relations Act yet presented.' The best example of sympathetic press treatment is seen in the various editorials that appeared the morning after Bonham-Carter's press conference held for the publication of the PEP Report (17 April 1967). Endorsements soon followed in the leader columns of: *The Times, The Guardian,*

The Observer, The Sunday Times, The Economist, The New Statesman, The Spectator and *New Society*.

32. Compare, for example, the views of Deakin, 1970; Hiro, 1971; Heinemann, 1972; and Katznelson, 1973; and, more recently, those of Miles and Phizacklea, 1984; Layton-Henry, 1984; and Banton, 1985 and 1987.

33. Sandys was reported to have made the following remarks: 'The breeding of millions of half-caste children would merely produce a generation of misfits and create increased tension'; see *The Daily Telegraph*, 25 July 1967. He was not censured, either by his party or by the Attorney-General for the possible breach of Section 6 of the 1965 Act relating to incitement to racial hatred. He was, however, speaking as a backbencher at this time, having left the Shadow Cabinet in 1966. The Sandys controversy came in the immediate wake of the arrest of Michael Abdul Malik, a leader of the Black Power Racial Action Adjustment Society, for allegedly stirring up hatred against whites in a speech made in Reading. Malik, in turn, had only spoken at the Reading meeting in place of the American Black Power leader, Stokey Carmichael, who had been made the subject of a banning order from Britain by Jenkins. The banning order strangely enough was served on the same day (26 July 1967) as both Jenkins' announcement of a new round of legislation and the first outbreak of serious rioting in Detroit, Michigan.

34. On 23 November 1967 the Prime Minister arranged for Jenkins to swap jobs with Callaghan who had been at the Treasury until then. The move owed a great deal to the Prime Minister's attempt to regain credibility for his government's economic strategy in the aftermath of the devaluation of Sterling barely a fortnight earlier.

35. His views are amply set out in Powell, 1969. For opposing views see Marris; 1968; Ennals, 1968; Steel, 1969; and Cable, 1969.

36. The Bill was formally introduced at its first reading in April 1968. It received its second reading on 23 April 1968 and went on to occupy the House's time until October 1968, involving no less than 13 standing committee sessions and a colossal 400 tabled amendments.

37. For an early assessment of the difference this structural change made to local community relations problems and practices see Butterworth, 1972.

38. For a full and lucid account of UP's birth in the simmering racial tension of early-1968, see Edwards and Batley, 1978: 25-33. The authors point out that Wilson's Birmingham speech in fact announced the new item of social policy on the basis of a few tentative proposals produced by his aides in Downing Street, and before many senior civil servants (notably at the Home Office) had heard about it.

39. See Jenkins, 1967, on the application of these ideas to the field of employment anti-discrimination law.

40. A radical critique of the local voluntary initiatives that lay at the heart of Jenkins' liberal hour strategy is provided by Nandy, 1967. In addition, a concurrent evaluation of the applicability of the ideas of the liberal settlement in a number of different policy areas - eg. housing, education, welfare, etc. - is found in a Fabian Research Series pamphlet published in July 1967; see Deakin and Lester, 1967. This pamphlet also contains Nandy's contribution cited above.

4 Race and local politics in Ealing Borough, 1965–86

Introduction

The purpose of this chapter is to provide an historical overview of developments in race and public policy in Ealing Borough (in outer-west London). Drawing upon primary and secondary evidence from the borough, I shall provide an account of the changing themes in the borough's experience of the interaction between race and public policy. The evidence shows that, for a considerable period following large-scale black immigrant settlement in the area, race-related issues were successfully marginalised and kept off the agenda of local politics and policy-making. Further, this marginalisation was achieved through a subtle, yet identifiable, attempt to deny credibility to race issues in local politics. However, a number of important socio-political, demographic and other factors existed at grassroots level in the borough, which served to raise the saliency of race issues. Forces external to the local authority's traditional policy-making concerns, compounded by an acutely competitive local two party system, began to exert significant pressure on local race-related public policy. Thus, by the mid-1980s, the pressures working to sustain a "mobilisation of bias" against the legitimacy of race-related issues had given way, at least partially, to a new era of quasi-racialised local politics and policy-making.

The chapter examines both how the conceptual framework of race-related public policy is created and, in particular, the way in which such policy subject matter is approached by dominant, agenda-setting policy actors. The chapter argues that policy is formulated and made within an environment that attempts to negate the specifically racialised aspects of the policy subject matter. Young (1985b: 286) has described this as a 'culture of inexplicitness', whilst Messina (1989: 21-78) uses the term 'the de-politicisation of race'. The latter in particular focuses too closely on the relationship between race relations and party political activity in explaining why local parties and politicians pursue so-called "colourblind" political strategies. In this chapter, I will document and explain not just this *narrow* political relationship, but also place it in the *broader* context of policy-innovation versus policy-maintenance in the local RPE.

The evidence shows that relations between major policy actors at certain moments in the period 1965-86 were reduced to near breaking-point. The wonder then is that any RPE emerged or managed to survive at all. In other words, the question remains, not *how* or *what* race-related public policy was pursued by the local authority, but rather, *did* it have a set of policies? The evidence suggests that, for the most part, it did not, and what is more, it was successful in turning the RPE into an arena of systematic "non-policy-making".

The chapter is composed of four main sections, each dealing with the tenure of successive Labour and Conservative administrations in Ealing. Firstly, the span of the "short" Labour administration from 1965 to 1968; secondly, the "short" Conservative administration of 1968-71; thirdly, the "long" Labour administration of 1971-78; finally, the "long" Conservative administration of 1978-86.

The "short" Labour administration, 1965-68

This early era is characterised by the problems faced by the newly-created local authority, the London Borough of Ealing (hereafter LBE), in dealing with the local settlement of large numbers of black immigrants mainly from the Indian sub-continent. Prior to LBE's creation in April 1965, immigrant-related matters had mainly been the concern of one of its various predecessor authorities, including Southall Borough Council (hereafter SBC). Unofficial - yet informed - estimates of the black immigrant population in Ealing circa 1965 put the figure at around 9,000, or just under 3 per cent (LBE, 1965d). Very few black immigrants were to be found beyond the district of Southall on the western edges of the borough. Describing the borough's immigrant population, the then Chief Medical Officer for the local authority wrote in 1967:

> For some years the Southall area has formed an attractive target for immigrants from India and Pakistan... There is a local tradition that the arrival of Indian immigrants began with one Indian ex-soldier who sought and obtained work from his former British officer who, after the war, was working for a local factory. The wages and standard of living obtainable attracted some of the Indian's friends and relatives who, in turn, influenced other compatriots. Unable to rent accomodation, they gradually bought up many houses...south of the Uxbridge Road. (LBE, 1967: 1)

Southall's legacy

LBE's main strategy at this time aimed to devolve as much responsibility over immigrant affairs as possible to Southall International Friendship Committee (hereafter SIFC). Established in 1963, SIFC represented the foundation of the local community relations movement.[1] The arms-length approach of LBE to the so-called "immigrant question" meant that it was continually referring matters to SIFC. This strategy was supplemented by an early attempt to liaise with the leadership of some Asian EMGs, most notably on issues relating to immigrant use of public services - eg. education and housing - as well as over the sensitive issue of alleged overcrowding of privately-owned residential properties (LBE, 1965b). A third element of this strategy concentrated on trying to forge a dialogue with central government about LBE's acute problems. This dialogue was with a view to negotiating a special funding relationship to help offset some of the financial burden of LBE's immigrant-related spending programmes. Thus, a great deal of time and effort was devoted within the LBE bureaucracy towards arguing its case before central government and other national executive bodies. LBE established its own Immigrants Committee of the Council during 1965. The Committee's initial job was to act as a go-between for the LBE Labour administration in its relations both with national bodies such as central government departments and NCCI, as well as with local bodies such as SIFC and leading EMGs.

The Labour administration was soon forced to defend itself (and individual ruling-group councillors) from the attacks of white community interests. These attacks were mainly from residents' and parents' groups protesting against both the rising immigrant presence in the area as well as the level of immigrant take-up of public services. LBE's defensive posture was crucial in guiding and influencing the political calculations of various policy actors (including many councillors) as to whether race should have a legitimate status in local politics. I shall look at each of these strands in the early history of the local RPE.

LBE and the community relations movement

The priorities of SIFC at this time stemmed mainly from its experiences between 1963-65 in bringing together various political and community élites in Southall. SIFC believed that the tensions created as a result of large-scale immigrant settlement in Southall could be satisfactorily resolved through a process of accommodation, co-operation and inter-élite liaison. Thus, having already set up a machinery for this liberal-orientred approach to local race relations, SIFC firmly believed the same principle could be extended to the whole borough and involve the active participation of the new, much larger, local authority. To this end, SIFC was instrumental in founding the new borough-wide Ealing International Friendship Committee (hereafter EIFC) in 1965.

During the summer and autumn of 1965, the new LBE administration held talks with the recently-established NCCI. The purpose of these talks was to obtain advice on the most suitable role for the LBE-funded staff of EIFC (LBE, 1965d). Shortly afterwards, LBE's newly-founded Immigrants Committee agreed to back a proposal to establish a Liaison Officer for EIFC. LBE's stated aim was to channel resources and attention towards EIFC as a frontline agency dealing with the borough's growing race controversies. In doing so, LBE was endorsing the broad spirit of the race and community relations initiatives of central government at this time. The spirit of the "liberal hour" experiment of Roy Jenkins et al. was clearly alive and operational at grassroots level in Ealing at this time.

SIFC had previously gained the goodwill and co-operation of leading EMGs such as the Indian Workers' Association (hereafter IWA) and the Pakistan Welfare Association (hereafter PWA). Though it was proving hard, EIFC was clearly keen to try to present a united front between itself and leading EMGs, especially in its early, as yet uncertain, relations with LBE (EIFC, 1966). However, continuing conflicts within Southall's Asian communities, coupled with recurring personality rifts and political factionalism, meant that EIFC's vision of being - and being seen as - a local umbrella body always seemed to remain beyond its grasp. Following its launch in 1965, EIFC lost no time in trying to involve itself in every aspect of local public policy towards black immigrants. Within a year, EIFC had developed and publicly presented its position on virtually all aspects of LBE's immigrant-related policies (EIFC, 1967: 1-4). Whilst the bulk of EIFC's concerns lay in immigrant welfare-related issues (such as language provision, housing difficulties, etc.), EIFC was nonetheless prepared to voice criticism of more controversial items of public policy. For instance, whilst accepting that LBE had to act on central government advice to disperse immigrant schoolchildren, EIFC's Secretary noted that:

> With the number of immigrants in this part of Southall still rising and the proportion of the host community declining, this policy is *bound* to become more and more difficult to operate. (EIFC, 1967: 1 - emphasis added).

On the equally thorny local issue of overcrowding, EIFC initially upheld LBE's right to intervene and enforce legal regulations.[2] However, this support was couched in terms of an equation which held that, if EIFC was in the business to defend equal rights for all citizens, it must also insist on equal responsibilities for all citizens (Gazette Series, 9 June 1967: 7). This line inevitably created ripples among many EMGs affiliated to

EIFC (EIFC, 1968a: 2-3). EMGs such as IWA emphasised the reasons behind immigrant overcrowding, and asked why EIFC was now prepared to side with LBE - and therefore against immigrant interests - on this key issue.

LBE's dialogue with EMGs

LBE's attempt to develop a direct channel of communication with EMGs in the borough was a more haphazard process. Unlike its relationship with EIFC, the relationship with EMGs was more prone to *ad hoc* confrontation on a number of issues, the most significant being the enforcement of overcrowding notices. EIFC offered EMGs a useful and convenient public platform, which they were unwilling to give up, in spite of their strong disagreement with both LBE policy and EIFC support for it. Moreover, EIFC was largely in the business of trying to bring EMG and LBE interests closer together. Thus, EIFC's reaction to the simmering overcrowding dispute was, not surprisingly, to try to avoid an estrangement between LBE and EMGs.

In addition, an important incentive existed preventing LBE from forging too close a relationship with leading EMGs. White, anti-immigrant, community interests were an important local political factor which many LBE councillors generally felt they could not afford to alienate. Thus, EIFC, rather than EMGs, was thought to be a more reliable and politically acceptable ally for LBE in its early participation in the RPE. The alternative was to risk the charge of having taken sides in local inter-race disputes on the side of the "immigrant", rather than the "host", community. This sensitivity to white community fears is seen most graphically in the 1965 call by the Conservative Prospective Parliamentary Candidate (hereafter PPC) for Southall, Barbara Maddin, for an immediate and unqualified ban on further local immigrant settlement (Gazette Series, 15 October 1965: 9).

Centre-periphery relations

The mid-1960s represented a period of intense national activity in formulating a framework for race-related public policy (see also Chapter 3 above). This process had accelerated sharply following the change of government in October 1964. Locally there was a mushrooming of activity in the period leading up to, and immediately following, local government reorganisation in April 1965. Stable central-local relations on immigrant-related questions had been originally nurtured through the then Minister of Education's visit to Southall in autumn 1963 (see also Chapter 5 below).

The main purpose behind LBE's co-operation with, and lobbying of, the centre was to promote additional funding for its immigrant-related local expenditure. Examples included the appointment of additional language teaching staff and public health inspectors to patrol the growth of overcrowded residential accommodation. The centre's motives, meanwhile, lay in trying to assess the scale of local problems, and to gain some feedback from its various proposed solutions to these problems. The best known example of central intervention was, of course, the 1963-65 local crisis over alleged immigrant-dominated classrooms in Southall - ultimately dealt with by a centre-inspired and subsidised dispersal policy (see also Chapter 5 below).

Both SBC (pre-1965) and LBE (post-1965) received a number of visits from junior ministers and others on fact-finding missions during this period. In March 1965, in the dying days of SBC, Harold Wilson's newly-appointed minister with special responsibility for immigrant affairs, Maurice Foley, led a delegation to inspect conditions in Southall.[3] Foley's main purpose was to examine the work done by voluntary agencies, such as SIFC and IWA, in order to report back on the possibility of supplying central funds for local community relations agencies (Gazette Series, 26 March 1965: 1). The ministerial visit also highlighted the attempt to try to bury race issues into the administrative process of local government. On the precise question of the new initiatives proposed by the centre to deal with acute educational, housing, and other local problems, Foley's reply on behalf of central government was that:

It is difficult for a borough of Southall's size to deal with immigrant problems, but as part of the new Ealing Borough, Southall could tackle integration with more powerful backing. (Gazette Series, 26 March 1965: 1)

In other words, central government held out no real prospect of dealing with these issues in terms of their specific racial significance. Any *race-specific* criteria for assessing the problems of Southall, let alone the solutions to these problems, were clearly beyond the scope of central-local liaison at this time. The bureaucratic upheaval that was scheduled to take place in London local government later that year was held to be the only likely way out of these problems (Gazette Series, 2 April 1965: 2). A change in the size and administrative structure of the local authority, rather than any specific policies it was supposed to pursue, was presented by both the ministerial delegation and LBE leaders as the only plausible policy response. Therefore, the Foley mission was not so much an example of race *policy-making* as of *policy-avoidance*.

Later in May 1968, LBE sent its own deputation to Whitehall to press its case to the Under-Secretary of State at the Home Office, David Ennals (LBE, 1968c). As a written submission from the deptuation argued, LBE was clearly of the view that immigrants were placing an intolerable financial strain on the borough:[4]

> The rapid growth in the numbers of immigrants... settling in Ealing...has created specific health, educational and other problems but there is of course a considerable social problem. It is the Council's view that this is a matter of national concern and that all areas of immigrant saturation, including Ealing, should be assisted without any suggestion of a "means" or "wealth" test!... Failing all else, the Southall area should be viewed in isolation, and not against the Borough as a whole, as an area which, to use the Prime Minister's expression, 'has reached its absorptive capacity in respect of new immigrants'. (LBE, 1968c: 1 and 4)

White anti-immigrant interests

White anti-immigrant interests constituted an important aspect of the RPE, not least because of the constraints they placed on the actions of other key RPE actors. Two main white community interests were launched at this time. The first was the Beaconsfield Road School Parents' Committee, formed at the time of the initial immigrant education controversy in 1963.[5] The other, also formed in 1963, was the much larger and more influential Southall Residents' Association (hereafter SRA).[6] Both, but particularly the latter, exercised formidable influence, first in Southall, and after 1965, in the borough as a whole. The views of a large segment of local white public opinion were often encapsulated in SRA's various pronouncements, public meetings, letters to the press, and deputations to council leaders.

In 1965 SRA was involved in a dramatic episode in Ealing local politics. In June 1965, LBE's Housing Committee split across party lines over a controversial plan to restrict the residential qualifications required of local applicants for LBE public housing[7] (Gazette Series, 18 June 1965: 1). A major public storm ensued in which six Labour members defied their official party whip and voted with the Conservatives not to allocate extra points to those living in overcrowded conditions (predominantly immigrants). The rebels found themselves temporarily expelled from the Labour Group on the Council. Explusion led to all six of them taking up Independent seats in the Council, and two of them subsequently fought and won seats as SRA councillors in 1968. SRA, voicing the anti-immigrant mood of many white Southall residents, reacted strongly to the row, calling for either LBE's new housing policy to be scrapped or the resignation of the Committee (Gazette Series, 13 August 1965: 1).

The episode illustrated SRA's tactics of deliberately identifying the failure to limit immigrant settlement in the borough as the root cause of the housing policy controversy. As SRA's President, A.E. Cooney, argued (in reply to an attack from Southall's Labour MP, Sidney Bidwell):

You cannot mend a burst tap if you don't turn it off. This town is overflowing and we urge an absolute end to immigration to this town with a dispersal plan. (Gazette Series, 18 March 1966: 1)

LBE's Labour administration was effectively caught in a no-man's-land between white working class support in the borough, and its own substantial support amongst the Asian community in Southall. The administration's solution was to keep a safe public distance from local EMG leaders, whilst at the same time attacking SRA in particular on the grounds of 'half-hidden racialism' (Gazette Series, 25 February 1966: 1 and 18 March 1966: 1).[8] A similar onslaught was waged against the British National Party (hereafter BNP) which had fielded candidates in local and parliamentary elections in Southall since 1962.[9]

In 1965 SRA affiliated to Ealing Federation of Residents' Associations (hereafter EFRA). EFRA had lobbied strongly against further immigrant settlement in the new borough (even though it was widely accepted that LBE did not possess powers to regulate such settlement). Between 1965-68, EFRA published two detailed reports on the effects of immigration in the borough (EFRA, 1965 and 1968; LBE, 1965c). The immediate result of these reports was to put pressure on LBE to be seen to be "doing something" about the borough's immigration problems. LBE responded by establishing an *ad hoc* Immigrants Committee of the Council; in addition, a special Immigration Section of the Health Department began to meet soon afterwards (LBE, 1965e).

1965-68: overview

Throughout this early period it appears that the liberal settlement-inspired philosophy of "community relationsism" had yet to gain momentum in the borough. LBE, the dominant actor in the RPE, was content to give greater attention to other strands in its race relations strategy. In particular, LBE members and officers were largely precoccupied with national politicians and public bodies on the one hand and local white community interests on the other. The notion of trying to regulate local race relations by devolving responsibility to a peripheral, non-town hall, organisation such as EIFC was rather novel and remained untested.

The period also demonstrates LBE's growing realisation of the enormity of the task facing it. Virtually every policy suggestion it made was soon superseded by events at the grassroots. The erosion of LBE's frontline position in day-to-day public debate and its capacity to keep abreast of the problem facing it, is a noticeable feature of this period. LBE appeared determined to steer a middle path through the race relations minefield, ever conscious of not being seen to take a high profile or take sides, or for that matter, being accused of ignoring the issue altogether. However, such a middle path of *policy inexplicitness* had a series of direct consequences in terms of the policies and measures pursued by LBE within the local RPE. (Discussion of these consequences can be found in Chapter 7 below).

The "short" Conservative administration, 1968-71

The period of Conservative rule in Ealing following Labour's defeat in the 1968 local elections represented far greater continuity than change. That is to say, many aspects of the early RPE that had been forged under the first Labour administration, were largely consolidated under the Conservatives. This basic continuity notwithstanding, it is possible to identify a number of diverging race issues beginning to emerge amongst various policy actors at this time. Such change is especially pronounced in relation to EMGs and their role in the local RPE. Furthermore, the evidence of the development of a local "community relationsism" ethos suggests that subtle changes in outlook were beginning to be reflected in other aspects of the RPE.

Following the establishment of the national Community Relations Commission in 1968, EIFC adopted the new title of Ealing Community Relations Council (hereafter ECRC).[10] ECRC's profile in the borough was increasingly oriented towards local campaigns. Meanwhile, the climate of race relations on the national political stage had clearly deteriorated following the 1967-68 Kenyan-Asian immigration crisis. This change of political atmosphere was at least partially reflected at grassroots level in the borough. A number of councillors publicly sided with SRA, EFRA and others, anxious that a new round of Asian settlement seemed imminent. ECRC's response was to adopt an ever higher profile in local public debate over the consequences of such settlement for LBE public service provision.

ECRC's more overtly interventionist line is best seen through its change of tone over LBE's policy of issuing overcrowding notices to (mainly Asian) households in Southall. Previously community relations activists had been willing to endorse this policy in the interests of being seen to treat all sections of the community equally. Equal rights, community relations activists had once argued, meant equal responsibilities (EIFC, 1967). In the run-up to the 1968 local elections however, ECRC leaders were prepared to voice stronger accusations over this increasingly controversial policy:

> It is difficult to avoid the conclusion that there is *official support* for colour prejudice in making direction orders to control overcrowding in Southall. We think that the application of this policy must inhibit the purchase of houses by immigrants outside the main area in which they are living. It inhibits voluntary dispersal and is not conducive to integration. (Gazette Series, 29 March 1968: 1 - emphasis added)

ECRC was effectively claiming that this controversial policy served to geographically restrict LBE's concern and responsibilities regarding local race relations. This claim implied that LBE's commitment to the development of race-related public policy would be similarly limited. The suggestion was that LBE's policy towards overcrowding was guided by a larger policy goal; namely, to halt the spread of race-related social problems, both geographically and, by implication, from areas of mainstream policy-making. The simplest way for LBE to halt the proliferation of these problems was to try to restrict the geographical spread of the borough's immigrant population.

The result of ECRC's higher profile was a gradual deterioration in its relations with LBE. Councillors' reactions to ECRC's phased bids for LBE subsidies and subsidies-in-kind (ie. accommodation, secretarial support, etc.) led to long, arduous battles being fought over relatively small sums (ECRC, 1969: 3). This deterioration was also reflected in a series of direct, personal attacks launched against ECRC's senior officer, Martyn Grubb, by a group of LBE councillors who felt he was primarily responsible for the politicisation of ECRC. One Conservative councillor protested that: 'He [Grubb]...spoils his position and embarrasses people by putting himself forward as a champion for one section of the community...like an immigrant pressure group spokesman' (Gazette Series, 19 July 1968: 1).

ECRC also faced vehement public attacks on its credibility and its right to act as the umbrella body it aspired to become. ECRC's counter-reaction was to further emphasise the distinctiveness of its contribution to local race relations. Above all, ECRC activists were aware of the need to resist attempts by LBE to marginalise ECRC by, for example, trying to establish a loosely-organised and less radical race "policy community" of its own. ECRC leaders claimed that neither ECRC's role, motives or priorities could be absorbed, let alone substituted, by the town hall. 'Our job', wrote ECRC's Chairman in June 1969, 'is not to duplicate their [LBE's] work. We should try to fill any gap in the field of community relations which cannot be filled by other organisations' (ECRC, 1969: 1).

The EMG contribution to the local RPE began to change during this period for three reasons. Firstly, the notion of a single, dominant EMG being able to represent and discipline the political interests of the whole Asian community in the borough began to waiver. Secondly, a number of religious and cultural community organisations in the Asian community began to assume quasi-political roles. The public campaign against LBE's controversial bussing policy led by IWA and ECRC attracted the active support of a whole host of EMGs (see also Chapter 5 below). Finally, the period marks the early willingness of some Asian community leaders to move a shade closer to the Conservatives in local politics. Previously the overwhelming majority of Asian EMGs and their leaders were assumed to be safe constituents of the Labour Party. There is a noticeable shift in local politics at this time towards a more plural form of party competition on race issues and the mobilisation of black support.

A number of splits and counter-splits emerged within IWA in Southall during the 1960s, resulting in several breakaway groups becoming involved in local politics.[11] From here onwards, it is no longer sufficient of think of an homogeneous set of EMGs playing a uniform role in the RPE. IWA began to sub-divide into a number of factions, though not all of these reflected personality clashes within the organisation alone (Gazette Series, 3 January 1969: 1). These factions also partially reflected differences within the Asian community regarding the association it should maintain with various radical, black movements of the day (Interview: former IWA President, 1985). At the height of the Kenyan-Asian crisis *The Financial Times* (8 March 1968: 20) wrote of the moderate IWA leadership:

> The IWA is actively involved in integration efforts. It seeks to protect its members' interests, not by isolating them, but by involving them in the community.

However, during the late-1960s new radical factions within IWA had managed to wrest away some of the executive's influence over the membership. In the executive leadership poll of April 1968 the competing slates presented the membership with a sharp contrast of political strategies (Gazette Series, 26 April 1968: 1). Moreover, six months earlier in November 1967, a small group of IWA leaders had been publicly rebuked by colleagues for their attempts to radicalise the organisation from above (Gazette Series, 10 October 1967: 1). The attempt to bring IWA into league with radical political groups had been firmly, if temporarily, slapped down.

Similar differences began to emerge within ECRC over its line on the black separatist movement. Intra-ECRC disputes over this issue demonstrated that ECRC itself was in a state of constant flux over its proper identity. The tactics of some LBE councillors included trying to link ECRC with the Black Power Movement, and the allegation rapidly became a familiar feature of LBE-ECRC negotiations over funding (Gazette Series, 6 March 1970: 5). For the most part, ECRC activists were content to ignore politely or to deny such ideological sympathies. However, differences emerged following a call by some ECRC activists for the organisation to place its opposition to black separatism on the record (Gazette Series, 17 July 1970: 5; 28 July 1970: 3; and 6 November 1970: 2). The pejorative Black Power accusation made by a number of Conservative councillors - which featured the name of "Malcolm X" as one of several alleged villains supported by ECRC - had undoubtedly cast a damaging smear on ECRC as a credible mainstream RPE participant.

Other smaller EMGs also began to participate at the fringes of local politics for the first time during this period. Most notably, a few Southall-based religious organisations intervened on several controversial local issues. For example, in 1972 Southall's largest Sikh *Gurdwara* (or temple), the *Sri Guru Singh Sabha* (hereafter SGSS), pledged itself to the ECRC campaign to reform LBE's bussing policy (Gazette Series, 12 May 1972: 7; Southall Rights/CARF, 1981). The intervention of such groups into local politics still remained more the exception than the rule however. More usually, such EMGs restricted their attention to those aspects of LBE's statutory duties that touched on their private status as local charitable organisations. For instance, during this period SGSS voiced far greater fury over LBE's road-widening proposals for a trunk road outside its *Gurdwara* premises, than it ever did over LBE's official dispersal policy! (Gazette Series, 26 December 1969: 1).

Meanwhile, the pace of the establishment and expansion of local EMGs was increasing (Gazette Series, 6 November 1970: 2). The RPE was soon to expand to accommodate the voices, if not always the interests, of many more EMG policy actors during the 1970s. However, the opening of these formal channels of participation in the RPE during the 1970s, did not necessarily mean that public policy outcomes were always liberal or progressive in tone. Indeed, the 1971-78 Labour administration marked one of the most racially-*illiberal* periods in the local politics of race in Ealing (see also the following section).

Local issues and the 1970 General Election

The relationship between local EMGs and the major political parties in Ealing underwent great change at this time. Hitherto, the bulk of Southall's Asian community had been closely aligned to the Labour Party. For example, according to a *Southall Gazette* opinion poll just prior to the 1966 General Election, Labour's support in the Southall parliamentary consitituency stood at 53 per cent, more than double that of the Conservatives at 24 per cent.[12] There is no reason to suggest that differential black-white support for Labour in this seat was significantly greater (or indeed less) than national or regional swings in support in the 1970 poll. Allowing for such swings, the (increasingly Asian-dominated) electorate of Southall remained loyal to Labour.[13]

However, beginning in the late-1960s, there is increasing evidence to suggest that Conservative support amongst certain EMG leaders was rising. The best known example was the recruitment of Dr N.S. Mangat who stood as the Conservative candidate in Northcote ward in the 1968 local elections. Although unsuccessful, shortly after the local elections he was invited by the victorious Conservative Group to fill one of the borough's aldermanic vacancies.[14] Further, by the time of the 1970 General Election, the enterprising Conservative MP for Ealing Acton, Kenneth Baker, was pioneering new territory in openly soliciting Asian votes in the borough: 'I think that many immigrants...are well aware of the advantages of voting Conservative' he said (Gazette Series, 6 June 1970: 7).

Earlier in 1966, Southall Conservatives had joined EIFC, and retained membership throughout the 1968-71 Conservative adminstration (Gazette Series, 7 October 1966: 1). However, the Conservative administration's relationship with the newly-renamed ECRC, despite overtures to some EMG leaders, remained luke-warm. Early in 1970 the relationship fell into a state of crisis, hitherto unknown in the local RPE. A group of right-wing, somewhat racially-illiberal, backbench Conservative councillors set out to check the 'menacing, spoiling and unrestrained' influence of ECRC using the weapon of finance.[15] Their tactics included the following thinly-veiled threats:

> If they [ECRC] continue to play politics, I will move that they have no grant at all next year. I would like to see their extinction. (LBE, 1970a)

> It does appear as if they [ECRC] are setting themselves up as a kind of protection committee for immigrants. (Gazette Series, 20 February 1970: 7)

> ECRC has no respect from the white community because of the way it does its business. It gives this impression - unlike CRCs in other boroughs. It is an immigrant pressure group. (Gazette Series, 6 March 1970: 5)

The line taken by the Conservative leadership, whilst less provocative, was nonetheless equally ominous for ECRC:

This Council and the Government are supplying funds to enable the CRC to bite the hand that feeds it, and to say to us...we are wrong in trying to help...the immigrant population by dispersing them in the borough. We supply the community relations council's needs. It is for us to administer the slap when it is needed. (LBE, 1970a)

The dispute coincided with the preliminary stages of the 1970 General Election campaign. Consequently, the issue was to become a microcosm of the local campaign's wider debate on race, fought, as it was, against the backdrop of an increasingly race-sensitive national campaign (Deakin and Bourne, 1970). Councillor K. Reeves, the Conservative leader and the Conservative PPC for Southall, stated during the campaign:

I think that Powell and Heath will win us the election... I would like to see overseas aid spent on the voluntary repatriation scheme... To be an immigrant must not become a privilege... My concern is that immigrants do not have enough cause for concern. They should be more concerned about educating their people about the English way of life... No new immigrants should be allowed to settle in this area, and the existing situation could be relieved through voluntary repatriation. (Gazette Series, 6 February 1970: 10 and 5 June 1970: 5)

A sharp reply ensued from the editor of the local press, not usually noted for his liberal position on race relations:

[Councillor Reeves'] speech will make many immigrants feel that this Tory policy was a substantial minus... Where Councillor Reeves is right, is in urging the need to make more resources available to tackle the problem. Local authorities do not have sufficient resources to pursue a real policy of integration, even if they wanted to... But better if we worked together towards solving the problems without speeches that can only arouse more fear in one section of the population and resentment in the other. (Gazette Series, 6 February 1970: 10)

IWA also joined in the argument, calling upon the Conservative Party to 'denounce [Reeves'] shameful racialist outburst' (Gazette Series, 20 February 1970: 1). Finally, Southall's sitting Labour MP, Sidney Bidwell, intervened in the fracas, claiming 'while there are racialists in the Labour Party, there are many more in the Conservative Party which runs the affairs of Ealing' (Gazette Series, 13 February 1970: 16). The long-standing, bi-partisan consensus to de-politicise the race issue in the borough looked, for a short period around 1970, to be in real danger of breaking down.

Limited intervention by LBE

One of the solutions put forward by LBE to resolve the increasingly-bitter dispute was to suggest incorporating ECRC into the bureaucratic machinery of the town hall. This move was ostensibly fuelled by LBE's constant fear of ECRC being at liberty to criticise any individual or organisation it pleased - including LBE - in the name of "racial justice". Such autonomy was clearly worrying to many among the LBE administration. LBE's short-term strategy was to try to associate ECRC with the label of extremism as much as possible. Thereafter, it was proposed to fill the unoccupied middle-ground with some form of LBE-sponsored and accountable community relations council (Gazette Series, 18 September 1970: 15). The LBE Conservative leadership were able to recruit the support of a quasi-political EMG, the Indian National Association (hereafter INA), thus giving the impression that ECRC perhaps lacked the full support of its most important constituency, the Asian community.[16]

The grant-aid dispute spilled over into a new argument over ECRC's autonomy

(LBE, 1971a). According to Councillor Tommy Steele (an ex-Labour, now SRA member), ECRC had betrayed its original *raison d'être* based on an assimilationist view of racial harmony: 'It was set up to integrate the immigrant communities with our own. I don't blame it for not being able to do so - no-one else has been able to' (Gazette Series, 8 January 1971: 5). Others could not see the value of having, let alone publicly funding, a body such as ECRC at all: 'Do we consider the work this community relations council does is valuable? I think the benefit the community in Ealing gets from this organisation is minimal' stated one Conservative councillor (Gazette Series, 8 January 1971: 5).

A backbench motion to suspend ECRC's subsidy fell by a majority of 8:3; instead, LBE's General Purposes Committee agreed funding for £4,500. The resolution was overturned by the full Council which, after a heated exchange, pegged the grant at the previous year's figure of £4,100 (LBE, 1971b). Unable to muster quite enough support to abandon its subsidy to ECRC, nor to absorb it in one attempt, LBE nonetheless served notice that ECRC's brand of community relations was deeply resented. According to one backbench Conservative councillor, ECRC represented a serious threat to the effective management of race in the borough:

> Even in giving ECRC a grant...we are taking a calculated risk in hoping that the majority of their members will ensure they keep an eye on the activities of those among them who are less well disposed, and realise their projects should help the borough - not further Marxist philosophy! (Gazette Series, 22 January 1971: 7)

1968-71: overview

The period of LBE's first Conservative administration ended on a poor note for race relations in the borough. Moreover, the prospects of establishing an effective and durable RPE appeared slim. The era had begun with a large degree of continuity in the relationship between various different policy actors in the RPE. However, as time wore on, a number of important contextual factors in the RPE began to change.

Firstly, EMGs in the borough began to occupy a multiplicity of political positions on various local issues concerning them. The solid link with the Labour Party in local politics could not be taken for granted as it once had been. Secondly, the number and variety of participant EMGs also began to grow. The leading EMG in Southall - IWA - went through a period of protracted internal factionalism, making it hard to build a cohesive Asian immigrant political bloc. Thirdly, the Conservative and Labour Groups also experienced change. For example, the 1966 split in the Labour Group had a significant long-term effect on party competition in Ealing. A number of the expelled members were returned in 1968 as SRA or Independent members, committed to a doggedly anti-immigrant line throught these years. Finally, there was a significant re-ordering of priorities within ECRC, resulting in a noticeable change of profile. The late-1960s marked a crucial watershed for the community relations movement. The spawning race relations "industry" brought with it a new wave of activists into ECRC, not to mention a number of new, more radical, policy goals onto the broad agenda of the RPE. The reaction of dominant RPE actors to these new goals - as well as towards ECRC specifically - was one of hostility. The result was a serious deterioration in their bilateral relations specifically, as well as in the tone and cohesion of the RPE more generally. The RPE bequeathed by the Conservative administration to its Labour successor in 1971 was very different in nature to that which existed in the borough barely three years earlier.

The "long" Labour administration, 1971-78

The change of administration in 1971 created great expectations of a new direction in LBE policy. The legacy of the previous Conservative administration had put a tremendous strain on relations between various RPE actors, notably LBE and ECRC. At a minimum, ECRC believed that its guerilla war with LBE - ostensibly over allegations regarding ECRC's political motives - would be superseded by a more constructive relationship with the new Labour administration. However, many of the early initiatives undertaken by both sides to try to forge a more constructive RPE, geared towards negotiation and collective decision-making, were undermined by the 1972 Ugandan-Asian crisis. Local politics during this episode degenerated into a facile and acrimonious argument over immigration statistics, thus serving to put the development of the RPE back a number of steps.

The 1970s represented an era in which the borough's social and racial problems multiplied significantly. Large, noticeable pockets of severe deprivation appeared on the borough's socio-economic map - especially in parts of Southall and Acton.[17] The racial consequences of this process were serious in two senses. Firstly, such deprivation also affected poor white communities, often reinforcing their initial anti-immigrant attitudes and, thus, their political outlook on local race issues. Secondly, these problems were proportionately concentrated in a handful of mainly black pockets of the borough - eg. Asian-dominated Southall and Afro-Carribbean-dominated Acton.

Labour's return to office

Following the 1971 local elections, liberal segments in the RPE such as ECRC and many EMGs clearly had high hopes for the new Labour ruling-group. Moderate EMG leaders in particular believed that a new Labour administration would ensure that race issues were not relegated to the backburner (Interview: IWA leader, 1985). As a discrete social issue area of the RPE, the district of Southall was singled out and treated with special attention by the incoming administration. As one prominent Labour councillor stated unequivocally: 'Southall will not be the left-out corner of the borough in the future...Southall and all its people will be central to the new Council's concerns' (Gazette Series, 11 June 1971: 12).

In the event however, the office of the two successive Labour administrations (1971-74 and 1974-78) proved to be an historical low-watermark in the climate of race relations in the borough. Race relations in Ealing began to deteriorate in the wake of the 1972 Ugandan-Asian influx, reaching a nadir in the period 1976-79. The situation was compounded by two further developments: firstly, the rise in support for far-right, anti-immigrant groups, reflecting a more universal increase in racial tension and violence; and secondly, the rise of *ad hoc* protest movements amongst Southall's Asian community - and Asian youth in particular - during the latter part of the decade. These developments were to place a further test on LBE's ability to steer a middle course through the minefield of worsening race relations at the grassroots. Moreover, the crises of the 1970s were to confirm the fears of LBE and others that race relations problems were too awkward to be debated openly and therefore had to be "managed" via domination of the RPE.

The changing face of Southall's EMGs

The 1970s also saw a gradual, though important, evolution in the types of EMGs active in Southall's social, cultural and political life. The previous decade had been dominated by IWA, with its own brand of social-welfare and cultural priorities for its members. The 1970s, in contrast, revealed two important changes. Firstly, IWA no longer dominated EMG representation in local borough politics in the monopolistic way it had done in the 1950s and 1960s.[18] Secondly, the range and types of EMG activity multiplied significantly, reflecting a wider spectrum of Asian political participation.

IWA's fall from prominence was undoubtedly exacerbated by a series of internal splits and disputes. These disputes were, in fact, dated back to the mid-1960s but increased in scale and temper during the early- and mid-1970s. Although often inspired by personality clashes amongst the leadership, they sometimes masked a more subtle feature of IWA's changing profile as a local pressure group (Interview: former IWA

President, 1985). This change came to a head during the organisation's executive election campaign of 1976-77 (Gazette Series, 12 August 1977: 6). The timing and scale of the electoral contest was doubly significant since it coincided with the 1976 crisis in Southall over disaffected Asian youth (see also pp. 63-5 below). IWA effectively shot itself in the foot at a moment when a number of new emerging Asian youth organisations were complaining about the excessive moderation and remoteness of IWA's incumbent leadership. The strategy of the winner of the presidential election, Vishnu Sharma, highlighted claims of the relative economic disadvantage suffered by the Southall community. His allegation of neglect, resonating loudly in the local Asian community, can be viewed as an early marker in a campaign taken up a decade later by the radical Labour administration of 1986-90. Sharma's 1977 victory suggested that the geo-political issue of "Southall's plight" had begun to be incorporated into the changing terms of debate of the RPE.

Other EMGs were anything but muted in their attitudes or actions, often opting to debate local race issues in a hard-hitting, controversial manner. For example, in January 1973, following the Ugandan-Asian crisis of the previous year, a small group called the British Indians Board (hereafter BIB) issued a damaging press release which was to lead to a major political row. BIB claimed that it had compiled a secret dossier of the past record and activities of 'known racists in the borough', including some prominent LBE members and officers (Gazette Series, 23 January 1973: 1). Shortly afterwards, IWA publicly split in response to a call from BIB for support on the issue. A majority of the IWA executive argued that the organisation was merely inciting racial hatred and local resentment through such behaviour. BIB eventually rescinded its threat to publish the dossier, but not before it had been demonstrated that IWA no longer commanded a monopoly of grassroots support amongst Southall Asians.[19]

LBE and central intervention

The 1970s was also a period in which Ealing Borough - and Southall in particular - began to receive widespread national attention because of its large immigrant population. Southall had frequently been in the limelight, receiving considerable media coverage for some years (eg. ITV, 1965; *The Times*, 26 January 1968: 7; *The Financial Times*, 8 March 1968: 20). Now it was the turn of LBE to be the focus of the attention of central government and national politicians, eager to inspect the realities of large-scale immigrant settlement.

During 1971-72, the borough was the subject of no less than three high-level, fact-finding visits. Firstly, in March 1971 Lord Windlesham, Minister of State at the Home Office, came to observe local conditions (LBE, 1971c). Secondly, in October 1972 the Secretary of State for the Social Services, Sir Keith Joseph, visited the borough to examine how LBE was coping with the Ugandan-Asian influx (LBE, 1972b). Thirdly, in June 1973 members of the Central Policy Review Staff "think-tank" visited LBE for a similiar purpose (LBE, 1973b). Earlier, in July 1972, LBE had sent a delegation of senior members and officers to the Home Office to argue that the borough should be exempt from any settlement plans for Ugandan-Asians (LBE, 1972a). Throughout these high-level discussions with the centre, LBE had consistently argued that it wished to see an additional, special funding relationship established to help meet the financial costs associated with its large immigrant population.[20] LBE argued that immigration was a national responsibility, and since it was shouldering part of the centre's responsibilities, it should be compensated for doing so. Moreover, LBE recommended that any new immigrant influxes ought to be dispersed beyond the borough. Compared with matters just a few years previously, LBE's position was clear-cut and coherently argued:

> In the Council's opinion, the granting of permission to enter this country to large numbers of people of Asian origin will inevitably result in an increase in the social problems of the population of Ealing. (LBE, 1972b: 2)

It was also entirely blameless in its determination to identify the centre as the villain of the peace:

> While we [LBE] are confident that the many problems can be overcome, we are anxious to put before you [the Social Services Secretary] the pressures under which local authorities are working, often as a result of government policies. (LBE, 1972c: 4)

At a broader level, LBE was able to argue that policy-innovation and/or reform of the RPE was something it could not enter into so long as the local immigrant population continued to grow. A stablisation in this population, claimed LBE, would allow it to begin to deal with the borough's serious social problems, such as overcrowding and dispersal. In the meantime, LBE's main purpose in the RPE was to argue for a restriction of numbers settling in the borough, and for the dispersal of those already settled (LBE, 1973b). This argument even went so far as some members and officers *actively promoting* an otherwise poorly-publicised Home Office voluntary repatriation scheme! (LBE: 1973a).

Thus, for a number of years LBE was successful in resisting pressure for change. Its defence was based on the selective use of a dual argument. Firstly, it was opposed to many of the proposed forms of change because of its philosophical attachment to "colourblindness" and an associated general policy stance, largely rooted in the prevailing liberal policy framework. Secondly, the politics of local government's funding relationship with the centre stood as a powerful "objective" obstacle to any meaningful policy-innovation in the local RPE. According to FitzGerald (1986a: 7):

> The context of increasing financial pressure [had] severe implications for the maintenance of existing services and militated strongly against their development or the consideration of any issues which might throw up new demand.

The Ugandan-Asian crisis, 1972-73

The single most important reason why the construction of a stable RPE foundered during the 1970s has to do with events surrounding the arrival of large numbers of Ugandan-Asian refugees during the summer and autumn of 1972. The widely-perceived "threat" posed by their local settlement scuppered virtually all progress made in a liberal-progressive direction during the preceding years. Furthermore, the new immigration crisis surfaced at a time when many other race-related issues already featured heavily in local political debate; for example, by July 1972 the anti-bussing campaign led by ECRC, IWA and others had begun to yield modest dividends.[21]

News of the refugees' arrival in the country was greeted with an massive outburst of local protest from the borough's party political leadership. On national television, LBE's Leader, Councillor J. Telfer, requested an urgent meeting with Home Office officials to put the case for the refugees' compulsory dispersal to areas beyond Ealing. And, in a letter to the Home Secretary published on the front page of the local press, the Town Clerk demanded that (Gazette Series, 18 August 1972: 1):

> Positive action for the dispersal of immigrants is needed if Ealing is not to face increased social problems... There should be inducements provided to prevent the development of ghettos of increasing size.

ECRC immediately began lobbying support for an emergency plan to assist the refugees' local settlement, urging that 'Ealing must not lag behind other authorities in the generosity of its response' (Gazette Series, 25 August 1972: 1; ECRC, 1972). Opposing ECRC's initiative, the Conservative Group tabled a motion calling on LBE to lobby the centre against the local resettlement of the refugees (Gazette Series, 1 September 1972: 6). A Labour amendment also argued for the refugees' resettlement elsewhere. The amendment merely softened the tone of the robust Conservative motion, suggesting that dispersal could be achieved via a policy of central financial inducements (Gazette Series, 8 September 1972: 1).

The response of the major local parties' to the crisis, in turn, incited IWA to launch a strong attack on them both. The IWA executive described the original Conservative motion as 'deeply racist', calling on Labour councillors to oppose it and abandon their own 'disturbing' amendment. At a quickly-arranged public meeting an *ad hoc*, IWA-chaired reception committee was set up, incorporating a number of leading ECRC and EMG figures on its steering body. The committee's chief aim appeared to be to challenge LBE directly on the issue of local refugee settlement (Gazette Series, 8 September 1972: 1).[22] At its inaugural meeting, the IWA President, A.S. Rai, strongly criticised LBE for not having taken the lead: 'This is their [LBE's] legal responsibility, ours is only a moral obligation' he stated (Gazette Series, 22 September 1972: 1). Moreover, Rai cited the findings of an investigation by the Institute of Voluntary Service which strongly criticised LBE's poor response to the estimated 1,000 refugees thought to have settled in the borough (Gazette Series, 29 December 1972: 1).[23]

An emergency full Council meeting was convened during early-September 1972 (Gazette Series, 25 August 1972: 1; and 15 September 1972: 1). This event was preceded and followed by a series of highly acrimonious exchanges between the various RPE actors. The eventual outcome was that the softer Labour amendment was passed, causing the ECRC chairman, Eric Barzey, to later complain bitterly that 'the Council has started to implement the theories of Enoch Powell!' (Gazette Series, 15 September 1972: 1).

The spill-over affect of the Ugandan-Asian episode was considerable. For example, citing the recent actions of both LBE and central government, in June 1973 IWA decided to unilaterally 'withdraw from all statutory and state-funded bodies' (Gazette Series, 15 June 1973: 1). Ironically, IWA's withdrawal policy amounted to ending its affiliation to ECRC because of the latter's (local) 'state-funded status'. However, Rai was keen to stress that: 'It is the policy of the Government and the Council we are objecting to, not the ECRC' (Gazette Series, 15 June 1973: 1). IWA's walk-out, in turn, stimulated similar action by a number of other EMGs affiliated to ECRC.[24] The cumulative result of these incidents was to sour the climate of race relations in the borough. The most widely reported of these incidents included the 'dossier of known racists' episode, the wave of resignations from ECRC, and, at Westminster, the House of Commons Select Committee on Race Relations and Immigration's recommendation to end bussing (see also Chapter 5 below). Capturing the mood of the moment, a local press editorial entitled 'Summer of Discontent' commented on the behaviour of ECRC and IWA respectively:

> The fact has to be faced that there is a growing two-standard society which is developing in this borough. It is essential that ECRC overcomes its problems and establishes itself as the guardian of all members of society. It is little use talking about the "racist white community" unless [ECRC] is prepared to admit to the "racist coloured community"... [For IWA] to cut themselves off and to threaten a coloured workers' strike, will only harden attitudes and set a question mark over the whole future of immigrants here and those who may yet wish to come. (Gazette Series, 29 June 1973: 8)

LBE-ECRC relations

Shortly after the Conservatives' 1971 local election defeat, the suggestion was made by Conservative Alderman Robert Hetherington that the time had come for LBE to 'take-over ECRC' and its functions (Gazette Series, 16 June 1971: 1). Not surprisingly therefore, Labour's return to office was heralded by ECRC activists as a potential turning point in the relationship between LBE and ECRC (Gazette Series, 11 June 1971: 12). As the decade proceeded however, there was little noticeable improvement in the relationship. The Ugandan-Asian (1972-73) and Southall youth (1976-78) crises certainly placed considerable strain on the relationship. Further, the evidence suggests that LBE's unwillingness to support an active and campaigning CRC, played a large part in the radicalisation of ECRC towards the latter part of the decade. Three issues reflected the state of their relationship: the two episodes mentioned above and the on-going dispute over bussing (see also Chapter 5 below).

During the early-1970s ECRC had placed itself at the head of the campaign against LBE's controversial bussing policy. Despite putting pressure on the previous Conservative administration to review the controversial policy, it had made little headway in its campaign. The initial reaction of the new Labour administration, however, was no more encouraging (Gazette Series, 30 July 1971: 1). The new policy was to retain the previous policy, although its status was to be reviewed periodically. The breakthrough did not come until 1974, when LBE finally conceded the principle that dispersal ought to be ended (Gazette Series, 19 July 1974: 7). However, any increase in the number of local school places in Southall was ruled out *before* 1978 (Gazette Series, 6 December 1974: 1).[25]

Meanwhile, pressure for ECRC to assume a more progressive and active role was rising from within its ranks. ECRC's reinstated Chairman, Barzey, warned that other policy actors - notably LBE - had managed to emasculate and contain both ECRC and the ethos of community relations on a number of fronts:

> We have lived and experienced the period of conciliation under the banner of civil rights; it has failed. We have seen members of the political parties working in community relations, and when they cannot win the organisation for the containment objective, they find reasons to leave. It is time that their actual role in community relations regarding the containment of immigrants' basic democratic rights was fully explored. (Gazette Series, 31 May 1974: 1)

ECRC had also proved to be a rather ineffective force during the Ugandan-Asian crisis. Apart from publicly labelling LBE's somewhat unwelcoming policy towards the refugees as 'Powellite', comparatively little was achieved by ECRC (Gazette Series, 15 September 1972: 1). In fact, the evidence shows that ECRC, rather than LBE, suffered the biggest short-term set backs in the political fall-out from the episode, eg. the 1973 IWA walk-out (Gazette Series, 15 June 1973: 1).

In the eyes of its radical and conservative critics alike, ECRC was beginning to be seen as *irrelevant* to local race relations. This view operated at two levels within Southall's Asian community alone. Firstly, among IWA and other traditional EMGs, this irrelevance was because of ECRC's indirect connection with both LBE and central government policy. This link - vastly exaggerated in any case - was increasingly seen as a threat to the black immigrant community. Withdrawal from ECRC was used as a convenient, if not entirely appropriate, outlet for this protest. Secondly, Southall's Asian youth became increasingly militant as a result of growing local racial violence at this time. Within this context, both ECRC and IWA were rejected and shunned on the basis of their conciliation-based channels of political activism. The sense of irrelevance and rejection was epitomised by the diminished credibility of both the traditional liberal policy framework in general, as well as the track-record of widely-perceived anomalies and grievances of the local RPE in particular.

The series of street disturbances in Southall in 1976 and beyond served to transform ECRC's relationship with both LBE and its EMG constituency. The growing level of *ad hoc* protest against the rise of far-right groups was incorporated into ECRC's long-standing criticisms of both LBE and the local police. In 1973, ECRC had commissioned an investigation into allegations of police harassment of local black youth; the report published at the end of the investigation indicated quite clearly that the issue ought to be placed onto the local political agenda.[26] In addition, the social problems of Asian youth were given new priority in ECRC's work. ECRC lobbied vigorously for additional LBE financial support, both for itself as well as for a number of special projects it had set up for black youth in the borough (Gazette Series, 6 August 1976: 12 and 21 July 1977: 1).

Whilst bodies such as IWA might have been slow off the mark in responding to the demands of frustrated Asian youth, ECRC showed itself to be more sensitive to these developments. Although ECRC and its traditional liberal policy framework had come under heavy criticism from the new wave of radical EMGs, it is clear that ECRC was determined not to be shut out of the RPE altogether. Clearly, it had become caught in something of a no-man's-land. On one hand, conflict over rival conceptions of community relations characterised its relationship with successive LBE administrations. On the other hand, its credibility amongst one of its natural constituencies, the Asian community, had also become strained, both in the eyes of its traditional EMG supporters as well as in the eyes of the new wave of radical EMGs. To that end, the tensions faced by ECRC were a reflection of the shortcomings of the philosophy of "community relationsism" applied in local politics.

The result of these events and changing circumstances was a re-evaluation by ECRC of its identity and role in the RPE. Although the costs may have included antagonism of LBE and the local police, ECRC clearly demonstrated that it was essential to review its own approach to the RPE. ECRC's introspection led to the adoption of a more progressive, campaigning profile beginning in 1976-77, in an attempt to regain its previous central - and relevant! - position in the RPE. As a result of the cumulative impact of the Ugandan-Asian and Southall youth episodes, ECRC's chances of rehabilitating its relationship with LBE were poor and unlikely to be revived. As ECRC's Treasurer commented in early-1977, the myth of a close LBE-ECRC nexus under a Labour administration had been exposed: 'During the last year we have found that the present [Labour] group controlling the Council is not better than any other' (Gazette Series, 21 January 1977: 3).

The basic ground-rules of the RPE were transformed substantially at this time. In the area of LBE-ECRC relations, more than in any other, the experience of the 1970s had dramatically challenged the nature of the local politics of race policy. The result was that at the start of the Conservative administration in 1978, ECRC arguably had more in common with local radical protest groups than with liberally-inclined sections of LBE. ECRC was now allied to radical, frustrated forces, and together they sought a dramatic reform in the borough's RPE.

Grassroots developments in Southall, 1976-78

Arguably the events in Southall during summer 1976 began a process that was to transform the character of local race relations and the RPE out of all recognition. Whereas previously a stable, if often ineffective, RPE had operated in the borough, the fall-out from this period questioned the legitimacy of both the prevailing RPE as well as aspects of the broader liberal policy framework. ECRC and IWA had previously participated in, and co-operated with, the LBE-dominated RPE. The events of this period caused them to re-evaluate their strategies.

In June 1976 a young Asian student, G.S. Chaggar, was murdered in Southall as a result of what was thought to have been a racist attack. Asian youth groups reacted to the Chaggar incident by launching a protest movement against racist attacks. Several organisations were established - dominated by the Southall Youth Movement (hereafter SYM) - to offer alternative channels of political expression and protest. The record of established bodies such as IWA was clearly thought to have failed. As a result of these developments, aspects of the prevailing local RPE were challenged and all but discredited for the first time since the mid-1960s.

The precise details of the events in Southall during this period are adequately documented elsewhere (Southall Rights/CARF, 1981; Messina, 1984). Similarly, the disturbances of April 1979 are well described by others (NCCL, 1980; Southall Rights/CARF, 1981). What can be said, however, is that the Chaggar incident and its immediate aftermath undoubtedly marked a milestone in both local *and* national race relations. The liberally-inclined Home Secretary, Roy Jenkins (in his second spell in the job), rushed to the scene to try to appeal for calm (Gazette Series, 11 June 1976: 1). Protest demonstrations, headed by a series of *ad hoc* leaders and committees, ran the real risk of spilling over into further disturbances. For example, the SGSS *Gurdwara* planned to stage a massive demonstration to show the unity of Southall against the threat of racial violence. ECRC's initial reaction, in contrast, was low key with its newly-elected Chairman, D.S. Chana, calling for a truce and 'return to normality' (Gazette Series, 11 June 1976: 3). Above all, established members of the local RPE emphasised that the incident should *not* be seen as a straight-forward black versus white conflict. Whatever else, things were not as they once were at grassroots level within Southall's Asian community. The anger and frustration, particularly of the younger members of the community, had been displayed. LBE and other RPE actors were left under no illusions about the scale and strength of grassroots feeling. According to a local press leader:

> The danger is that this one innocent student [Chaggar] may be turned into a martyr; a symbol of oppression; a reason for defiance and protest... This must not be allowed to happen. (Gazette Series, 11 June 1976: 8).

Once the immediate disturbances had ended, ECRC lost little time in attempting to capitalise on events and the perceived needs of black youth. For example, it relaunched a bid for £50,000 worth of funding from the Community Relations Commission for a multi-cultural youth centre. In the wake of the disturbances, the initiative was now warmly received by a number of councillors and the local press. ECRC leaders argued that only a body such as ECRC, rather than EMGs such as IWA, could help to fill the vacuum in the leadership of black interests in the RPE (Interview: ECRC leader, 1986). As Grubb argued: 'The grievances of Asian youth are expressed in terms of...a lack of confidence in the leadership provided by their leaders' (Gazette Series, 6 August 1976: 12). A few months later ECRC put in a bid for an increased LBE grant - rising from £11,000 to £15,000 - claiming that this was essential to 'avoid further street troubles'. 'Not everyone' stated an earlier ECRC Chairman, 'is convinced of the need to avoid trouble' (Gazette Series, 21 January 1977: 3). ECRC's implicit message was to warn of the greater likelihood of direct political action by the new wave of Asian youth organisations. Grubb meanwhile noted that these organisations' general refusal to affiliate to ECRC was a worrying sign for community relations in the borough (Gazette Series, 21 January 1977: 5). ECRC, therefore, was determined to use the climate engendered by the disturbances both to improve its position, and to redirect the attention of others in the RPE.

The ECRC warning was further reiterated by SYM following the end of the trial of those accused of the Chaggar murder. SYM now presented itself as the figurehead of alienated black youth. A fundamental generational schism had opened up which was likely to dominate both Southall EMG's internal political activity and Southall EMGs' external participation in the RPE. A local press editorial reflected on the newly transformed situation:

> With one demonstration, they [ie. Southall's youth] had managed to do what their parents and community leaders had failed in years of letter writing, dignified protest and tame meetings with officials from governments and councils. Little wonder that the young speak of last year's [ie. 1976] events as something of a victory. (Gazette Series, 6 May 1977: 6)

The realisation that young Asians were capable of taking things into their own hands was not lost on EMG establishment figures. IWA, in particular, was left responding to, rather than spearheading, events in Southall politics. Former IWA President Rai conceded that 'they [ie. Southall's youth] used the opportunity to vent their feelings. We [ie. IWA] tried to act as a bridge between youth and white society, but we found ourselves in an awkward position' (Gazette Series, 6 May 1977: 6).

The emergence of SYM and other groups signalled a new era of alienation and protest in Southall politics which was to prove to be of great importance in the RPE through into the 1980s. According to SYM's Director, B.S. Purewal, the new channels of activism opened up by SYM merely exposed the effective bankruptcy of existing IWA-dominated channels:

> After Chaggar almost everybody jumped on the bandwagon and said the incident highlighted various problems. The fact is that nobody has learnt any lessons. Nobody has gone out of his or her way to do something about the problems of young people. If something like Chaggar happens again the young people will not just demonstrate against the police. They will show their hostility towards all these organisations that claim to be trying to help them. (Gazette Series, 13 May 1977: 5)

Perhaps the most immediate result of the events of 1976 was the new style of leadership elected to serve IWA in the following summer. After an extended seven year term of office under the moderate - and often confused - leadership of A.S. Rai, Vishnu Sharma was elected as the new IWA President with a massive mandate.[27] Sharma's election signified a new direction for IWA. For although Sharma had been elected to the IWA executive on and off since the late-1950s, his 1977 platform was unique and uncompromising in its criticism of the existing state of local borough politics in general, and LBE's attitude of "colourblind" indifference in particular. He declared that Southall had been systematically neglected by successive LBE administrations. His response was to turn IWA into an active campaigning organisation, less concerned with Southall's own internal issues, and more sharply focused on the quality of Southall's public services from both LBE and central government. "Fair shares" served as an off-the-cuff slogan for his strategy. He explicitly challenged the received wisdom of more than a decade of stalled policy-making in the RPE:

> I believe they [ie. LBE] have neglected the area... We are always being told that the town has gone downhill because of the large black population. I don't believe that for a minute... We are certainly going to fight vigorously for a better Southall. (Gazette Series, 12 August 1977: 6)

Sharma's also stated for the first time IWA's willingness to co-operate, rather than compete, with SYM. His "Broad Alliance" strategy received wide media coverage. A local press editorial characterised the strategy in the following terms:

> The IWA for the last seven years has been low-key in its approach to the affairs of Asians in Southall and has kept its activities very much "within the family". The IWA under Sharma promises to shed any such insularity and to call upon the impatience and frustration of youth, declare its grievances and to speed its programmes. (Gazette Series, 12 August 1977: 6)

The net result was that, beginning in the late-1970s, a new brand of black political activism started to make its presence felt in the RPE. LBE came under heavy criticism from the new wave of EMGs attempting to either redirect or reform the RPE. Relatively little was achieved through this more confrontationalist dialogue during the first term of the Conservative administration elected in 1978. The 1982 re-elected Conservative administration however, responded in a more positive manner, not least as a consequence of the urban riots in Southall during 1981.

1971-78: an overview

The 1970s were undoubtedly a period of immense change in local race relations. The Ugandan-Asian refugee and Chaggar episodes put great pressure on the existing RPE. However, through a skillful combination of domination and the denial of legitimacy to rival voices, LBE was largely successful in keeping the local political agenda free from detailed discussion of its own track-record on race. In 1986 an independent researcher wrote of the 1971-78 Labour administration's record on race and public policy:

The Conservatives took control in Ealing in 1978 and inherited little more from Labour than the educational initiatives begun some ten years previously. Much of the major development in local authority policy has taken place *since* 1978... Labour in Ealing [between 1971-78] had *not* been a pioneering authority in any sense. (FitzGerald, 1986a: 4 - emphasis added)

LBE was assisted in this process by a number of factors. Firstly, as ECRC discovered, the community relations ethos came in for heavy questioning, both from within and beyond its ranks. Secondly, LBE was able to neuter the impact of ECRC's criticisms by arguing that community relations ought to remain outside the realm of conventional party competition. For this reason, full legitimacy for ECRC and its work always remained elusive. Thirdly, the weak profile of leading EMGs such as IWA - particularly following the 1976 crisis - meant that they were easily dominated in the RPE. Finally, LBE was highly successful in defending its record of policy-maintenance in the RPE, eg. on dispersal. Its capacity to maintain existing policies was aided by a combination of ideological imperatives (eg. the attachment to "colourblind" rules-of-thumb) and the wider policy process (eg. central funding restrictions and administrative difficulties).

The politics of "non-policy-making" seemed to characterise the RPE under two successive Labour administrations spanning seven years. The Conservatives returned to office in May 1978 facing a bleak and deteriorating RPE. Unlike the previous change of administration in 1971, expectations for the future remained low. Within months, the RPE was to enter a new and even more difficult period of crisis.

The "long" Conservative administration, 1978-86

The new Conservative administration took over at a time of exceptional change and volatility in local politics in Ealing Borough. The decade had begun with Conservative Alderman Hetherington predicting that it would take a long time to deal with the borough's 'immigration problem' (Gazette Series, 16 June 1971: 1). By the decade's closing hour, his vision had, to say the least, been borne out.

The borough had undergone a lengthy search for a clear direction on race relations. Between 1978-86 other factors continued to disrupt the attempt to find a sustainable path through the minefield of race-related public policy. Moreover, these disruptions were occasionally serious enough to signal a broader deterioration in race relations nationally. These disruptions provided LBE with powerful ammunition in its attempt to manage the RPE. Bias against RPE reform or policy-innovation was frequently mobilised in the borough *without* the direct intervention of LBE.

The Conservative's return to office

In addition to grassroots developments in race relations, the question of the political and ideological complexion of the LBE Conservative administration during this long period must be taken into account. Relations between policy actors within the RPE were further weakened as a result of the extreme polarisation of forces in local politics. At a party political level, there is little mistaking the widening gulf that crept into relations between the Conservative administration and its Labour opposition. This gulf, to some extent, helps to account for the visible radicalisation of the Labour Party in Ealing from the late-1970s onwards. Labour's shift leftwards embodied a new progressive position on race which sought to challenge the conceptual basis of the prevailing RPE.

Party-specific factors began to make a larger contribution to the RPE during this period. Whereas in earlier years a large measure of cross-party *consensus* existed on race - if only through its de-politicisation - a contrasting inter-party *dissensus* begins to emerge in the late-1970s. The evidence is sketchy to support any hypotheses concerning the electoral impact of the breakdown of the race consensus (Messina, 1985a). However, it is clear that the parties' respective moves away from the centre-ground on race contributed to a sharper debate over the conceptualisation of race in the RPE by the 1980s. This sharp contrast of outlook on race is illustrated by the respective comments of two leading Labour and Conservative councillors (speaking in 1986). According to one Labour member:

> Our highest priority within our new policy is to change attitudes, including our own, and we recognise the deep-seated racism of previous Labour Councils in Ealing, dominated by white men in particular. (Interview: Labour councillor, LBE, 1986a)

And a Conservative member stated:

> We [ie. the Conservative group] have always tried to ensure that there is no racial prejudice in the Council. But you have to recognise that there are at least two ways of going about doing that. There's Labour's way, which involves quotas and lowering standards and so on, in order to pull in more... minorities. And there's our approach which says that "everyone's equal" and should be treated on the merit of their application. (Interview: Conservative councillor, LBE, 1986a)

Further turmoil in Southall, 1979-81

The Chaggar incident of summer 1976, more than any other, dramatically awakened RPE participants to the extent of discord amongst Southall's Asian youth. The sense of local crisis was accentuated by further disturbances in Southall during the late-1970s and early-1980s. The best known examples were the April 1979 disturbances in connection with a National Front (hereafter NF) electoral rally in Southall, and the street disorders of the "hot summer" of 1981. It is worthwhile examining the former in greater detail.

The new Conservative administration had been voted in on a "hands-off" ticket to keep LBE's intervention in the RPE to a minimum. LBE was neither prepared to undertake positive reforms, nor to entertain suggestions of giving public subsidies to those wishing to challenge the legitimacy of race-related public policy altogether. The role of LBE in the prelude to, and aftermath of, 23 April 1979 graphically illustrates the discriminatory and damaging consequences of LBE's non-interventionist, "colourblind" philosophical policy stance. The initiative was left instead to other policy actors.

Following an alarming rise in racial tension during 1977-78, LBE had taken an uncharacteristicly interventionist line and voted to withold use of Ealing town hall for a NF booking (Gazette Series, 21 July 1978: 1).[28] The decision was a controversial one, and a number of Conservative councillors, citing ideological arguments relating to freedom of speech, voted to honour the NF booking. Nine months later during the spring 1979 General Election campaign, LBE was again forced to deal with the same thorny issue. On this occasion, the NF leadership cited electoral law in support of its right to hire public premises for a nominally-public election meeting. The issue was particularly provocative since the booking requested the use of Southall's old town hall (located in the heart of Southall's main commerical district). LBE narrowly voted to uphold the application, in spite of the counter argument to request the police to ban the meeting as a threat to public order.[29] The NF meeting inevitably fuelled local passions, and a groundswell of protest quickly emerged. ECRC and IWA, although weakened by the events of 1976, unhesitatingly began co-ordinating the protest campaign. Almost inevitably, the NF meeting indirectly resulted in an unprecedented level of street disorders in Southall. Frantic activity by numerous local EMGs and individuals to convince LBE to reverse its decision proved fruitless. These moves also included multiple requests for the Home Secretary's intervention and even a telegrammed appeal from the IWA President to the Prime Minister.[30]

The episode demonstrated two important features of the RPE. Firstly, it revealed the extent to which LBE was prepared to pursue its "hands-off" policy, despite the serious provocation to local race relations associated with such a stance. Secondly, it exposed the minimal real influence of EMGs, ECRC and others to present any sort of veto in the local RPE. The RPE was unmistakably dominated by LBE's control over key levels of decision-making, and the April 1979 episode demonstrated this central fact. Instead, LBE exercised its right of veto and excluded other RPE interests from its decision-making process. LBE was not faced with a routine RPE issue involving, typically, the budgetary process or LBE-ECRC relations. Instead, the evidence suggests that the major conflict between LBE and its protagonists involved rival conceptions of the RPE and the liberal policy framework behind it (see also Chapter 8 below).

Crisis in LBE-ECRC relations

The cumulative result of events between 1976-81 was to place great strain on LBE's relationship with ECRC. Other RPE policy actors also became disillusioned with the role played by LBE. However, it was ECRC that chose to take the most combative line with LBE. ECRC activists strongly believed that LBE was flying in the face of all the evidence that indicated it should begin moves to reform the framework of the RPE as well as some of its more controversial policies. LBE-ECRC relations had, of course, been strained on many occasions before. The main difference now lay in the view held by many ECRC activists that race relations in general - and not just ECRC alone - were being deliberately undermined and marginalised by LBE's policies and unilateral actions. In other words, ECRC's fear was for the fabric of local community relations when, for example, it found itself under heavy attack for its part in the April 1979 crisis. Further, familiar LBE charges that ECRC was trying to extend its jurisdiction into local politics were forthrightly challenged by ECRC as a smokescreen to hide LBE's own hand in the violent conflict. ECRC's Chairman, Chana, argued that his organisation was motivated by a concern for community relations, rather than its own narrow position:

> ECRC is broad-based and has to take account of the feelings of that broad-based membership. I cannot accept that this [ie. the April 1979 NF episode] was not an issue which involved ECRC. It would be impossible to sit back and do nothing when the National Front was meeting in our area. (Gazette Series, 18 May 1979: 3)

In taking a firmer stand, particularly following April 1979, ECRC took a number of risks. For one thing, it risked a split in its own ranks between those members in favour of extending ECRC's campaigning profile, and those members fearful of the penalties of such behaviour. A split did indeed occur at this time, revealing a divide between ECRC's officers and executive (Gazette Series, 18 May 1979: 3). It centred on the narrow, yet symbolic, question of whether ECRC should participate in a highly-charged march mourning the loss of the life of an anti-NF protestor, an east London teacher named Blair Peach, during the disturbances. ECRC can have been under little doubt that LBE's response was likely to be the by now familiar threat of financial excommunication. At a specially convened full council meeting less than a month after the disorders, backbench Conservatives launched an attempt to hold a financial ransom against ECRC. Supporters of the motion claimed that:

> In the light of its [ECRC's] contribution to the picketing of Southall police station and irresponsible behaviour at the riots, Ealing Council should withdraw its grant.

> ECRC is supported by grant-aid from this authority and has once again bitten the hand that feeds it by using the money to promote unnecessary fear in the hearts of those people it was created to assist. (LBE, 1979b; Gazette Series, 18 May 1979: 3)

For its part, ECRC remained largely unrepentant. Grubb, for instance, wrote to Metropolitan Police Commissioner McNee stating that the Southall community 'did not trust the police at the present time' (Gazette Series, 18 May 1979: 1). Sharma, also a leading figure on ECRC's executive, announced that, if the police wanted further information about unsolved incidents, then they should come to Southall since the community was in no mood to approach the police! (Gazette Series, 18 May 1979: 1). ECRC was the leading force in setting up an *ad hoc* group simply called the Co-ordinating Committee to provide financial help for those charged with offences. The Committee chose to deliberately shun the Conservatives and only invited representatives from the Labour and Liberal Parties, claiming quite bluntly that: 'The Tories caused the situation in Southall. We hold them to blame' (Gazette Series, 25 May 1979: 3).

LBE's behaviour had served to unite moderate and radical factions within ECRC. The common view was that, on this occasion, LBE's non-interventionist line was little more than provocative neglect (Interview: ECRC leader, 1986). As Chana argued convincingly in a lengthy letter to the local press:

> All this could have been avoided if the borough council had had the courage to make the right decision. All this...because the leader of the Council believes in abstract "free speech". The special council meeting showed the ignorance of some its members...based on prejudice and malice. This is not the sort of behaviour I would expect from our elected representatives. (Gazette Series, 25 May 1979: 6)

In sharp contrast, LBE adopted a harder line, voting in a heated debate to 'commend the police for their courage and patience during the Southall riot' (LBE, 1979b). The increasingly embittered Labour side responded with a counter-motion condemning LBE for sanctioning a meeting that proved to be well-short of the public election meeting it had been billed as. Labour Councillor P.S. Khabra, also a leading IWA figure, spoke of the desperation of Southall: 'A great human tragedy has taken place and I cannot understand why the Tory Group does not appreciate the situation' he said (Gazette Series, 18 May 1979: 3).[31]

Odd skirmishes between ECRC and LBE persisted throughout 1979-80. These exchanges usually involved raking over the events of April 1979, and the role of the police in particular (ECRC, 1979). Late in 1979, another public row erupted over the terms of reference of a proposed enquiry into the riot by the National Council for Civil Liberties (hereafter NCCL). ECRC had made great play of this investigation, claiming that NCCL had no local axe to grind and would therefore produce an impartial account of the incident. However, the police's refusal to co-operate with NCCL was condemned by ECRC, provoking yet another round of LBE-ECRC exchanges (Gazette Series, 12 October 1979: 1). The eventual published NCCL report stressed the sense of outrage felt by the Southall community which few politicians were willing to respect in the wider political battle over the riot:

> [No-one] appears to have perceived the necessity for saying something to allay the feelings of alienation produced in the Southall community or even express an understandinh of the affront which the day's events had caused. (NCCL: 1980: 14)

The first real casualty of this deterioration in relations was ECRC's grant application for the following year. LBE openly used the fall-out from April 1979 to twist ECRC's financial arm to try to get it to moderate its public profile. Early in 1980, LBE's Policy and Resources Committee voted to cut ECRC's grant by £4,000, unless ECRC could match this amount through its own fund-raising efforts (LBE, 1980a).[32] LBE-ECRC relations were thus plunged into a new crisis (Gazette Series, 25 January 1980: 1; LBE, 1980b and 1980c). ECRC was to remain out in the cold, cut off from LBE funding, for a period of three years until 1983. The situation forced ECRC into a position of financial strain, though this did not appear to emasculate its political voice in any way. It continued its attacks on LBE, no longer showing caution for fear of being financially penalised.

Finally, the local dispute soon filtered into the national spotlight. ECRC's alleged "extremist" reputation even produced an interjection from the junior minister at the Department of the Environment (with responsibility for race relations affairs) and Conservative MP for Ealing Acton, Sir George Young:

> The CRC should try to communicate and identify itself with the bulk of citizens in Ealing, instead of focusing exclusively on a small - and I fear diminishing - audience. The success of race relations in the Borough over the next 10 or 20 years will not depend on what is written in *Ealing News* [ie. ECRC's journal], but on the opinions, views and commitment of ordinary people... Many people in Ealing see ECRC as a group of intolerant, left-wing, anti-police activists subsidised by local rate-payers. ECRC can of course continue with this policy, but if they do, they cannot be expected to be subsidised by the rate-payers. (Young in *Ealing News*, 1980: 4)

The rise of the radical Left

The period 1978-82 is also significant because it marks the emergence of a new, polarised brand of local politics in Ealing. Arguably, the drift away from the consensual centre-ground on race occurred within both the Labour and Conservative Parties - nationally as well as locally (Layton-Henry, 1978; Messina, 1985a and 1989; Saggar, 1991b). However, the emergence of radicalism on race issues is more noticeable in Labour's ranks, with significant long-term consequences for the RPE in the borough.

Both Labour and Conservative LBE administrations in the 1960s and 1970s presided over an evolving RPE which retained stronger elements of continuity than change. From the viewpoint of ECRC and many EMGs, significant redirections of policy were as unlikely under Labour administrations as under Conservative (Interview: Labour councillor, LBE, 1986b). However, grassroots developments in Southall, beginning with the Chaggar incident in 1976, began to alter the party political framework within which race was discussed in the borough. Further, the April 1979 and summer 1981 disorders plainly served to widen the gulf between RPE interests. Serious discussion of local race relations issues was little more than a sham by the early-1980s. Instead, the RPE was increasingly becoming an arena for the expression of conflict over fundamental aspects of the liberal policy framework. These conflicts, in a sense, had always been subliminal to RPE debates since the 1960s. The main difference was that, not only had they been resurrected, but Labour and Conservative politicians had began to divide over these fundamental questions.

Another contributory factor was the changing make-up of Labour politicians and activists in the borough dating from about the time of the party's 1978 defeat. One observer, Grubb, later recalled that the new Labour opposition group had visibly come under the influence of a more self-consciously liberal faction of councillors (FitzGerald, 1986b). Many had been elected for the first time and were not exclusively from Southall wards.[33] This process was further accelerated during the 1982 local elections when Labour narrowly failed to win office. By the time of Labour's return to office in 1986, large numbers of comparatively young and outwardly radical Labour politicians had been selected or re-selected in winnable wards (Interview: Labour councillor, LBE, 1986c).

Prelude to major RPE reform

The period between the 1982 and 1986 local elections was one in which tremendous community-based pressure was exerted in trying to bring about RPE reform in Ealing. The image of LBE in local race relations had been subjected to extensive criticism since the late-1970s. Nonetheless, the Conservative administration was re-elected in May 1982 largely as a result of national electoral trends. Race relations remained a central area of local conflict, in which LBE was increasingly up against the combined forces of all other RPE actors. By the early 1980s however, LBE was showing signs of a more imaginative approach to the RPE. The long period of unbudging policy-maintenance was gradually replaced with a small measure of flexible innovation on one or two fronts. The motivation behind LBE's change of approach was, at least partially, to do with perceptions of socio-electoral change in the borough. In the view of influential members of the Conservative administration, the earlier inflexible stance of avoiding all discussion of policy-innovation and reform was thought to be an increasing liability (Interview: Conservative councillor, LBE, 1986b).

Furthermore, the autonomous, self-help initiatives of various community groups in Southall suggested that, if necessary, the umbrella role of ECRC could be selectively by-passed. LBE embarked on a gradual shift towards a policy of becoming involved in these developments, clearly preferring to be in a position of some influence, rather than remaining aloof and unresponsive (Interview: Southall UCA leader, 1985). The scope of the RPE was therefore expanded for the first time to encompass many self-help community projects, not least to reinforce LBE's role in them.

There are a number of illustrations of LBE's change of tack. One example is LBE's response to the summer 1981 disorders in Southall. Unlike the April 1979 disorders, these events were generally surrounded by a much smaller public display of acrimony between different RPE actors. Although the police were involved in both incidents, the accusations and counter-accusations concerning their role were markedly fewer and less hostile. Consequently, the efforts of both sides to set up a Home Office-sponsored Police Liaison Committee (hereafter PLC) in 1982 were not as doomed to failure as they might have been earlier (ECRC, 1982). The tone of ECRC's position on the police's role was altogether more conciliatory:

> Our aim was to try to set up a framework which would allow us to co-operate with the police and the Conservative Council... Of course they [ie. the Conservatives] are going to defend whatever the police do, but at least they weren't having to defend a police riot - as they did in 1979. (Interview: ECRC executive member, 1986)

LBE's more self-consciously constructive outlook was motivated by two factors. Firstly, there was pressure from the centre for LBE to bring ECRC and EMGs into the consultation process on certain aspects of LBE policy-making. For example, the Home Office's revised (1982-83) guidelines for S.11 spending required LBE to actively consult these interests (Home Office, 1982 and 1983; ECRC, 1983a and 1983b). ECRC's decision to co-operate with the PLC initiative, albeit cautiously, was another reflection of the improvement in relations (Gazette Series, 9 April 1982: 1). This improvement notwithstanding, mutual suspicions remained, and are lucidly illustrated through a comparison of the views of a backbench Conservative councillor with those of a senior ECRC officer on the police accountability issue:

> ECRC's anti-police attitudes in particular only alienates them from the main population in Ealing. Their behaviour in 1979 and 1980 was disgraceful, showing themselves bent on criticising the police on every possible occasion. I just hope they've learnt from that, and that they'll try to support the police in the very difficult job they have to do. (Interview: Conservative councillor, LBE, 1986c)

> In order to be a truly tripartite committee between the police, the local authority and the community, the committee must allow full discussion and participation. This has not happened so far. We want to develop the idea of an independent police monitoring group in the borough... The committee was formed in response to the riots when violence blew up between the police and young

people. The Council's attitude is defensive because the voices of anger have been excluded from the committee. (Gazette Series, 24 December 1982: 3 and 25 February 1983: 13)

Secondly, LBE was under pressure to show interest in numerous local initiatves to try to improve the climate of race relations (ECRC, 1983b). LBE's 1982 agreement to begin subsidising a handful of new community group projects in Southall reveals a limited but important step in its resolve to become more involved in community development issues, if not necesarily in race-specific issues. A good example is seen in LBE's partnership with IWA to redevelop the latter's Dominion Cinema premises in Southall as a major local community and leisure complex (Gazette Series, 19 February 1982: 5). This project was costed at approximately two million pounds and involved bi-lateral capital investment by both LBE and the Department of the Environment.[34]

Continuing "colourblindness"

It is important to remember however, that these initiatives were modest and consciously limited to non-race-specific issues. In many other areas, continuation of previous themes shaped the RPE. LBE's own internal decision-making machinery was an area the Conservative administration were determined to keep well beyond the scope of RPE discussion. In late-1983 the Conservative administration reacted strongly and negatively to the growing calls from Labour councillors for LBE to initiate a special race relations or equal opportunities sub-committee of the Council (Gazette Series, 2 December 1983: 7). Once again, the contrast between the political parties on this proposal could not have been sharper. According to a prominent Labour councillor:

> The degree of attention to the requirements of ethnic minorities is minimal. This is an important issue which the Council has steadily ignored. (Gazette Series, 2 December 1983: 7)

And, a Conservative councillor retorted:

> I doubt very much if race relations in other boroughs are better than ours. There is an obsession with colour and with divisions of race. This sort of motion is trying to perpetuate this...division. (Gazette Series, 2 December 1983: 7)

Two further examples can be cited to illustrate LBE's unwillingness to open up its own internal decision-making structures and processes to the so-called "race dimension". Firstly, LBE successfully stood out against strong pressure for it to adopt some form of ethnic monitoring. Heavy pressure for it to do so had been exerted by, among others, ECRC, the Labour Group and staff trade unions such as NALGO (Gazette Series, 16 December 1983: 5). Perhaps more than any other proposed reform, ethnic monitoring symbolised LBE's offical policy line of "colourblindness", and its proposed adoption was seen in principle as directly affecting LBE's own in-house policy and practice. According to recent independent research:

> The official policy adopted by the Conservative administrations of 1978 and 1982...has been to oppose ethnic record-keeping on the grounds that it would be discriminatory. Certainly...it is unclear how many of the ruling group accept the fact of racial disadvantage. (FitzGerald, 1986a: 4)

Secondly, between 1984-86 LBE successfully resisted even stronger local demands for it to formally adopt an equal opportunities statement of policy. LBE was under pressure from ECRC, the Commission for Racial Equality, the Department of the Environment, and others to use the Commission's 1984 Code of Practice for Race Relations as the basis for such a policy adoption. The Conservative Leader, Kenneth

Kettle, stated the nature of LBE's opposition to the proposal: 'We object to monitoring. It's offensive to label people and register them according to their colour' (Gazette Series, 20 January 1984: 4).

The reasons cited in objection to such a policy encapsulates the twin bases of the "colourblind" policy-maintenance position of LBE, so successfully defended during this period. The first was ideologically-centred on the alleged discriminatory nature of such a measure, allowing LBE to challenge its necessity. The second was articulated as a rational judgement of the utility of the proposal, focusing on the prohibitive cost of running a skeleton ethnic monitoring programme (estimated around £45,000 per annum). Its refusal to comply, however, rested mainly on the former reason rather than the latter. The administration's ideologically-motivated opposition to the proposal was so strong that it even resulted in Conservative councillors over-riding the strong practical recommendations of the LBE Town Clerk to comply:

> In any future case, unless your Officers can show compliance with the new Code, it seems likely that neither the courts nor the industrial tribunals will be convinced...that the Council's employment selection procedures were adequate to prevent discrimination. (LBE, 1983: 1).

LBE's refusal to debate these issues as legitimate areas of reform only served to convince critics that the town hall not only practiced racially discriminatory policies in effect, but also in intention. Critics now saw and openly referred to LBE as an island of racial injustice in a surrounding multi-racial sea. For example, in early-1984, a local Southall journal provoked a furious row with LBE councillors and officers, when its investigative feature on LBE's Social Services Department reported that:[35]

> Ealing has established a reputation as one of the most racist and reactionary boroughs in London. The Council's refusal to adequately meet the needs of a multi-cultural Southall are clearly demonstrated in education, housing, health, unemployment, and social services. (*Shakti*, 1983: 17)

Conclusion

Between 1965-86 the dominant interest in the RPE - LBE - was largely successful in maintaining and defending its own position of dominance. LBE's dominance was the central factor in defending the status-quo. In short, policy-maintenance, rather than policy-making or innovation, was the order of the day.

The period began with high expectations of new directions in race-related public policy, and proceeded with ever-greater grassroots, community opposition to large aspects of LBE's policy and practice. Educational dispersal (see also Chapter 5 below) together with public housing are both notable examples of policy spheres where policy-maintenance was the standard practice of LBE. These policies had serious distributional consequences for local public resources, reflected in the growing level of resentment towards the LBE administration.

However, the question remains: how was LBE able to affect and maintain such a situation? The situation arose and persisted mainly as a result of five key factors. First and foremost, the legacy inherited during the mid-1960s by the newly-created LBE, meant that race was already seen as a "problem" area placing great demands on the local policy-making process. LBE was therefore easily able to "manage" race policy within the RPE using a set of criteria not normally acceptable in local politics. A number of white, anti-immigrant interests were placated through the adoption of specific policy measures that restricted black-white contact and competition for public resource allocation, be it in housing, education, or whatever. Bussing, for example, began as a move to be seen to be "doing something", but soon developed a momentum of its own far-removed from its original aims (see also Chapter 5 below).

Secondly, over the course of this period, LBE became increasingly sophisticated in its use of the concept of legitimacy as an abstract rule-of-the-game. The participation of other policy actors in the RPE was selectively sanctioned through the use of this concept. Thus, LBE would often switch attention away from detailed discussion of specific policies, and towards questions about the right of other policy actors to participate in the mainstream RPE. This practice served to distract the attention of bodies such as ECRC and IWA away from detailed examination of LBE's policy record and criticisms thereof. Existing policies and practices were thus successfully and routinely shielded from systematic inspection and evaluation.

Thirdly, RPE interests such as ECRC and various EMGs were periodically beset by internal power struggles and other such distracting disputes. LBE, although not immune to internal splits, suffered relatively less in this sense. On the sole occasion when LBE's credibility was damaged by such a split (ie. the 1966 housing qualification dispute), the result was to strengthen the hand of local anti-immigrant interests in the RPE.

Fourthly, LBE was persistently able to claim that it was unable to engage in wholesale reform of its most controversial policies since its hands were tied by the centre. For example, additional central funds to alleviate Southall's dearth of local school places or council houses were not forthcoming. Moreover, using a familiar Conservative quasi-ideological argument of financial prudence, the 1978-86 administration flatly refused to fund such reform out of an increased rate levy. The 1971-78 Labour administration, lacking a similar ideological defence, instead argued that central spending restrictions meant that there would be no early departure from further policy-maintenance, however regrettably.

Finally, LBE was able to mobilise bias and maintain its often difficult policy stance by selectively introducing fundamental conceptual questions into narrow policy discussions. For example, the rival conceptualisations of race of different RPE participants was frequently cited as the basis of broader discussion over the acceptance of the traditional liberal policy framework. Small-scale disagreements over specific policy proposals quickly and all-too-frequently erupted into major conflicts over the framework and goals of race-related public policy generally (see also Chapter 8 below). LBE's commitment to the underlying terms of the liberal settlement meant that attempts to focus on race-specificity in local public policy were routinely treated with short shrift. The mobilisation of bias in the RPE is witnessed in LBE's steadfast refusal to adopt any of the various race-specific demands of other policy actors throughout this period, be it in respect of ethnic monitoring programmes, recruitment procedures, grant-aid to community groups, hostility towards bussing, Sikh religious schools, or whatever (see also Chapter 5 below). In other words, wherever LBE was able to side-step the question of the differential racial consequences of public policy, it did so.

Notes

1.   In June 1963 the idea of setting up some form of committee to discuss the impact of immigrants on Southall was first mooted. The initiative came from the Southall branch of the Transport and General Workers' Union and was then taken up by the Hayes and Southall Trades Council; see Gazette Series, 15 June 1963: 1.

2.   These were in the form of overcrowding notices under the following items of legislation: 1957 Housing Act (S.90); the 1961 Housing Act (S.11, 15, 16, and 19); and the 1964 Housing Act (S.73-90).

3.   The appointment was largely the result of the shock waves set off by the Smethwick episode earlier in the 1964 General Election. For a full account of Foley's appointment and tasks from March 1965 onwards, see Deakin, 1970: 104 and 113.

4.   According to the brief presented by LBE members and officers to Ennals at their May 1968 meeting, the cost of staff employed or to be employed as a result of the borough's large immigrant

population, was estimated at £209,800 for the 1968-69 financial year. Up to 50 per cent of this amount could be set against S.11 funding. LBE was referring to some 148 identifiable posts, 145 of which were directly employed by the Education Department. LBE's written submission concluded: 'What does seem reasonably clear is that exceptional measures will have to be adopted involving some local authorities in exceptional expenditure'.

5. Beaconsfield Road School Parents' Association was set up in summer 1963 with the express purpose of trying to limit the number of black immigrant schoolchildren attending the school. This action, together with the publicity received by the Association, heralded the start of the dispersal episode, initially operated by SBC and then by LBE. An *ad hoc* group of parents of children attending the school were invited to attend a special meeting with the Minister of Education, Sir Edward Boyle, held *in camera* at the school in October 1963; see Gazette Series, 19 October 1963: 1.

6. SRA had its origins in the Palgrave Avenue Residents' Association, established in August 1963. Its first Secretary was Margaret Penn who was also Secretary of SRA. She was to later resign from SRA amid accusations of the organisation being a "front" for racialists; see Gazette Series, 31 August 1963: 1.

7. The Conservatives proposed a motion calling for a 15 year residential qualification for applicants to be admitted onto the LBE council housing waiting list. The controversy, however, lay in an additional clause of the motion which sought to apply this extended qualification to "immigrants" (undefined) alone, thereby creating a differential policy for the residential qualifications required of blacks and whites respectively. Non-immigrant, indigenous applicants were required by the motion to have lived in the borough for only 5 years. Allowing for the revolt, the Labour ruling group were eventually able to defeat the motion by a slender majority of just 3 votes. For further details about the rebellion and explusion of the five Labour members, see Southall Rights/CARF, 1981: 27.

8. In early 1966 it was revealed that the SRA Secretary, Grace Woods, was also an officer of a body called the Racial Preservation Society.

9. Between 1962-68, BNP contested nearly all the local and parliamentary elections held in Southall. Their best result, by far, came in May 1963 when BNP fielded candidates in the two wards containing the highest immigrant concentrations in SBC. Both candidates managed to push the Conservatives into third place with an average 28 per cent share of the vote.

10. The change of name in 1968 was closely linked with a formal revision of its role and relationship with the newly-created Community Relations Commission; see Hill and Issacharoff, 1971.

11. IWA suffered numerous internal rows and splits during the 1960s. In March 1966, IWA (Great Britain) attempted to suspend the Southall branch because of the attempt by its executive to revise its consitution unilaterally and to register IWA as a Friendly Society for financial purposes; see Gazette Series, 4 March 1966: 1. In October 1967 a row erupted following allegations of financial imprudency; see Gazette Series, 6 October 1967: 1. Later in November 1967, a damaging split occured over the public support given by an executive member delegate - S.S. Gill - to a "Black Power"-inspired motion presented at a CARD meeting. Gill was expelled from the executive for his actions and was later elected as LBE's first black councillor (Labour) in the May 1968 local elections; see Gazette Series, 24 November 1967: 1; and 31 May 1968: 1.

12. In March 1966, a week before polling day in the 1966 General Election, the *Southall Gazette* carried out an *ad hoc* opinion poll in various different parts of the town. Three sampling points were used: the Broadway, Lady Margaret Road and King Street. The aggregated results, together with the actual returns on polling day, are given below:

Table 4.1 *Voting intentions of Southall electorate, 1966 General Election*

	Opinion Poll	General Election
Lab.	35 %	53 %
Con.	24	39
Lib.	5	-
BNP	2	7
d.k.	34	-

Source: Gazette Series.

13. During the period 1965-86, Labour dominated Southall, as well as the western part of Ealing Borough in general. The only occasion when Labour suffered substantial defeat was in 1968. On this occasion, the Conservatives recorded a landslide victory, leaving Labour with just five seats in the whole borough. In addition, two SRA candidates were returned in Southall wards. The details of Labour's strength in the four Southall wards (each returning three members) are as follows:

Table 4.2 *Labour and non-Labour representation of Southall wards, 1964-86*

	1964 [a]	1968	1971	1974	1978	1982	1986
No. of Lab. seats	9	2	12	12	11	12	12
No. of non-Lab. seats	3	10 [b]	0	0	1	0	0

[a] The first LBE elections were held in May 1964 one year in advance of local government reorganisation and the creation of LBE in April 1965.
[b] Includes 2 SRA councillors (ex-Independent and ex-Labour).
Source: author's calculations.

14. In May 1968 a prominent local Asian GP, N.S. Mangat, stood as a Conservative candidate in Northcote ward in Southall. Despite a well-publicised and colourful campaign, Mangat only finished fifth in the poll. The Conservatives had, nonetheless, gained control of LBE for the first time by a massive 53:7 majority in full Council. A week after the election Mangat was named as one of the Conservatives' five nominations for Aldermanic vacancies, precipitating a storm of criticism from, among others, Gill who had in fact topped the poll in Northcote; see Gazette Series, 17 May 1968: 2. Mangat served as Alderman for the next five years. In early 1973, his name was associated with the emergence of a new, highly-vocal EMG called the British Indians Board. In 1973 the Board was reported to have complied a "blacklist" of "known racists" in the borough and threatened to publish the relevant names; the "blacklist" included names of police officers, Aldermen, and LBE officers and members. Inevitably, a major public row erupted over the use of such tactics. Most importantly, Mangat was the subject of an immediate disciplinary inquiry by the Conservative Group executive. Mangat was asked to resign; he refused and was expelled instead on four counts of misconduct including the "blacklist" affair. He continued to serve after his expulsion but as an unwhipped Alderman; see Interview: Conservative councillor, LBE, 1986b; Gazette Series, 23 January 1973: 1; and 2 February 1973: 1.

15. ECRC's existing grant from LBE in 1969-70 was £4,100. In early-1970 it submitted an increased bid of £4,400 for 1970-71. This bid was rejected by the General Purposes Committee who voted to peg the grant at £4,100 and was upheld by the full Council; see LBE, 1970b and 1970c.

16. In September 1970 a meeting between the executive of the Indian National Association (hereafter INA) and the Conservative Leader, Alderman Hetherington, received wide local publicity; see

Gazette Series, 18 September 1970: 15. At this meeting, the Association's support was pledged to the Conservatives' proposal to incorporate ECRC into the functions and machinery of the town hall. The meeting resolved that the first move in this process would be to ensure that ECRC's senior officer was an appointment of the LBE General Purposes Committee. Unfortunately, very little is known or obtainable about INA's membership, background and leadership.

17. Full details concerning the relative deprivation of Southall and Acton - on the western and eastern edges of Ealing Borough respectively - are provided in a document published by Ealing Housing Aid Service. In particular, the quality and quantity of housing stock was shown in the report to be markedly poorer than in other parts of the borough; see EHAS, 1980.

18. For a short history of IWA, including the largest and best-known Southall branch, John's study for the Institute of Race Relations is unmatched in detail. This study gives some attention to the perennial splits in the organisation, and highlights the social as well as political reasons behind centre-periphery tensions in IWA; see John, 1972.

19. Interestingly, the Board does not appear to have played any further part in local Southall political or community life after the 1972-73 "blacklist" affair. By the mid-1970s, Mangat had also gradually dropped out of the limelight; see interview: former IWA President, 1985.

20. In correspondence with the Social Services Secretary, Sir Keith Joseph, LBE demonstrated that any increased central spending on local government social services did not necessarily translate into higher spending by authorities such as LBE. This was because such spending was formula-related, based on the Rate Support Grant. LBE argued that it received considerably less than the national average Rate Support Grant subsidy of 58 per cent. In 1972-73, LBE's expenditure was £34 million. However, since this expenditure was offset against various other grants received by LBE, its Rate Support Grant subsidy was just £10.4 million (as opposed to £19.7 million had it attracted Rate Support Grant to the extent of other similar boroughs). LBE's argument, therefore, was that any central monies targetted for authorities facing large-scale, immigrant-related expenditure ought not to be channelled through additional Rate Support Grant, but rather through programmes such as S.11.

21. An emergency meeting was held between LBE councillors and officers, and senior Department of Education and Science and Department of the Environment officials on 19 July 1972. LBE pressed the case for maximum central government aid to allow it to build two new schools in Southall with 640 places. These schools were to be ready by the 1974-75 school year and not subject to the 40 per cent immigrant quota set for other Southall schools; see Gazette Series, 21 July 1972: 1.

22. The reception committee set up by IWA, ECRC, EMGs and others to help receive the expected influx of Ugandan Asian refugees was named the West Middlesex British Ugandan Relief Committee. Its unanimously-elected President was Rai (also President of IWA), and it met at the IWA-owned Dominion cinema for the first time in September 1972.

23. The Institute of Voluntary Service compared the records of four London boroughs to the Ugandan Asian influx (Ealing, Camden, Brent and Wandsworth). The Institute estimated - from a variety of poorly-cited sources - that 1,000 such refugees had probably settled in Ealing. It criticised LBE's poor response to the crisis, in comparison with the actions taken by the other local authorities examined.

24. The IWA-led walkout was obviously a very damaging blow for ECRC, so soon after the uproar over the Ugandan Asian refugees. It precipitated the resignations of at least two other affiliated EMGs: the Afro-Caribbean Society and the Indian Overseas Congress. In addition, Barzey, ECRC's Chairman, resigned in protest against the retrospective implementation of the 1971 Immigration Act.

25. In December 1974, at a LBE full Council meeting, the Education Committee Chairman, Michael

Elliott, announced that the dispersal system would be extended from 11 to 12 year olds at the start of the new term in September 1974. Elliot reported that, even if all LBE's schoolbuilding plans were agreed to by central government and went ahead as planned, then only another 1,280 places could be created in Southall by 1978. He sugested that this was the earliest date by which the dispersal system could be ended.

26. The Pullé Report was commissioned by ECRC in conjunction with the Runnymede Trust in 1972. Stanislaw Pullé, a visiting scholar from the US, was asked to investigate a catalogue of complaints ECRC had received and logged from young Asians and Afro-Caribbeans about alleged mistreatment by the police in Southall and Acton. The cases stretched back over a number of years and had largely been left un-investigated, either by ECRC or the police itself. In short, the report concluded that clear evidence of police abuse and harassment existed in a number, though not all, of the cases looked at. It went on to make a number of suggestions as to how better police-immigrant relations could be fostered in the borough, based on the active involvement of ECRC, LBE Social Services Department, and the management of the police force; see Pullé, 1973.

27. The 1977 IWA elections were the first held since 1973 despite a constitutional requirement for biennial elections. The Rai leadership was deeply unpopular at this time for its comparative low profile in local politics. A genuine feeling existed throughout Southall that IWA under Rai had not met the needs of Asian youth during the Chaggar episode of the previous summer; see interview: IWA leader 1985; interview: Southall UCA leader, 1985; interview: Labour councillor, LBE, 1986b. In the circumstances, therefore, it was surprising that Rai was able to secure as many votes as he did. The final result of the Presidency poll was: Sharma=1,706 votes versus Rai=1,407 votes.

28. On 21 July 1978 the full Council met to debate a motion to refuse to allow the National Front to use or hire LBE premises. The vote taken was an unwhipped one, with a majority upholding the non-booking policy (by 35:28 votes).

29. A full account of the respective arguments for and against use of the 1936 Public Order Act to ban the march and meeting is provided in the report prepared by the National Council for Civil Liberties; see NCCL, 1980. The report was the work of the Unofficial Committee of Inquiry set up by the NCCL following the disturbances and was chaired by Professor Michael Dummet of the University of Oxford. The report noted that a spontaneous protest march on 22 April 1979 - the day before the NF meeting - had attracted some 5,000 people and had involved little or no violence. The protests of the following day however, resulted in approximately 340 arrests and over a hundred injuries. Many of those arrested and charged subsequently appeared before magistrates courts long distances from Southall (the most common being Barnet Magistrates Court in north London); this practice served to further undermine Southall's relations with the police and became a heated issue throughout 1979-80. The report also rebutted the widespread view that the disturbances were caused by outside "extremist" elements, suggesting instead that the heavy-handed style of policing was at least partly to blame.

30. In addition to the ECRC telegram to the Prime Minister, IWA leaders also sent messages to the Prime Minister and Home Secretary seeking their intervention; see interview: former IWA President, 1985.

31. Khabra, always known for his forthright contributions, had previously gone further by stating to the national and local press that the events of 23 April 1979 had reminded him of the gas chambers of Nazi Germany. He was, needless to say, speaking metaphorically.

32. In January 1980, following eight months of heated exchanges between ECRC and LBE, the former's grant for 1980-81 was slashed by £4,000 to £18,300. In order for ECRC to receive a fully restored grant at 1979-80 levels, LBE laid down a requirement that ECRC had to find matching funds to the level of their reduced LBE grant; see LBE, 1980a and 1980b.

33. This impression is based on a transcript summary supplied to me of an interview of Martyn Grubb who was the senior officer at ECRC for 13 years until early-1980; see FitzGerald, 1986b.

34. The Environment Secretary, Michael Heseltine, visited Southall on 26 February 1982, in order to view the proposed site at which the IWA-owned cinema would be demolished and rebuilt as a leisure and community centre. He chose the occasion to announce that his department had agreed in principle to provide up to £1.8 million in capital funding for the project.

35. In late-1983 a local Southall journal, *Shakti*, ran a strongly-worded feature on the LBE Social Services Department. The article, rather loosely-based and sketchy in its evidence, argued that LBE was guilty of 'institutional racism'. The article claimed that the Department's Director lacked interest in service delivery for ethnic minorities. The outcome was a major row between LBE and the journal's editor. The episode reflected the extremely poor relations that existed between both sides based, as it was, on mutual suspicion and hostility; see *Shakti*, 1983.

5 Educational dispersal in Ealing, 1957–81: a case study

Introduction

The question of whether a school classroom ought to accommodate upwards of a third of Asian immigrant schoolchildren does not immediately strike the casual observer as being the sort of issue at the core of race-related public policy. Indeed, such an administrative concern may seem trivial in comparison with some of the more visible and potentially volatile race issues of the past thirty years. Issues to do with housing and employment, to say nothing of inter-race and police-immigrant tensions, are the most common conceptions of the impact of race on British politics and public policy since 1958.[1]

But such impressions may mislead. In its own way - and for reasons outlined in this chapter - the issue of Asian schoolchildren in the classroom was to crystallise the reaction of a white-dominated local political system to the concept of a multi-racial society. This reaction can be seen both in terms of local political debate as well as in the broad direction of local public policy to deal with the putative "problem". Over a ten year period beginning in the late-1960s, as much inter-racial animosity and political energy was expended in a frontline west London borough,[2] as had been previously witnessed in Notting Hill or Nottingam. Moreover, as the policy debate moved on through the 1970s, Ealing's bussing dispute came to rank alongside the racial problems of places such as Smethwick, Wolverhampton and Bradford.[3]

Educational dispersal policy,[4] as practiced by Southall Borough Council (hereafter SBC), and its successor, the London Borough of Ealing (hereafter LBE), was, in a sense, about a concern for the future integration of the white and non-white communities. The concern came in large part from an implicit recognition of the significant problems associated with the settlement of large numbers of Asians in the town from the mid-1950s onwards. The fear generated by their arrival - and unavoidable call upon local public services such as education and housing - could have led to a variety of policy responses.[5] This chapter seeks to provide answers to two crucial questions concerning the response of policy-makers to the challenges of racial and ethnic pluralism: why did the policy process lead to dispersal?; and why did it not result in a segregationist or a *laissez-faire* policy?

The choice of the bussing issue is significant for this study in at least three related senses. Firstly, the issue - more than any other - helps to summarise the nature of the public policy debate on race that took place in the borough for a large part of the 1965-86 period of this study. In Southall the issue was part of a series of inter-related controversies over what the town's newspaper persistently labelled as 'the immigrant problem'. These controversies spanned residential overcrowding, public health standards, local jobs, linguistic barriers, and so on. Local education policy - and the dispersal question in particular - became the symbolic focus for many of these tensions and controversies. For this reason, bussing provides us with an excellent case study.

Secondly, dispersal provides interesting signals about the conceptualisation of race in the local RPE. A dynamic analysis is required that explores and contrasts the dominant themes of the RPE in the early-1960s as compared with the mid-1980s. In other words, whilst it may be tempting to view dispersal with contemporary eyes as peculiarly reactionary or discriminatory, the policy was, in its day, at the fore of integrationist thought and practice. If the conceptualisation of race is an important ingredient of the liberal policy framework, then this factor ought to be reflected in the bussing example.

Thirdly, bussing provides an excellent illustration of the forces leading to, and sustaining, minimal responsiveness by public policy agencies to external pressures. In other words, bussing amounts to a case study in protracted policy-*maintenance* by a local authority in the face of considerable pressure for policy reform. One of the most significant factors in the maintenance of the policy was the ability of key policy actors to successfully control the areas of legitimate RPE debate. The mobilisation of bias in the RPE meant that the debate over bussing systematically avoided examination of the serious distributional affects of existing policy across different racial groups. The continued life of bussing is explained in these terms, and its eventual abandonment transpired only once attempts were made to bring such distributional questions back into legitimate RPE debate.

The chapter is composed of five sections. The bussing episode, both as an issue and as a policy, *in toto*, stretches over more than twenty-five years. There are four fairly distinct phases in the policy life-cycle, each of which form the basis of the discussion: firstly, the *adoption* of the policy by SBC between 1957-65; secondly, the successful *operation* of the policy by LBE between 1965-71; thirdly, the *maintenance* of the policy between 1971-78; fourthly, the *abandonment* of the policy between 1978-81. Fifthly, the chapter considers the implications of the bussing policy example for local race-related public policy. The chapter concludes that the local authority ignored, diverted or otherwise took no notice of non-white service delivery demands. The policy outcome of the RPE amounted to little short of the non-recognition of non-whites interests in the local political system. Messina (1984 and 1989) has claimed that interests of black people were allowed too 'slip between the cracks' of the political system. The chapter argues that his characterisation misses the point in focusing on party competition-centred explanations. Instead, the invisibility of black interests appears to have had significantly more to do with the underlying framework within which local race policy was fought over - a framework inspired and guided by the liberal settlement of the 1960s.

Policy adoption, 1957-65

The arrival of large numbers of Commonwealth immigrants from the mid-1950s onwards placed new and uneasy strains on local public services in many parts of Britain. In the case of Southall, the presence of Asian schoolchildren in local schools remained on a fairly modest scale until the 1950s. Southall's immigrant population was mainly made up of working men for most of the first decade of settlement; the great majority had come as labour migrants whose families only arrived following a number

82

of years of separation. The modest Asian school-age population was set to rise dramatically as a consequence of family reunification and the high fertility rate of the relatively young immigrant community (Southall Rights/CARF, 1981: 11-22; Interview: former IWA President, 1985).[6]

During the period until 1965 local government responsibility in the Southall district rested with SBC. Education was in the hands of the Education Committee of Middlesex County Council (hereafter MCC) at a strategic, guiding level. The specific educational arrangements for Southall's schools were presided over by Southall Divisional Education Executive (hereafter SDEE), a body appointed by SBC but also accountable to MCC Education Committee.[7]

The linguistic question of Asian pupils' fluency in English first appeared in a report prepared by Southall's Divisional Education Officer presented to SDEE in January 1957 (SDEE, 1957a). The report identified the problem of linguistic adjustment, and it was proposed to set up special language classes in a single primary school for up to 30 pupils. The issue was discussed solely within the terms of reference of an administrative decision by SDEE acting on specialist advice given by its officers. The Executive acted on the recommendation in March 1957 and shortly afterwards a small unit run by a specialist language teacher was established at North Road School (SDEE, 1957b; Gazette Series, 9 March 1957: 1). A policy decision had been taken to direct a proportion of the education budget - albeit minute - towards a discrete, race-related programme. There was no wider debate on black immigration. The decision had not been significantly influenced by any consideration of the pros and cons of segregated or integrated public education (common in the United States at that time). Within a few years, the issue of the education of immigrant schoolchildren would be virtually indistinguishable from broader debates about race and immigration public policy.

The legacy of the 1950s

The numbers of Asian faces continued to grow exponentially in Southall classrooms during the late-1950s. There are no reliable figures for their numbers on SDEE's roll-call during the 1950s. However, it is likely that from an overall Asian population of between one and two thousand, the school-age population would have been of the order of a few hundred (Interview: former IWA President, 1985). SDEE statistics from 1960 show that ten per cent (or 750) of Southall schoolchildren were classified as "immigrants" (Southall Rights/CARF, 1981: 31). Four years later in 1964 this figure had risen to fifteen per cent (or 1,130).

From 1957 through to 1963 relatively few political developments took place in relation to immigrant education in Southall, other than the gradual expansion of the 1957 language fluency scheme. At the same time, however, the growing numbers of Asians settling in the town led to rising anti-immigrant sentiment expressed from a variety of sources. In particular, public service provision issues relating to the newcomers had begun to edge onto the local political agenda during this period. Ominously, the local press ran a full page special feature on the fissions caused by the desegregation of schools in the United States following the Little Rock episode in late-1957 (Gazette Series, 14 September 1957: 7). Few, if any, would have predicted that a similar controversy would arise closer to home in SDEE's attempts to steer a middle path between segregated and integrated schooling.

In 1963 SBC and SDEE faced the problems of race and education on their own. There was little tangible help available from outside bodies, let alone the possibility of a cross-borough solution to the growing crisis. With the issue of local government reform in Greater London only just beginning to emerge onto the national political agenda, there was little hope of an early solution being found beyond the immediate capacity of SBC and SDEE. In fact, although there was minimal anticipation of local government reform in public debate at the time, in early-1963 SBC was a little over two years away from amalgamating with two neighbouring boroughs to form a new larger local authority, LBE. Education, like most other borough council services, was to be reorganised such that the old SDEE would be disbanded. Responsibility would then pass to the local education authority run by the new LBE Education Committee. Meanwhile, SDEE's overall policies were accountable to the Education Committee of MCC (the county to which Southall belonged). A meeting of MCC's Education Committee was held in February 1963 in order to plan the sharing of both resources and commitments between the reorganised Executives (MCC, 1963; Gazette Series, 16 February 1963: 8). Through the discussion, the implications of reorganisation soon became apparent, with a minority of representatives registering alarm over the future requirements of Southall's immigrant schoolchildren. Consequently, a deputation was sent on behalf of MCC's Education Committee to press the Minister for Local Government and Housing, Keith Joseph, for help. It proposed establishing several smaller, "mini" local education authorities as one method of limiting the so-called 'immigrant education problem' posed by Southall. It achieved nothing.

The 1963 BNP catalyst

Meanwhile, the linguistic problems said to be associated with the education of Asian immigrant children were beginning to receive increasing local public attention. At a public meeting organised by SDEE in February 1963, its chairman, Councillor W.E. Jones, outlined different aspects of the Executive's response to immigrant education difficulties (Gazette Series, 16 February 1963: 5). Once opened out for public discussion, the main themes of the mostly-white gathering's concern were two-fold: firstly, the need for a greater degree of segregation in the classrooms to ensure that "sub-standard" English did not infringe white schoolchildren's educational opportunities; and secondly, the financial cost of special language tuition for immigrant pupils. On both points, Councillor Jones evaded clear or reassuring answers, except to acknowledge that SDEE was liaising closely with the IWA's cultural sub-committee, though it was not clear to what purpose.

The real precipitant for the massive row over immigrant education that was to follow came in April-May 1963. The British National Party (hereafter BNP) singled out two Southall wards in which it fielded two candidates in the spring 1963 SBC local elections. Standing on an explicitly anti-immigrant platform, both candidates did remarkably well in the May 1963 poll: in fact, one managed to push the Conservative candidate into third place with an impressive 28 per cent share of the vote.[8]

The election was undoubtedly the first real race-specific electoral contest in Southall in which the immigrant - or indeed anti-immigrant - card was openly deployed by a local party. It was significant for at least three more reasons. To begin with, it was the first time an extreme far-right - and allegedly fascist - political party had contested an election in Southall's history. Furthermore, the BNP breakthrough came in Hamborough ward containing the highest concentration of black immigrants in the town.[9] But more importantly still, it was responsible for laying down the markers within which many future white anxieties on aspects of immigrant settlement would be vented - eg. allegations concerning co-racial education, overcrowding, disease, etc. As one of the BNP candidates put it:

> We are particularly concerned about health standards which are being affected by gross overcrowding. The education of our children is being retarded by the numbers of coloured youngsters in the schools. I believe they should be kept in certain areas of the country. (Gazette Series, 27 April 1963: 1)

The campaign had two primary results in terms of local politics; these were pushing in opposite directions. On one hand, BNP's presence incited a volley of anti-fascist reaction on the part of the political establishment (both Left and Right) in Southall. Southall's Labour MP, George Pargiter, launched a scathing attack on BNP describing them as 'sinister fascists', comparing their "Keep Britain White" slogan with the anti-semitism of Nazi Germany (Gazette Series, 4 May 1963: 4). On the other hand, BNP served to crystallise a wide variety of fears held by the white community about their new black neighbours. At a superficial level, this fear was reflected in BNP's strong electoral showing. But, more importantly, the evidence suggests that Southall's political establishment was placed on the defensive over immigration. White interests in Southall could, for the first time, legitimately voice their concerns and expect to be heard seriously, both by their representatives and political élites generally. Thus, the anti-immigrant lobby was both condemned and recognised at one and the same time. In Pargiter's words: '[Asian immigrants] bring with them their social habits and their standards do not conform to our standards...but voting for the BNP does not settle anything' (Gazette Series, 25 May 1963: 1)

The 1963 BNP vote may not have settled anything but it did, for the first time, bring black immigration, and related issues to do with public service provision, firmly onto the local political agenda. Ironically, it was the topic of children to which Pargiter turned as evidence for his conclusion that the BNP triumph had been a freak abberation unlikely to be repeated, and that the solution lay in the "colourblind" world thought to exist in the classrooms of Southall. The MP continued: 'I have not heard of any colour prejudice problem in the schools because there is no colour bar among children' (Gazette Series, 25 May 1963: 1). He may well have been right. But he was not to know that it would be in the name of those same schools that so much of the early conflict over race in local politics would take place.

Ministerial intervention

In July 1963 the issue received renewed attention when the local press ran a headline story entitled 'Growing Problem of Educating Immigrant Children' (Gazette Series, 6 July 1963: 1). The report contained details of a special emergency meeting called by the headmistress of Beaconsfield Road School to respond to the alleged fears of white parents concerning the growing numbers of Asian children in the school. The Mayor of SBC and SDEE representatives were also present at the well-attended meeting, which was chaired by SDEE chairman, Councillor P. Southey.[10] A few days later SDEE met to consider the strength of feeling shown by white parents at the *ad hoc* school gathering (SDEE, 1963). SDEE restricted itself to exploring possible solutions that would maximise the sense of being seen to be "doing something". The Executive decided to send a deputation to discuss Whitehall's potential role in finding a solution with the Minister of Education, Sir Edward Boyle.

SDEE placed a four-point exploratory plan before the Minister (SDEE, 1963). This plan reveals a great deal about SDEE's broad approach to the problem. Two of the four points were largely administrative alterations. The remaining two points were more far-reaching: to seek a ministerial view on (white) parents being allowed to transfer their children to schools outside their (presumably immigrant-concentrated) catchment areas; and to solicit support for special status resources for SDEE's immigrant education difficulties. These represented both a call for dispersal in some form, as well as a new expanded criteria enabling local government to receive additional central government allocations for its education budget. The dispersal element of the plan remained ambiguous and indirect at this stage. The emphasis lay on the notion that it would be *parents*, rather than education authorities, who would opt to transfer children from one school to another for *non-educational* reasons. Moreover, the process would be a voluntary matter and no mention was made of compulsion or discrimination. The burden of action at this early stage clearly rested with disgruntled white parents.

The underlying concern of white parents (to which SDEE felt it was responding) was that white schoolchildren were becoming "swamped" by immigrant schoolchildren. The latter's putatively poor linguistic ability and "alien" cultural background were said to have a detrimental affect on the educational standards of the former. As one Labour councillor argued:

> I might say speaking for the majority of members that we feel it would be a sad day for Southall from a social and educational standpoint, if Beaconsfield Road School ever became an all-Indian school. That is why we are asking for the support of the County and the Minister. (Gazette Series, 6 July 1963: 1)

In August 1963 the first Southall deputation (made up of SBC and SDEE leaders, and led by SDEE chairman, Councillor Southey) met with Boyle. The background to the deputation was one of constant press reports of alleged Asian overcrowding, street brawls, unhygienic living conditions, *ad hoc* parental demonstrations against immigrant schoolchildren, and so on. Moreover, SBC was under constant pressure to step up its campaign of prosecution against overcrowding by Asian householders.

There appears to have been two distinct, yet intertwined, themes in the Council's collective, cross-party response to these various issues. On one hand, councillors were keen to be seen to be taking the issue seriously, conscious that public feeling was increasingly hostile to their previously perceived soft line, particularly on overcrowding. A senior Labour councillor pleaded that:

> I am not complacent about the situation and nor is the Health Committee. It is suggested that we treat this matter with kid gloves in case we are accused of racial discrimination and given a colour bar tag. But we are doing our utmost about the situation... We want to find out all the problems and weaknesses, and then take them to the Minister. (Gazette Series, 27 July 1963: 1; SBC, 1963)

On the other hand, however, councillors repeated optimistic rhetoric that time and goodwill would produce the results sought. These results, presumably, would be measured as a change of "character" and "behaviour" among local Asian immigrants. Another Labour councillor spelt out the terms of the integration equation:

> Although we should help the immigrants in every way, they must also help themselves and attempt to conform to our ways. Until they learn to live like us, I don't think we can have peace in this borough. (Gazette Series, 27 July 1963: 1; SBC, 1963)

The deputation's visit to Whitehall amounted to something of a litmus test of whether SBC or SDEE could actually do anything at all about the immigrant question as a whole. It received wide and favourable local (and national) press coverage, thereby successfully creating a sense of concern and activity. General support for the first two points of the preliminary plan were signalled by the Minister; the third (and most important) point received a good hearing; whilst the fourth received no comment at all. The biggest publicity victory, however, was in convincing Boyle to pay a return visit to Southall in order to inspect conditions on the ground for himself, and to discuss the dispersal option further.

A week prior to the Ministerial visit the whole immigrant education issue flared up yet again. This time it revolved around SDEE's plans for a new specialist language unit and reception class for a group of 18 immigrant schoolchildren at Lady Margaret Road Infants School (Gazette Series, 12 October 1963: 1-2). The 18 were to be bussed to the school from their various catchments areas across Southall, having failed to secure admission to local infant schools due to lack of capacity. The decision to bus these children was more than an *administrative* decision in response to overfull classrooms. Technically, a homogeneous ethnic group had been classified together by SDEE as suitable for inter-school transfer (ie. bussing). There was no scope within the decision either for their accommodation into a variety of overflow schools, as might have been the case for their white counterparts without places. Neither was there any scope for them to be admitted into the mainstream classes of their new school. This decision was doubly significant since there was no evidence that these 18 pupils had come from immigrant-dominated schools; as infants, of course, they were in fact starting their schooling!

Nonetheless, the rising "moral panic" over education standards anticipated among white parents at the school, meant that SDEE had opted in advance to segregate the bussed pupils. Thus, the decision looked like a bussing policy *and* a segregation policy at one and the same time. Despite that, the Asian pupils' arrival was greeted with hostility by white parents. In the words of a spokesman for white parents at the school, the public debate on immigrant education was at a nadir:

> We are also concerned about their social behaviour because we understand that they do not know how to use toilets properly, not having had experience of them. (Gazette Series, 19 October 1963: 3)

The return ministerial visit took place in October 1963. Apart from its fact-finding aim, its purpose was to address a specially-convened meeting of (white and black) parents. Interestingly, much of the advance publicity in the local and national press made great play of Boyle's personal opposition to the segregation option, ie. a white-only and black-only schooling system. Instead, it was reported that the Minister favoured a simple white-majority solution. The implications of how to achieve such a majority - namely through bussing - were not mentioned at this stage. Meanwhile, SDEE instructed its Divisional Education Officer to conduct a comprehensive ethnic census of the Southall school population. Its results would form the basis of drastic revisions of SDEE's catchment area maps. These catchment areas, in turn, would be the basis of a dispersal plan acceptable to the Minister (Gazette Series, 14 September 1963: 1).

The broad outcome of Boyle's visit was two-fold. Firstly, white parents were given a range of assurances, both general as well as specific, by the Minister's dispersal plan. Secondly, the visit set in motion a series of trilateral talks between SDEE, MCC Education Committee and the Ministry of Education on how to turn the plan into a practical programme. Although formal segregation had been labelled as a non-runner, discrimination on grounds of race continued to play a role. It would be a much subtler role, involving racial quotas for what were thought to be "overly-dark" sending schools and "overly-pale" receiving schools. Boyle sensed that the policy had a chance of working insofar as it addressed white fears over standards. To Asian parents present at the meeting, he said:

> Parents might suffer some inconveniences; some children might have to go to schools that are not nearest their homes. But, in the end and in the best interests of your children's education and future, I hope you will accept this plan.

The Minister went on to fuse together the liberal concept of integration with the more palliative concept of dispersal:

> It would be wrong and dangerous to establish what in effect would be segregated schools. In the long run, the integration of the immigrant and domestic populations must be eased, and not hindered. As part of this plan, the proportion of coloured children in the school should not exceed the *educational danger-point* of one-third. (Gazette Series, 19 October 1963: 1 - emphasis added)

White and black community interests

The months of August and September 1963 witnessed the birth of Southall Residents' Association (hereafter SRA). Its inception came about as a result of three simultaneous petitions from separate groups of white Southall residents presented to SBC. The largest of these came from the Palgrave Avenue Residents' Association, featuring some 640 signatures with an aim to 'keep at least one part of Southall "white"!' (Gazette Series, 31 August 1963: 1). Palgrave Avenue Residents' Association and its *ad hoc* spokeswoman, Mrs Margaret Penn, were to later form the core of SRA. More than any other single grassroots community organisation, SRA was to have, in the months and years to follow, a major influence on the formation of a race-specific local political agenda. This agenda was achieved via its campaigning profile on issues such as the sale of private houses to Asian immigrants, the compulsory purchase of so-called 'immigrant-vulnerable' properties by SBC, and a more decisively segregationist SDEE policy on the immigrant education controversy.

IWA had also been closely involved in the October 1963 ministerial visit. Its leaders were keen to play a positive role in the developing RPE, and this was reflected in their initial stand on the dispersal plan. The consensus Boyle was trying to achieve around dispersal clearly extended as far as the IWA leadership. The support given by IWA lent an important degree of credibility to the plan, allowing its supporters to convincingly argue that it would both defeat the extremists of BNP, SRA and others, as well as promote the liberal goal of racial harmony. Commenting on a short meeting between IWA leaders and the Minister, one IWA leader, P.S. Khabra, pronounced that:

> It was a very successful meeting. We stressed the necessity of spreading our children out to all the schools and the Minister seemed to agree...his views satisfied everyone concerned including the IWA. (Gazette Series, 19 October 1963: 1)

So confident was Boyle of his dispersal plan, he even suggested that, were it to be the subject of a hypothetical House of Commons vote, it would be endorsed by no less than three-quarters of all MPs. By coincidence, a month later in November 1963, the House of Commons was to get its own chance to debate a motion on 'Racial Discrimination in Schools'. This debate provided the Minister and his supporters with a second and larger platform from which to argue the dispersal case. 'A school with more than one-third immigrants changes its character and cannot give a true introduction to the British way of life' stated Boyle to the House (H.C. Deb. 685, 27 November 1963, Cols. 438-44).

The controversy had, by late-1963, pushed the town and the general immigrant education issue into the fore of national debate over immigration. Consequently, a number of other local authorities (including Birmingham facing similar difficulties in Boyle's former Handsworth constituency) declared themselves to be reviewing their policies.[11] In February 1964 the Leader of the House of Commons, Selwyn Lloyd, visited Southall to give an address on the race and immigration question. He argued that the only alternative to the dispersal policy was a segregation policy: 'Segregation is not the answer - in the long term it only brings many of its own problems' he urged (Gazette Series, 15 February 1964: 17).

Amalgamation as a dispersal policy solution

Between 1964-65 other major developments were taking place involving local government reorganisation in London.[12] The first elections for the new LBE were to be held in May 1964, with the new body taking over a year later in May 1965.[13] The framework within which local political debate took place in Southall was increasingly structured by the impending abolition of SBC and its amalgamation with the neighbouring boroughs of Ealing and Acton. It was against this backdrop that the dispersal question was debated and implemented during 1964 and early-1965.

With the largely SRA-orchestrated public debate still raging, an important development took place during January 1964 which dramatically altered the direction of the dispersal policy debate. SDEE unanimously resolved to approach its neighbouring boroughs on the possibility of dispersing Southall's immigrant school-age population throughout the new LBE, ie. into Ealing and Acton schools. This proposal was a precautionary move; cross-LBE dispersal would only be carried out in the event of an 'escalation of the crisis in Southall schools' (Gazette Series, 11 January 1964: 1; SDEE, 1964a). Nonetheless, the larger local government framework of the new borough's education authority was clearly seen as a possible way out.

During early-March 1964, the Education Committee of Ealing Borough Council (one of the three predecessor bodies to LBE) met to discuss the SDEE proposal. Any decision was deferred pending further talks and exploration of the plan with SDEE. The forthcoming reorganisation was little over a year away. The sooner SDEE could arrive at an agreement in principle with its Ealing and Acton counterparts, the more likely it was that the whole issue could be successfully defused. Defusing the issue was undoubtedly a major consideration in the motives and actions of SDEE and SBC members and officers at this time. Those not as yet convinced of the urgent need to find a practical solution to the crisis were adequately reminded by the results of the two sets of local government elections during spring 1964.[14] In addition to securing a working majority in the first LBE poll, Labour also won all 4 Ealing seats in the first GLC elections.

At the April meeting of SDEE, its chairman, Councillor Southey, reported that all reception classes for immigrant schoolchildren set up in Southall were now full. The forthcoming amalgamation of Ealing, Acton and Southall seemed the only obvious short-term way out of the quandary. It was also reported that Ealing and Acton had been asked to form reception classes of their own to take overflows from Southall. An 'educational danger-point' had already been reached in one school, but Southey insisted that SDEE 'was keeping a watchful eye on this problem...and special steps are being taken to ensure that the position does not deteriorate' (Gazette Series, 11 April 1964: 7; SDEE, 1964b). The 'special steps', it turned out, were nothing more than trying to squeeze extra numbers into the already-full reception classes in Southall.

For much of 1963-64 there had been a consensus between both major parties in Southall on the immigrant education issue. This consensus extended to many other aspects of local race relations, from overcrowding to public health to integration initiatives. It was perhaps only a matter of time before this fragile inter-party consensus was shattered. The May 1964 inaugural LBE elections provided the catalyst, when Conservative sentiment - from beyond Southall itself - became openly critical of existing and proposed policies. In April 1964 an Ealing Conservative councillor, Robert Hetherington, made a well publicised speech to Ealing Young Conservatives in which he claimed that Labour-run SBC had been guilty of a 'softly, softly' approach on overcrowding by immigrants in the past. Further, he attacked the new alleged alliance between the Labour Party and IWA in Southall during the LBE elections. This alliance, he claimed, was added testimony to the view that the Labour Party could not be trusted 'to defend standards of public health...when they are willing to come to electoral pacts with people who do not respect these standards' (Gazette Series, 18 April 1964: 7). The implications of Hetherington's intervention were two-fold. Firstly, the cosy bi-partisan consensus on the race issue was showing signs of coming undone. Secondly, if proponents of the dispersal option had thought that the LBE amalgamation would offer a simple and low-cost route out of the problem, then the sentiments expressed by Hetherington seemed to suggest that it was likely to be a much more complex process than first imagined.

Labour's control of the new LBE was based on small working majority.[15] Although race played a role in the campaign, the huge electoral cost to the Labour Party anticipated by Hetherington, SRA and others, failed to occur. Labour's control of LBE would at least provide the dispersal lobby - comprising SDEE, SBC, IWA, Boyle, etc. - with a favourable political framework within which to try to make the proposal operational.

By July 1964 SDEE itself had come to describe the reception class programme as 'near crisis point' (Gazette Series, 11 July 1964: 1). It disclosed that the number of Asian children in one school - Beaconsfield Road - had passed the one-in-two mark. SDEE was now busily engaged in trying to find an alternative temporary solution to ebb the tide whilst the cross-borough dispersal option still remained on the drawing board. Its response was to launch a press statement and public campaign to encourage white parents to transfer their children to that particular school in an attempt to reduce the immigrant concentration.[16] Ambitious as this suggestion may have seemed, it represented a reversal of the philosophy of the proposed bussing policy: white children, and not their black counterparts, were to be the *principal* policy subjects. Concomitantly, SDEE were keen to minimise potential white fears over educational standards, and resolved that, for the duration of this initiative at least, no further Asian schoolchildren would be admitted to the junior section of the school (Gazette Series, 11

July 1964: 1; SDEE, 1964c). Further, the Executive agreed to begin transferring all new junior-age Asian children from the Beaconsfield Road School catchment area (now barred from the school) to the North Road School catchment area. Thus, a *de facto* small-scale dispersal programme had begun.[17]

Additionally, SDEE announced that it was investigating the possibility of introducing a limited reception programme at the town's only grammar school. SDEE leaders were, however, eager to stress that 'this will not stop English children obtaining Grammar School places' (Gazette Series, 11 July 1964: 1; SDEE, 1964c). The Executive also agreed to publish a special report on its work on immigrant education to be distributed to interested parties (with white parents being the key target). Reassurance that SDEE was able to cope with the problem were its main themes.[18] According to Councillor Southey's remarks on the report:

> From time to time we have been criticised for our actions. This should let people know what is going on. The report was issued because of our concern over Beaconsfield Road School...but I think we have the problem under control. However, the problem will continue to be with us for a number of years. (Gazette Series, 11 July 1964: 1)

LBE policy adoption

At the beginning of 1965 LBE amalgamation was only three short months away. Pressure was mounting for LBE to agree to SBC's dispersal proposals.[19] In January 1965 the Middlesex Schools Medical Officer's report for 1963 was published. Interestingly, it was concerned less with strictly medical aspects of the immigrant education question, than with the broader question of Southall's response to the arrival of large numbers of immigrants. To the surprise of few, the fears of white community interests were at the top of the report's priorities:

> In providing the right environment for immigrants it is of the first importance that the interests of *local children* should not be allowed to suffer, and the sympathies of *local parents* should not be alienated. (MCC, 1965 - emphasis added)

The new LBE Education Committee convened in late-February 1965 in order to finalise an education programme and budget for the council year beginning in April 1965.[20] Much of the programme involved continuation of the capital spending plans of its predecessor education bodies, including an expansion of SDEE's reception class programme. The new LBE Chief Education Officer stressed to the Committee that any dispersal policy remained on the drawing board at this stage.

In March 1965, SDEE received its final report from its Immigrant Education Sub-Committee (SDEE, 1965). Once more, it made clear its recommendation to its successor body (ie. the new LBE Education Committee) that a fully co-ordinated dispersal programme ought to be adopted immediately. At this final meeting just a few days before amalgamation, Councillor Southey began his final report with a wider message directed to the new education authority:

> With the merger of the three boroughs...it should prove an easier task to disperse the children, and we have asked the new authority to give the problem their early attention. (Gazette Series, 26 March 1965: 13; SDEE, 1965)

The new LBE Education Committee was made up of a Labour majority, and was made up of members from the across the merged borough. In fact, the Southall presence on the Committee was limited to a single Labour member. Before it, stood a mountain of recommendations from its predecessor bodies, central government ministers and local politicians. With the exception of the ruling-group's manifesto pledge to see through a new comprehensive schools policy, the dispersal proposal stood out as the most pressing and controversial policy decision facing the new committee. It was against this backdrop that the new Education Committee resolved at its first meeting to begin a programme of 'dispersing Southall's excess Asian schoolchildren' (LBE, 1965a). Beginning in the autumn term of 1965, these children would be transferred to the "paler" schools towards the north, east and south of the new larger borough. Bussing had begun.

Policy operation, 1965-71

Although bussing originally had its roots in the 1960s race consensus, its differential impact on the Asian community soon undermined its legitimacy in Southall. A massive and protracted popular campaign to reverse the policy beginning in the early-1970s was unable to secure its abandonment until almost a decade later. The question of interest here and in the following section then, is not so much concerned with *why* the policy became unpopular, as with *how* LBE administrations were able to successfully maintain such a universally-controversial policy.

Support for the policy

Following the creation of the new LBE in April 1965 a note of optimism could be detected in the borough's race policy debate. This optimism centred on LBE's larger size and the scale of its resources being better matched to the nature of the policy problem. This sentiment was captured during a further ministerial delegation to Southall in March 1965, this time led by Maurice Foley, the Labour Government's newly-appointed minister with special responsibility for problems of race and immigration. Following his visit, the Minister spoke of the *administrative* cure for Southall's race difficulties:

> It has been difficult for a borough of Southall's size to deal with immigrant problems, but as part of the new Ealing borough, Southall can begin to tackle integration with more powerful backing. (Gazette Series, 26 March 1965: 1)

Only a brief local press editorial questioned whether LBE would be any more suitably equipped to find the solutions that had previously evaded Southall alone. It stated: 'Southall residents will closely watch developments made by the new borough to tackle these long-standing immigrant-related problems' (Gazette Series, 2 April 1965: 2).[21]

The composition and outlook of the RPE varied considerably over certain issues between the mid-1960s and mid-1980s (see also Chapter 4 above). On the dispersal issue, those in favour of the solution were able to cite the crucial endorsement of the Asian immigrant community itself. Such support remained fairly substantial as measured by the IWA leadership's endorsement between 1963-69. Central government, too, sought and highlighted the co-operation of immigrants themselves. By the time of the publication of the 1965 White Paper, dispersal was presented as an effective and desirable aid towards helping Asian children to integrate into British society (Cmnd. 2739).

Equally important was the suggestion that dispersal was essential to avoid resentment by white community interests. At this point, the fear centred exclusively on white parents' concerns about educational standards. A Circular published in 1965 by the Department of Education and Science added weight to the widely-held view that white children were being educationally held back:

> It will be helpful if the parents of non-immigrant children can see that practical measures have been taken to deal with the problems in the schools, and that the progress of their own children is not being restricted by the undue preoccupation of the teaching staff with the linguistic and other difficulties of immigrant children. (DES, 1965)

Later, the focus would begin to change - both locally and beyond - towards the view that dispersal was nurturing a white backlash in schools and communities otherwise far removed from immigrant concentrations. That is to say, white, anti-immigrant interests became more concerned about keeping all-white schools as all-white, rather than helping mainly-black schools reduce their black concentrations below Boyle's 'educational danger-point' of one-third.

The early impact of dispersal

A number of drawbacks associated with dispersal quickly became apparent. It is significant that they affected those groups and interests most closely involved in the operation of the policy, namely the Asian community in Southall. Dissatisfaction here centred on the differential impact of the policy. Asian parents became conscious of the destabilising results of extended journeys to and from distant schools, as well as the selective bussing of Asian schoolchildren only. Further, ECRC and IWA became increasingly aware that social or racial integration may in fact have been undermined, rather than promoted, through dispersal. Deakin (1970: 176) reports that:

> Immigrant pupils could arrive in a group and spend the day in a special class, to return in their bus after mixing possibly even less with English pupils than if they had remained in their high density local school.

Additionally, by July 1965, dispersal had already begun to cause resentment among white parents and residents in the receiving areas of the borough. In one sense, the original problem concerning the fears of white parents in Southall had merely been exported to other parts of the new borough. A petition on behalf of parents at a Northolt primary school in the northern part of the borough complained that 'the immigrant children will not be fluent because they persist in not using English at home...therefore, the teachers have to explain to them what "our" children already understand' (Gazette Series, 16 July 1965: 4).

The bussing policy was clearly proving difficult to implement in those parts of the borough where Asians children were being sent. LBE's Education Committee therefore agreed to a proposal in the same month to double the one-third maximum limit of immigrant children to two-thirds at the much-troubled Beaconsfield Road School. In addition, the one-third rule was revised to a 40 per cent maximum to be selectively employed in other LBE schools (Gazette Series, 23 July 1965: 2). However, SRA Secretary, Grace Woods, argued on a television documentary on bussing that: 'It is pretty obvious that people have reason to be worried...you'll see the danger of the local school becoming an all-Indian school'.[22] LBE was now being criticised by white, anti-immigrant interests both in Southall and beyond. The move appeared only to encourage the idea of all-black or all-white schools at precisely the moment when LBE had more generally embarked on a dispersal programme to avoid such "ghettoisation".

The dispersal policy served to sharpen the lines of division between white, anti-immigrant interests in the rest of Ealing Borough on the one hand, and the policy's sponsors in the RPE on the other. During the early years at least, the greatest opposition to dispersal continuously came from white, anti-immigrant interests, resentful of the presence of new Asian faces in "their" Ealing or Acton classrooms. Within Southall, the successful dispersal of black schoolchildren from local schools only encouraged SRA to begin campaigning for a similar solution in other fields. The main goal, of course, was to secure the adoption of dispersal of immigrants in general, away from the already-high concentration in Southall and towards low density areas. For example, in June 1966 SRA launched a campaign calling for such a policy from central government, targetting the Prime Minister nationally and the LBE Council Leader locally. This proposed policy would be carried out through non-complusory arrangements involving central government mortgages being given to those black families prepared to lessen Southall's concentration (Gazette Series, 24 June 1966: 1).

The LBE Labour administration at this time felt it was operating a bi-partisan bussing policy. There is little overt evidence to suggest that it did not have the full support of the frontbench of the Conservative Group. However, on the related issue of encouraging a more general dispersal of immigrants, there were signs of contrasting front and backbench party views. In March 1967 a motion was debated by the Council from a rebel Labour member, Councillor Tommy Steele, calling on LBE to do more to 'stop Southall becoming a ghetto'. Crucial support for the motion was received from Conservative Councillor Hetherington, who specifically argued in favour of 'further financial aid and more extended legal powers for the effective pursuit of a policy...to control the local displacement of local white people' (Gazette Series, 17 March 1967: 1). The motion was defeated by 6 votes, with sharply contrasting voting between the Labour and Conservative Groups. This vote suggested that there was a difference of view over the purpose of the existing dispersal policy. A spokesman for the Labour Group attacked supporters of the motion claiming that 'anybody who thinks like them would not be satisfied with anything except shipping all the immigrants back to India' (Gazette Series, 17 March 1967: 1).

Interestingly, the Conservatives were far from alone - and indeed found new and unexpected allies - in their arguments for the general dispersal of immigrants. During the first few meetings of Ealing International Friendship Committee (hereafter EIFC) in 1966-67, its senior officer, Martyn Grubb, pressed a similar case for general dispersal. He emphasised its co-operative, non-compulsory nature, but nonetheless was endorsing an option first mooted by SRA. At EIFC's first annual general meeting in June 1967, a Fair Housing Group was established to try to help immigrants to disperse across the borough. The concept of dispersal had become a legitimate policy option in the RPE, albeit for a number of different reasons and despite the absence of legal and other powers to effect such a general policy. On the bussing issue specifically, EIFC increasingly took on a reactive stance, keen to placate white fears of Southall becoming an all-Asian neighbourhood. Throughout the mid-1960s EIFC implicitly recognised that Southall had an immigrant "problem" which, as part of its solution, ought to be "exported" to other predominantly white areas. EIFC argued that bussing was necessary to relieve the chronic situation in Southall, and sought a policy of containment. For example, at the same annual general meeting, a proposal to bus white children from other parts of the borough into Southall schools was quickly and succinctly trounced by the EIFC executive led by Grubb:

> This has certainly been looked into very thoroughly. But it is not acceptable... To pursue this suggestion at this time would, I have to tell you, be nothing short of *political dynamite*. (Gazette Series, 16 June 1967: 1 - emphasis added)

Herein lay evidence for a fundamental confusion over the primary purpose of dispersal: was it an *instrument* of a broader race relations policy, or was it a *goal* of such a policy? Evidence reinforcing this confusion was littered throughout the policy debate.

Bussing called into question

The Asian school-age population in Ealing continued to grow at a very fast rate. During early-1968, LBE Education Committee reported figures for 1966 showing that some 6,600 children (out of an overall LBE school roll of 41,000) were defined as immigrants; some 2,400 of these were to be found in Southall alone (Gazette Series, 8 March 1968: 1; LBE, 1968a). This dramatic jump in numbers resulted in the Education Committee's sub-committee on immigrant education suggesting that 'the time has come to offer an all-immigrant school' (Gazette Series, 15 March 1968: 1; LBE, 1968b).[23] The policy was beginning to cause serious difficulties in its operation.

From about as early as 1968 there is evidence to suggest that bussing was being called into question by various policy actors. This reconsideration can be seen on two counts. Firstly, it was unpopular among the Asian families it affected, and secondly, it was beginning to be seen an inappropriate solution to the wider policy goal of racial integration. By the 1967-68 school year a handful of Asian parents were refusing to allow their children to be bussed to schools beyond Southall. However, the impact was negligible, since mobilisation of their *ad hoc* protests failed to materialise into a concerted anti-bussing campaign. More than 1,000 Asian children were being bussed each morning (Southall Rights, 1981: 32-3). An IWA activist later recalled that:

> Although we all knew of cases of some parents who didn't want to have their children bussed, they didn't amount to very many. The rest just went along with it, partly because they felt they were powerless to do anything, so what was the point of keeping their kids away they thought, and also because the IWA hadn't said anything critical about bussing. If anything, many of these Asian parents felt they were stuck with having their children bussed simply because the IWA had supported it so strongly only a couple of years earlier. (Interview: IWA activist, 1985)

Resentment over bussing continued to gather pace. By the late-1960s, grassroots sentiment against the policy was sufficiently strong for IWA to reconsider its position. The issue was persistently raised at IWA executive meetings throughout 1968 and finally culminated in a redirection of official policy in spring 1969 (Interview: IWA activist, 1985; Southall Rights/CARF, 1981: 33). Following a change of executive after the April 1968 IWA elections, the new IWA Secretary, H.S. Dhillon, described the 40 per cent quota rule as 'amounting to discrimination'. The policy, he argued, 'denied basic equal rights to immigrant parents to make the choice of school for their children...enjoyed by white parents' (Gazette Series, 3 May 1968: 1). A formal campaign to press for the ending of bussing was launched by IWA in 1969. Despite a spell of acquiesence to the policy lasting for almost five years, IWA had amended its position and showed itself to be reasonably responsive to its membership.

Moreover, it was becoming obvious that dispersal was failing to address its original aim of trying to provide a more ethnically-heterogeneous learning environment for Southall's Asian schoolchildren. The bussing statistics for 1966 revealed by LBE's immigrant education sub-committee caught many by surprise in the sheer scale of the increase in numbers of Asian schoolchildren. On a practical level, the sub-committee's call for the selective abandonment of the one-third Boyle quota reflected its view that bussing could no longer solve the basic problem of numbers. Instead, the idea of predominantly Asian schools no longer invoked opposition on educational grounds as it had automatically done during the early-1960s. The sub-committee in fact spoke of 'such a school that would become the pride of the immigrants' (Gazette Series, 15 March 1968: 1; LBE, 1968b). In the event, the suggestion was quickly quashed by LBE's Immigrant Advisory Committee (a separate body comprising Education Committee members and various teachers and head-teachers) - (Gazette Series, 22 March 1968: 1). LBE was not, as yet, prepared to publicly concede the serious weaknesses many others had already pointed to in the policy.

Having rejected the idea of allowing the one-third/two-fifths rule to be relaxed, LBE's Education Committee set up a working party on the education of immigrant children. LBE may not have been prepared to undermine its own policy but it was prepared to turn to central government for assistance. The working party produced a report in March 1968 calling on the Department of Education and Science to introduce a special grant towards transportation costs and, in the wake of the Kenyan-Asian crisis, to generally discourage further immigration to Ealing (Gazette Series, 5 April 1968: 10). Further, the report suggested an extension of the dispersal policy by requesting neighbouring education authorities to accept some of LBE's 'overflow Asian schoolchildren'. Rather than responding to opposition from the Asian community, bussing was in fact set to expand to cover more Asian children in more and farther catchment areas.

Mounting pressure for reform

The final event marking this turning point against bussing came with the launch of a public campaign by EIFC. Mounting grassroots pressure had produced a *volte face* in EIFC's ranks over the issue. In May 1968 the EIFC representative on the Advisory Committee argued that the policy was 'discriminatory in nature, interpreted as being based on colour prejudice...and builds colour consciousness at an early age' (Gazette Series: 10 May 1968: 1). A gradual phasing out of the policy was recommended by EIFC, together with a return to the traditional concept of neighbourhood schooling. Concomitantly, EIFC published a detailed report based on a study of various aspects of local education policy and their impact on immigrant schoolchildren (EIFC, 1968b). This document tried to draw together many of the advantages and disadvantages of the dispersal policy, concluding that, given its selective implementation, it could no longer be defended on strictly educational grounds. LBE's reaction was to try to defend its dispersal policy. Help from central government was sought in order to boost the scale of resources devoted to dispersal (Gazette Series, 31 May 1968: 7). By improving the programme and expanding the catchment areas, LBE felt that it could hedge the growing tide of criticism. LBE received word in May 1968 from the Department of Education and Science sanctioning its plan to maintain and expand its dispersal programme. Provisional approval was given by the centre to partially offset dispersal's transportation costs through the newly-announced Urban Aid Programme (Gazette Series, 12 May 1968: 15).

LBE's attitude towards ideas of reform was reinforced - and possibly hardened - following the May 1968 local elections.[24] The new Conservative administration pursued a line of continuity, both in the policy commitment and in the approach towards its critics.[25] Critics of the policy - including EIFC and IWA in particular - found the legitimacy of their contributions to the RPE questioned. The RPE discussion over bussing was to degenerate during the early-1970s into mutual accusations of mistrust.[26] This mistrust, in turn, served to further entrench LBE in its determination to avoid reviewing, let alone reforming, the controversial and by now deeply-resented policy.

In 1969 the newly-established House of Commons Select Committee on Race Relations carried out two study visits to Southall in order to examine some of the problems being faced by the Asian community and local authority. The dispersal programme was a central feature of their visits and subsequent report. Among the evidence the Select Committee received was that of the Department of Education and Science who now argued that Government policy no longer clung so tightly to the notion of dispersal (H.C. 413 - I). Written evidence from the Department stated: 'A rigid policy applied from the centre would not only be a derogation of [local] authorities' freedom but would be educationally unsound' (H.C. 413 - II). The official blessing that first SBC and then LBE had originally received from central government was diminishing rapidly.

Meanwhile, early in 1970 the local press reported the first case of open defiance by an Asian family against compulsory dispersal - the Sindu case. A delegation from the Race Relations Board soon became involved in the case thereby generating a great deal of press and media interest (Gazette Series, 6 February 1970: 1). The response of the chairwoman of LBE's Education Committee, Councillor B.J. Howard, was swift and aimed at minimising damage: an immediate transfer was organised. In the space of a few weeks, a single act of opposition had captured the imagination of both the Asian community and its anti-bussing supporters. This event marked a key milestone in terms of raising public awareness in the Southall Asian community, with Asian parents increasingly prepared to use direct action in order to try to end the controversial policy. Finally, other influential individuals began to denounce the bussing policy. These included ECRC's senior officer, Grubb, (Gazette Series, 17 July 1970: 5) and the borough's only Asian councillor, S.S. Gill (Gazette Series, 31 July 1970: 1). Southall's Labour MP, Sidney Bidwell, also intervened in the affair, calling for a complete review of the policy to be set up by LBE (Gazette Series, 13 February 1970: 16). His commitment to the anti-bussing lobby undoubtedly came at a crucial moment for the campaign.[27] However, Bidwell's critics - including his Conservative opponent in the June 1970 General Election - charged that his intervention was merely a short-term ploy to attract Asian support at the polls.[28]

In sharp contrast, the policy now appeared to command ever-increasing support among the SRA membership. SRA's chairman, Woods, stated: 'I think dispersal has been a major factor in relieving tensions. That is why I want to keep it' (Gazette Series, 7 August 1970: 11). Clearly, the debate over bussing had become highly polarised. LBE's own dispersal policy now only commanded the open support of far-right, anti-immigrant organisations, whose full legitimacy in the local RPE was far from assured. Meanwhile, the policy was fiercely opposed by EMGs and others, whose views and demands had yet to see the light of day in local public policy decision-making.

The policy debate surrounding dispersal had turned dramatically in the space of a few years. By the early-1970s, supporters and opponents of bussing could be easily identified, locked in open and fundamental conflict, in sharp contrast to the more subtle, mixed picture of anti-segregationists and liberals who had combined to originally sponsor the policy barely a decade earlier. The vision of the liberal middle ground, based on a policy goal of racial harmony in which dispersal was an important policy instrument, was barely visible in local politics in Ealing.

Policy maintenance, 1971-78

A new Labour administration was elected in May 1971 with a massive 20 seat majority. Attention soon focused on Labour's new initiatives and reforms for local race relations. Asian voters in Southall had been canvassed hard for their support and, it was commonly agreed, had been partially responsible for the sizeable majority. Indeed, in its combined victories of 1965, 1971 and 1974, Labour had only ever lost one seat in Southall (Messina, 1989: 89). A local press editorial claimed that:

> It does show that the Indian voters are supporters of the Left - perhaps by tradition - and the Conservatives have a lot of convincing to do to overcome this handicap. (Gazette Series, 14 May 1971: 2)

Expectations that the new administration would turn its attention to reforms in bussing and related anomolies were heightened through the early comments of its leader following the election (Interview: former IWA President, 1985). 'Southall will not be the left-out corner of the borough in the future' stated a senior Labour Councillor to a gathering of a cross-section of Labour's Southall EMG supporters (Gazette Series, 14 May 1971: 1). The Secretary of the Indian Social Club, S.S. Johal, in turn, reported the expectations of his membership and many other Asian EMGs in clear and precise terms:

> My members do not agree with the dispersal policy for immigrant schoolchildren, although they accept it as practical policy for the time being in the hope the Labour Council would be looking into it. (Gazette Series, 11 June 1971: 12)

According to an IWA activist, the assumption was that the policy would be wound up under the new administration or not at all:

> After having supported the Labour Party at the elections, most people naturally thought they would seriously listen to Southall's opposition to bussing. It was the least that everyone expected, including most of the Labour councillors... Just about everyone now agreed that bussing wasn't satisfactory any more and that it should be ended. Everyone, we thought, included Labour. If the Tories had just spent three years defending the policy, it was obvious that only Labour could be relied on to end it. Everyone...accepted that, and accepted it was only a matter of timing. (Interview: IWA activist, 1985)

Shortly afterwards, the new LBE Education Committee chairman, Councillor Michael Elliott, announced that the controversial policy was being reviewed. However, its short-term termination was ruled out, and instead, to the surprise of many, he spoke of the benefits bussing had brought: 'It meant the immigrants were not isolated...and had the opportunity to mix with English children'. Moreover, he continued: 'We have never looked on this as a wonderful thing, but we have faced the situation and said it was the best available' (Gazette Series, 30 July 1971: 1). By committing the administration to a status quo on the policy, the educational and race-related arguments against it were effectively shelved. Bussing, therefore, had now become an issue of educational practicality.

A survey conducted by LBE during May 1971 had revealed that some 2,000 children were involved in the daily dispersal programme, travelling, in many cases, up to 10 miles per day. Moreover, the cost of the programme was heavy and escalating at over £10,000 per annum (Gazette Series, 30 July 1971: 1; LBE, 1971d). A report prepared later in 1971 by the Chief Education Officer, Reginald Hartles, showed that the number and proportion of immigrant-classified children in LBE schools were projected to grow by more than one hundred per cent over the following ten years. From 9.6 per cent in 1966, the proportion in 1971 had risen 21.9. per cent; this figure, claimed Hartles, would reach 45 per cent by 1981 (Gazette Series, 22 October 1971: 20; LBE, 1971e). Councillor Elliott cited these figures as evidence to show that the designated policy problem was growing at a pace faster than any Council administration could deal with. This argument seemed to give support to the view previously expressed by Hartles, who claimed that LBE simply would not be able to cope with the increase. Grubb however, on behalf of ECRC, was not prepared to accept this conclusion: 'I see no reason why Ealing cannot cope with this increase' he said (Gazette Series, 22 October 1971: 20).[29]

The bussing issue had begun to dominate the Labour administration's priorities in the Council Chamber as well. A full Council meeting in July 1972 voted to continue with the dispersal policy, although concessions were made by the administration in pledging to start building two new schools in Southall (eventually creating 640 places). The unabated rise in the numbers of Asian schoolchildren meant that dispersal had reached its full capacity. Whilst many schools in the borough beyond Southall were full, there remained a chronic shortage of school places in Southall itself. Councillor Elliott conceded that: 'We have reached a watershed in our education policy' (Gazette Series, 21 July 1972: 1).

LBE leaders had come to realise that dispersal was only workable on a small, modest scale involving a minority of the school roll. The numbers they now faced necessarily meant that, for logistical reasons alone, dispersal was virtually unworkable. The years of single-minded pursuit of the bussing option by successive administrations had resulted in a serious neglect of the provision of school places in Southall itself. Old schools and classrooms were closed down, whilst the building of new ones was not contemplated, let alone initiated. Councillor Elliot's plan for 640 new places now sought to address that problem, albeit very modestly and belatedly. Thus, for separate logistical reasons (ie. the cumulative shortage of school places in Southall that had resulted from a moribund school building programme), the policy could not be abandoned. Significantly, the two planned schools would not be subject to the traditional 40 per cent quota, and therefore would be truly neighbourhood schools.[30] LBE, however, appeared to be facing in two directions at the same time: it remained firmly committed to its bussing policy, whilst concomitantly admitting that it needed to be reformed through building new neighbourhood schools in Southall. 'We still firmly believe', stated Councillor Elliott more than a year into the new administration's term, 'that there are sound educational advantages in dispersing immigrant children' (Gazette Series, 21 July 1972: 1).

The mood of local community relations activists was also beginning to reflect impatience. In 1971 a leading ECRC executive member, Eric Barzey, warned that:

97

Five years ago we could think that we had time on our hands. If we do not work decisively at this stage there is no solution other than catastrophe. The only trouble [with bussing] is that these children are little black Englishmen. By sending these children outside Southall we have established they are aliens. (Gazette Series, 24 September 1971: 15)

It was only a matter of time before ECRC would positively and actively commit itself to the anti-bussing campaign. At an ECRC meeting in March 1972 Grubb successfully carried a motion which called for 'the progressive and speedy return to neighbourhood schooling for all children in the borough'.[31] He continued:

The dispersal policy...is essentially a divisive policy. Although its intention is to create a balance in schools, in practice it denies parents the freedom to choose where they want their children educated. (Gazette Series, 10 March 1972: 1)

The last occasion on which ECRC had taken a public stand on dispersal was in 1968 when a report it had prepared had come down heavily in favour of the policy. In just four years ECRC had come full circle and was now strongly committed to terminating the policy.

The Conservatives were also beginning to have a change of mind on bussing. During a well publicised 1972 by-election in Glebe ward in Southall, the Conservative candidate, Gillian Goold, stated that she stood against the policy.[32] She argued that the basis for this turnaround lay in trying to preserve a 'degree of normality' in the rest of Ealing's schools (Gazette Series, 21 April 1972: 3). The underlying theme appeared to have shifted from whether Southall schools *should* be all-black schools to whether the borough's schools at large *could* be kept all-white. The LBE administration was coming under attack from all sides over its bussing policy, though for very different reasons. Curiously enough, it was a leading local Southall Conservative politician who initiated his party's opposition to bussing within the Council chamber. N.S. Mangat, an Asian Alderman who had attained prominence since 1968 (see also Chapter 4 above), launched a strong attack on the Labour administration's policy of continuation. Specifically, he attacked LBE's March 1973 proposal to spend a further £200,000 to expand capacity for bussed Asian children in Hanwell schools, whilst severe shortages of school places existed in Southall (Gazette Series, 9 March 1973: 1).

The local press also critically examined the growing furore over bussing. In a June 1972 editorial it was acknowledged that the policy's days were numbered:

Dispersal means a policy of expediency: the day will come when it can no longer be sustained. It is towards that day the Council must plan, beginning with the provision of adequate schools and amenities for the whole school-age community in Southall. (Gazette Series, 2 June 1972: 6)

Finally, it was reported that even the senior echelons of central government (namely the then Secretary of State for Education, Margaret Thatcher) had swung around in favour of ending bussing during summer 1971. According to a story that appeared in the national and local press, a Department of Education and Science spokesman stated that: 'This represents a change of thinking by the department...and it is backed by Mrs Thatcher' (Gazette Series, 30 July 1971: 1).

The Select Committee investigation

A major blow to the Labour administration's attempts to retain and possibly expand its dispersal policy came in summer 1973 with the publication of the House of Commons Select Committee on Race and Immigration's report on race and education (H.C. 405 - I). The Select Committee had undertaken a detailed study on the general issue in late-1972 and gathered substantial evidence through the first half of 1973. The report dealt at length with the dispersal question and concluded that, for a variety of reasons, its practice in Ealing (and elsewhere) ought to be ended.[33]

The report highlighted the increasing difficulties of trying to operate a local education policy based on dispersal by racial category. The weaknesses of the policy were clearly spelled out through the evidence collected by the Committee's investigation, and rested on four key points. Firstly, the rationale behind LBE's policy appeared to bear very little resemblance to that behind the policy's original formulation and adoption more than a decade previously. Crude numbers, in other words, meant that the policy was no longer working to achieve its original goals. This point was implicitly conceded by LBE, whose long-term policy, according to Councillor Elliott's evidence to the Select Committee, was to 'provide schools basically in areas of need and to...only retain dispersal for the present time' (H.C. 405 - III: 349). In the short-term, however, Hartles argued that various spoiling factors prevented a more fundamental review: 'The intention of the Council to restrict the volume of dispersal was defeated by the influx of Ugandan Asians into the Borough at the end of 1972' (H.C. 405 - III: 315).

Secondly, it was clear that LBE, whilst aware of educational disadvantages associated with the policy, was not prepared to act and begin a fundamental review of its policy. Hartles conceded that:

> I think that while people would still see the advantages...originally set down for dispersal, they are more aware of the disadvantanges, and so the balance of opinion is fairly fine. (H.C. 405 - III: 347)

Councillor Elliott, whilst acknowledging certain drawbacks, went further in his endorsement of the controversial policy:

> We would recognise that there are very grave disadvantages. Perhaps in this the initial arguments in favour of dispersal have to some extent been overlooked. We have been able, I believe, greatly to the benefit of all the children in our schools, to create very largely a multi-racial environment within our schools. (H.C. 405 - III: 348)

Despite the drawbacks, Elliott and others still believed in the basic aims of the policy. His argument was that he stood for a policy which was against the greater evil of segregation - an argument pitted with great effectiveness by Boyle ten years previously. Elliott stated to the Select Committee: 'We are not eager to see segregated schools on a racial basis come into existence' (H.C. 405 - III: 348).

Thirdly, on LBE's own admission, on a practical level dispersal could not be abandoned given that thousands of (Asian) children relied on it for their daily education. As Hartles made clear: 'We have so many immigrant children being dispersed from their home areas that we could not possibly educate them if we did not disperse' (H.C. 405 - III: 346). Two and a half thousand children were subject to daily dispersal from the Southall area. Based on figures presented to the Select Committee by Hartles, only an additional 800 places were planned in Southall neighbourhood schools (H.C. 405 - III: 315). At this (optimistic) rate, Hartles conceded during cross examination, the policy might still be with the borough by the 1980s. In the event, his somewhat uneasy prediction turned out to be the case.

Finally, the Select Committee faced a torrent of evidence from Ealing-based community organisations such as ECRC and IWA underlining the opposition of the Southall Asian community to the policy. For instance, Ian Potts, a well-known moderate ECRC education committee member and Conservative representative, expressed ECRC's and others' resentment of the complusory nature of the policy: 'We would not argue that nobody should be bussed; we would argue that they should not be *forced* to be bussed' (H.C. 405 - III: 380 - emphasis added). Based on evidence from an ECRC-convened public meeting to discuss bussing in Southall, Grubb reported to the Select Committee that: 'Every speaker from the immigrant side spoke against dispersal...I do not say that this is completely representative, but the overwhelming

evidence is against' (H.C. 405 - III: 381). The suggestion was not readily accepted b
LBE witnesses who argued that: 'considering the numbers of children involved, th
numbers of individual protests...is remarkably low' (H.C. 405 - III: 347). ECR
retorted - somewhat patronisingly - that on bussing, like many other public polic
issues, the Select Committee should be aware that:

> Asian parents tend to accept things that come from authorities like the educatio
> department of the borough...and do not make the protest that an English pare
> or community would make. (H.C. 405 - III: 382).

Protracted policy-maintenance arguments

The main arguments in defence of the race-related aims of the dispersal policy we
articulated during the early years of the 1971-78 Labour administrations. Beyond 197
however, the bussing issue essentially centred on the logistical and practical facto
standing in the way of its termination and replacement by some form of neighbourhoc
schooling. As Hartles had testified to the Select Committee:

> We would now be in favour of dispersal on purely practical grounds. Due
> the lack of school buildings to take the number of pupils, the authority wou
> not be able to educate them unless they were dispersed. Dispersal at th
> moment is inevitable. (H.C. 405 - III: 349; Gazette Series, 1 May 1973: 1)

LBE found itself in a corner. It was neither able to wholeheartedly pursue and expand
policy which, it had long since conceded, needed reform; nor was it fully able t
commit itself to the ending of the policy on the grounds of not having any alternativ
facilities to educate several thousand Asian schoolchildren.

In the period until the 1978 change of administration only minor adjustments a
apparent, both in the dispersal policy and in LBE's position. LBE periodicall
reaffirmed its general commitment to the policy whilst investing limited resources in
opening a few new schools in Southall (Gazette Series, 19 July 1974: 7). Howeve
plans only existed for an extra 1,280 places by 1978 - in other words less than half th
places required for dispersal to no longer be necessary. Nonetheless, LBE gradual
moved towards a formal commitment - actually given in late-1974 - to end bussing
soon as it was able to do so (Gazette Series, 6 December 1974: 1). This commitme
failed to guarantee a timetable for the termination of the policy, since LBE itself cou
not predict the rate of progress of its planned school building programme.[34]

Earlier, in a surprise turnaround, the authority agreed to grant full co-operation to a
enquiry by the Race Relations Board (originally set up in 1972) into its bussin
programme (Gazette Series, 25 October 1974: 1).[35] The Kogan Report prepared fc
the Board was published in July 1975 and concluded that dispersal was very probabl
illegal under the terms of the 1968 Race Relations Act (Kogan, 1975). In late-1976 th
Board announced that it was seeking to bring a discrimination test case against LB
under the 1968 legislation - a move strongly welcomed by ECRC, IWA and othe
opponents of the policy (Gazette Series, 3 December 1976: 1). The Board's attempts
conciliate with LBE to find a negotiated solution to end bussing had apparently faile
Prosecution, and a further polarisation of forces, seemed inevitable. That said, th
report's substantive conclusion came as a welcome surprise to LBE, in that th
quality of the education that immigrant children were receiving, the author reporte
was 'an exemplary attempt to help children assimilate successfully into Britis
education and society' (Kogan, 1975: 25). The result was that the received wisdom o
the educational implications of bussing suddenly appeared as murky as ever. Bo
bussing and the report's conclusions were open to differing interpretations by LBE an
its critics (Gazette Series, 28 November 1975: 16).

The salience of bussing as a symbolic focus for wider opposition to LBE's rac
related policies grew rapidly at this time. The issue came to be a metaphor for popula
community-based campaigns against not just LBE, but the town hall's domination

the RPE and the underlying liberal policy framework as well. As in the early-1960s, education - and the dispersal question specifically - became a litmus test for many of the wider tensions and controversies surrounding local race relations issues. The evidence from the early-1960s showed how a number of anti-immigrant groups and individuals focused on the education issue as a means of trying to mobilise support for more radical, segregationist-type policy solutions. Liberal policy actors had seen the resolution of the original controversy in favour of bussing as a tactical victory for the broader liberal policy framework for race and community relations which was beginning to take shape.

The climate for race relations in Ealing had begun to change dramatically during the mid-1970s (see also Chapter 4 above). The label of 'racist-inspired neglect' soon became associated with the once-encouraging Labour administration, not least among wide sections of Southall's Asian community. Bussing and its discriminatory impact on Asian children was seen as representative of LBE's impervious position towards Southall and its Asian community. The rapid polarisation of RPE policy actors meant that this perspective was particularly common among the plethora of new, radical Asian community groups that sprang up in Southall from 1976 onwards.[36] According to an *ad hoc* spokesman for a radical Asian youth organisation:

> For a long time people tried to argue with the Council to get them to change their minds on bussing. In our view, it didn't get them anywhere. On one hand, the Council made a lot of noises about how bussing was going to end, and on the other they did nothing about it. To us that showed their discrimination against Southall...[because] it's not just segregation that means discrimination. By putting a low priority on building local schools and trying to give Asians the choice whites took for granted, that particular Labour Council showed they weren't interested in us at all. (Interview: Asian youth group leader, 1986)

Bussing was now a reflection of the polarisation of the local politics of race. As one radical black community organisation put it in its account of contemporary Southall history: 'Through bussing the education of black children became a separate and inferior process' (Southall Rights/CARF, 1981: 32).

Policy abandonment, 1978-81

By the late-1970s, bussing had been a feature of Ealing's education policies for a decade and a half. The policy had persisted through seven difficult years of Labour rule between 1971-78. As an item of strict educational policy, dispersal had been under attack for more than ten years and had been abandoned in terms of the Labour administration's *philosophical* commitment since December 1974. In practical policy terms, however, the administration's *political* commitment remained fully behind the controversial policy. The move to finally wind up dispersal was initiated and executed under a radical and controversial Conservative administration (first elected in May 1978).

Between 1978-81 a number of decisive factors combined to secure the policy's demise. These developments took place both on the periphery of the dispersal question as well as in terms of its actual mechanics. The combination of these events had the effect of firstly, renewing, if not escalating, the sense of popular opposition to the policy, and secondly, increasing the pressure on the new Conservative administration to find a speedy solution to the problem. Three pivotal factors can be pointed to. Firstly, the comparatively new debate on multi-cultural education centred on the future of a well-known specialist school; secondly, the call for autonomous, publicly-subsidised Asian "separatist" schools; and thirdly, the significant expansion of the school building programme in the western, mostly Asian-dominated, part of the borough.

During the 1970s a number of other developments had taken place in education policy in the borough relating to black educational needs. In particular, a short but impressive record of curriculum development for multi-cultural teaching had been nurtured in a handful of Ealing schools. Events relating to two of these schools between 1978-80 highlighted the continuing sensitivity of the relationship between race and education.

Developments at the Cardinal Wiseman Roman Catholic High School and Twyford High School during this period served to bring the dispersal issue back into focus. By the early-1980s, a variety of options for local education policy for a multi-cultural borough such as Ealing were on the table. Some, more than others, related to the policy objectives of the liberal framework: a good example was the new multi-cultural education policy sponsored by LBE. Yet, even here, the evidence reveals the extent to which the earlier consensual support for the liberal framework had seeped away - both in its general conceptualisation of race and in its specific policy objectives.

During late-1977 and early-1978 the Labour administration proposed to cut back its significant public subsidy for Cardinal Wiseman High School, a leading local Roman Catholic grant-aided secondary school. With a declining school roll, it was suggested that the school could be merged into the mainstream, non-denominational school system. Immediately, a bitter public row broke out. A number of Conservative councillors tabled a motion condemning the move as 'deeply offensive to parental choice' (Gazette Series, 30 December 1977: 3). The Conservative prospective parliamentary candidate for Ealing North, Harry Greenway, forthrightly denounced the proposal. He asserted that the proposal denied (mainly white) Roman Catholic community the educational choice allegedly already enjoyed by the borough's ethnic minority communities. Moreover, he argued, the authority's recent willingness to begin experimental funding of selected EMGs was in sharp contrast to the withdrawal of aid to the school. The consequences, Greenway hinted, would be felt in the borough's race relations:

> This is dangerous stuff because people object to being obliged to finance minority racial groups to pursue their own cultures while being denied the right to pursue their own Christian culture. In my opinion [this is]...a situation which could create the sort of backlash which could damage race relations very seriously. (Gazette Series, 30 December 1977: 3)

Separatist religious schooling

The issues at the centre of the Cardinal Wiseman episode were reproduced in 1980 in the controversy over Twyford High School. In this case, however, the battlelines were even more sharply drawn. A radical Conservative administration presided over the borough at this time.[37] Developments during its first couple of years in office suggested that it was determined to block special race-specific funding programmes, both in educational policy (eg. the Twyford case) as well as elsewhere (eg. its relations with ECRC - see also Chapter 4 above).

The fate of Twyford High School in the early-1980s embodied long-standing debates in the borough over religious, denominational education policy. Situated in Acton in the east of the borough, the school attracted a large black (mainly Afro-Caribbean) school population and had become renowned for its innovative approach to multi-cultural education. From late-1978 onwards, the Conservative ruling-group let it be known that they supported the principle of establishing the first grant-aided Church of England school in Ealing (Gazette Series, 1 November 1978: 1; Interview: Conservative councillor, LBE, 1986a). A tentative campaign was launched by ECRC to oppose LBE's plan, even though the school targetted for the plan had not been specifed at this stage (Gazette Series, 16 February 1979: 2).[38] Within a few months, Twyford had been selected by a special LBE Education Committee meeting which gave approval to a Church of England bid of £1.7 million for the school (Gazette Series, 27

April 1979: 1; LBE, 1979a).

Once again, a furious public row clouded the borough's race relations. Critics argued that Twyford's redesignation for religious schooling was strongly opposed by staff, parents and pupils, and therefore was highly inappropriate (Gazette Series, 27 April 1979: 8). The Labour Party's National Executive Committee even intervened in the row, calling on the Archbishop of Canterbury to withdraw the controversial bid in the interests of racial harmony in the borough (Gazette Series, 25 January 1980: 1). Locally, the Labour Group Leader, Councillor Elliott, attacked the decision as an attempt to turn a successful multi-racial school into an essentially mono-racial, and therefore segregated, school. More significantly perhaps, another Labour councillor claimed it would 'create division amongst religious groups in the borough and encourage other religious groups to push for their own schools' (Gazette Series, 27 April 1979: 1).

This remark was a reference to the growing calls from the borough's Asian communities - predominantly the Sikh community - for LBE assistance in setting up their own religious-based schools. Although its plans were rather nebulous, the Conservative Group had begun giving tentative support to the idea of Sikh schools as early as November 1978.[39] In January 1980, a local Sikh *Gurdwara* tried to force the issue by presenting LBE's Education Committee with a deposit of £25,000 to buy a Southall secondary school it had targetted.[40] The bid was considered by the Education Committee in the following month but, once again, the pressure for Sikh schools (from by now two Sikh *Gurdwaras*) was frustrated (Gazette Series, 8 February 1980: 1; LBE, 1980a). LBE's blatant failure to fully embrace the "Sikh School" proposal quickly became a contentious local issue. An IWA leader, Khabra, complained that 'they could hardly oppose a Sikh school in view of their support for a Church of England school' (Gazette Series, 1 November 1978: 1).

The Twyford and "Sikh School" proposals, therefore, became enmeshed very quickly. The Labour Group had consistently tried to oppose any proposals to sell off either school. Its opposition stemmed from a number of sources, including *inter alia* a principled stand against religious schooling, opposition to the sale of public assets, and its support for the concept of multi-racial education. However, the most politically awkward of these reasons was clearly the latter. Its long-standing support for dispersal had also been based on this loose commitment. Yet its own dispersal policy between 1971-78 had yielded a succession of bitter political fights and deep resentment within the Asian community. The Conservative Group were similarly caught facing in a multitude of directions. Loose support had been given to the principle of religious schools but, in reality, this had only amounted to tangible assistance for the Church of England bid. Inevitably, a deep sense of double standards underscored the allegations made by both radical and liberal critics that the Conservative administration was pursuing a discriminatory education policy.

In short, therefore, the "separatist" schooling issue may be placed alongside the long-standing bussing issue as evidence of the collapse of both the assumptions and goals of the liberal policy framework.

Expansion of Southall's education facilities

Under ever-increasing pressure from anti-bussing groups, LBE agreed to start construction of two new large secondary schools in Southall in early-1978 (Gazette Series, 27 January 1978: 5). However, in November 1978 the new Conservative administration confirmed that it intended to pursue a policy of continuity. Dispersal was to be phased out slowly but could be expected to be operated on a significant scale until 1981. For the first time, LBE had spelt out a more than tentative timetable for the termination of bussing. In addition, the building of another primary school in Southall was announced. This new school was to be financed out of LBE's own capital expenditure, off-set by reduced capital programmes elsewhere (Gazette Series, 17 November 1978: 5).

Between 1974-79 LBE's Labour administration had persistently lobbied central government for additional capital resources (Gazette Series, 6 December 1974: 1 and 6 February 1976: 3). In the main, its requests for capital funding had been largely unsuccessful. Its limited primary school building programme (for two schools or approximately 1,200 places) had been financed out of its own existing education capital budgets. Any further school building under the Conservatives to try to reduce the shortage of places in Southall would equally have to be funded in-house by LBE.

Against this financial backdrop, LBE's new Conservative administration planned to begin winding down its bussing programme in the hope of reaching a target equilibrium between children and places within two to four years. LBE had successfully secured substantially increased central government subsidies to help off-set its considerable expenditure for black immigrant-related special education programmes, eg. English language tuition posts (in addition to the subsidies it received for the by-now huge bussing programme). According to Home Office figures, between 1974-78 LBE had received some £4 million in such subsidies - through the S.11 programme - as part of a total 'immigrant education- related current expenditure of £5.25 million' (Gazette Series, 27 January 1978: 5).[41]

The escalation in racial turmoil at this time had resulted in a series of sharp exchanges between Asian and Southall interests on one hand and LBE on the other (see also Chapter 4 above). Many of these feelings concerning Southall's alleged neglect were embodied in the views of an Independent Councillor, Shambu Gupta, elected in May 1978 for a Southall ward (Gazette Series, 10 August 1979: 4). LBE, he complained, was 'trying to run down Southall and turn it into a ghetto, separate from the rest of the borough' (Gazette Series, 20 July 1979: 1). Ironically, in spite of years of popular, community-based, anti-bussing campaigns, a number of his supporters cited the planned return to neighbourhood schooling as further evidence of LBE's determination to geographically contain the borough's black population. "White-flight", in short, was now the charge levelled at LBE as the only reason why dispersal was being phased out. In the short-run, however, the intervention of the Gupta campaign into the long-running bussing saga, only served to further tangle the educational, political and other arguments over the maintenance of the policy.

Following an accelerated school building programme during 1979-80, most of Southall's schoolchildren were successfully placed in local Southall schools by early-1981. At the close of the school year in late-July 1981, LBE's Education Department confirmed in writing to a Southall Labour councillor that the bussing programme would not resume in the following term (Mukherjee, 1982). Bussing had finally come to an end.

Conclusion

At one level it seems obvious that bussing was the product of a combination of the heavy migration of Asian settlers to Southall, and the high birth rate of the Asian community. The dramatic expansion of the Asian population, mainly in the western part of the borough, exceeded all realistic projections of its likely future growth. In Ealing's secondary schools alone, the proportion of 'immigrant classified' children rose from just under one in ten in 1966 to almost one in two by 1981. Further, the actual scale of the daily bussing operation soon reached a massive and seemingly absurd scale. For example, in the early-1970s the House of Commons Select Committee learnt that: the dispersal programme cost over £100,000 per annum (1971 prices), three-quarters of which was off-set by Home Office S.11 funds; it involved the daily movement of over two thousand (or 6.6. per cent) of the borough's primary school population; and that these figures were planned to increase by half as much again within four years. More than seven years later, as the bussing programme began to be wound down, nearly 3,000 schoolchildren were still being dispersed daily at an annual cost of over one million pounds and involving a bill of £54,000 for coach escorts alone!

However, an explanation for the dispersal policy based on demographic factors is insufficient. Four other factors are essential for an adequate understanding of the adoption and subsequent development of this unusual and selective item of public policy.

Firstly, it is perhaps no coincidence that education was the *symbolic focus* for so many local tensions and controversies over race. Further, in terms of the emerging race-related public policy agenda, it is arguable that education was - and has stubbornly remained - the litmus test for all local public services (see also Chapter 8 below). FitzGerald (1986b) writes:

> For of all local services, education, perforce, touches the lives of far and away the largest number of local residents. Even if black pupils were seen as making no special demands within the education service (or if their demands were ignored)...the fact that, in schools, almost the whole of the relevant age-cohort of the white population was forced into the sort of close and regular contact with the same age-cohort of the black population which whites in all other age groups avoided, created a situation in which wider tensions were bound to surface.

Educational policy has undoubtedly been one of the more difficult policy sectors to operate. To a large degree, "successful" policy is measured by the terms of "acceptable" policy: that policy option which commands the greatest - though not necessarily universal! - degree of agreement and co-operation amongst key policy actors. In this sense, for the overwhelming bulk of the period examined, the dispersal option represented a half-way-house solution. It began as a policy solution that commanded the support of a vast cross-section of policy actors. However, even allowing for its unmistakable decline in support, the policy was one which was defended on the basis of its preference over other options such as segregated education. It is certainly the case that demographic trends eventually meant that the borough could no longer avoid de facto segregated schhols. But the point of the dispersal policy was that it aimed to avoid such an outcome and, on this basis, was generally viewed sympathetically as the liberal option of integration and mutual tolerance. Its success-of-sorts was therefore the outcome of its normative though reluctant acceptance.

Secondly, the education-dispersal issue should be viewed in the *context* of the broad range of race-related public policy issues that local authorities have gradually come to preside over. The statutory duty to provide education for all children between certain ages is long established. Town halls have to fulfil their statutory obligations, irrespective of their wider political stance towards local ethnic minority communities. In contrast, in the areas of public housing or social services it has proved more difficult to operate policies of *total exclusion*, denyng ethnic minorities access to these public services. That is not to say that education and other public services are not susceptible to discriminatory or partial implementation; rather that local government has had opportunities to ignore or side-step the race dimension in some areas of public service delivery more than others.

The standard or quality of public service provision has tended to vary enormously. Whilst local authorities have found no easy way around black people's obvious right to and demand for public services, all sorts of strategies have been erected to prevent black people from receiving an equal quality of public service provision compared to their white counterparts. Education in Ealing between 1965-81 is a case in point. The local authority simultaneously executed its statutory duty to black parents to educate their children, whilst ensuring that white parents received an overall better quality of education for their children.

The initial demand for special language tuition provoked a specific policy response - dispersal. The local education authority could not fulfil its statutory duties unless this demand was met. Once race-related factors were introduced into this fairly inflexible framework, it became virtually impossible for the local education authority to avoid confronting and succumming to white parental pressure to "safeguard" white educational standards. Such pressure, quite clearly, was little more than a cover for widespread animosity towards the Asian community at large.

Thirdly, we need to consider whether bussing was the *integrative* measure it was commonly thought to be in the 1960s, and if so, in what sense. As little as five years after its launch, it was less widely accepted as the liberal-sponsored policy instrument it was supposed to be. Moreover, it was openly labelled by a wide range of policy actors as discriminatory - as well as illegal - by the mid-1970s. Why?

In the period 1957-65 bussing was originally proposed as a moderately integrationist measure, something of a compromise between segregationist and *laissez-faire* options. However, observing the impact of the policy over a longer spell, it can perhaps be seen more as a radically integrationist move on two grounds. Firstly, by extending the range of schools where white parents could potentially argue that immigrant children were having a disruptive effect, dispersal risked broadening white, anti-immigrant protest. Secondly, part of the explanation for the eventual abandonment of dispersal was that it had created fears amongst white parents in other parts of the borough. Ironically, its original rationale had been to allay white fears. Moreover, it is arguable that the absence of a dispersal policy would have resulted in a far quicker "white flight" from Southall than was the case. Therefore, by forcing borough-wide integration, dispersal helped to arrest the pace of the eventual "ghettoisation" of Southall.

Was bussing a radical policy born of a principled commitment to the liberal ideal of integration, or was it a reactionary compromise aimed at appeasing a growing tide of white hostility? The evidence here suggests that it was both an ideal and a compromise - simultaneously. In the short-run, the primary locomotive forcing immigrant education onto the local political agenda was a fear of white resentment, as embodied in the 1963 BNP episode. Once on the agenda, it is interesting to see the way in which policy-makers placed such white community interests alongside the educational requirements of immigrant children themselves. In this setting, the Boyle-led campaign tried to formulate a compromise, in which dispersal and *laissez-faire* supposedly represented the interests of each side respectively. This solution, however, amounted to a significant distortion of the picture of grassroots pressures in Southall since the evidence shows that the dispersal proposal was keenly supported by the Asian community's leadership at its inception.

It is not safe to assume that the Asian community's support for bussing was naïve. The community's initial support was based on the belief that Asian children were not receiving the supposed full benefits of British education. Bussing, then, was seen as an acceptable solution in response to such anxieties. The policy was not widely perceived at this time in terms of its differential quality of education. The subsequent modification of the Asian community's position should therefore be viewed as a gradual shift of emphasis towards the preservation of cultural identity, as well as a recognition of the second-rate quality of education imposed on their children. This shift climaxed in the post-1976 era, following the discriminatory and bitter experience of integrationist policies such as bussing.

The policy can be interpretted as both integrationist and reactionary at one and the same time. This view rests on the argument that bussing's support among Southall Asians alone is an insufficient basis for its liberal-integrationist characterisation. The major rationale behind the formulation and implementation of the liberal policy framework for race relations at this time, was an avoidance of fundamental questions on race and public policy. In a sense, therefore, the climate or 'culture of inexplicitness' (Young, 1985b: 286) in race policy issues can be dated from the early-1960s.

Fourthly, a tentative *life-cycle* for the policy can be sketched showing the movement in the surrounding debate on race and public policy. The initial phase was largely devoted to the consideration of alternatives. Allied to the rise of liberal values and aims in the policy framework for race, the major policy actors endorsed the dispersal option. Beyond that, in the period to 1971, the dominance of the liberal policy framework was reflected locally in Ealing in the generally successful operation of dispersal. The major part of the 1970s was a period in which the underlying values and assumptions of the liberal policy framework came under increasing criticism and strain, as witness in the ebbing away of crucial EMG and CRC support. Finally, the local education authority's policy decisions, time and time again from the mid-1970s onwards, were oriented not so much towards ending bussing and replacing it with neighbourhood schooling, but rather towards continuing with the controversial policy and, over time, allowing it to be superseded by events.

Therefore, the dispersal example provides us with a case study of how the traditional liberal policy framework, despite initial successes, came under increasing strain and moved towards a point of near-crisis. Established liberal "rules-and-norms" about the RPE, quite clearly, were no longer sustainable by the late-1970s, and were being challenged by various progressive and radical perspectives. The breakdown of the liberal policy framework is a theme returned to in the concluding chapter.

Notes

1. The year 1958 marks a watershed when race perhaps first became an issue of widespread public concern in the aftermath of the Notting Hill and Nottingham disturbances. In Southall, prior to the immigrant education episode, the main immigrant-related issues were housing and relations with the police.

2. Prior to local government reorganisation in spring 1965, the town of Southall was presided over by Southall Borough Council. The authority was amalgamated with Ealing Borough and Acton Borough Councils in 1965 - both also Middlesex boroughs - to form the Greater London Borough of Ealing.

3. These towns have become well known as a result of racial tensions during the 1960s. Smethwick leapt to prominence during the 1964 General Election following the overtly racist campaign of the Conservative candidate and subsequent MP, Peter Griffiths; see Deakin, 1965. In addition, during the 1960s Wolverhampton's transportation executive was embroiled in a bitter dispute over the wearing of turbans by its Sikh employees; see Beetham, 1970.

4. The terms "dispersal", "educational dispersal policy" and "bussing" are used interchangeably in the chapter.

5. The best documented case of a local authority's deliberate attempts to disperse black immigrant households through its housing policy - thereby restricting their concentrations - is that of Birmingham City Council. For further details see Flett, 1981.

6. For differing accounts of the early period of black immigrant settlement see EFRA, 1965 and 1968; LBE, 1965b and 1965c; and Southall Rights/CARF, 1981. In May 1958 an IWA press release spoke of just 400 Indians in Southall. In comparison with other estimates, this figure is probably an under-statement of numbers.

7. The early part of the immigrant education debate was set against the backdrop of Labour control at two levels of education policy-making affecting Southall, ie. divisional (Southall) and county (Middlesex). MCC's Education Committee contained a Labour majority following the April 1958 MCC elections; see Gazette Series, 19 April 1958: 1. Concomitantly, Labour also won control of SBC in May 1958; see Gazette Series, 10 May 1958: 1.

8. The result of the May 1963 poll was that there was no net change in the parties' representation on SBC. The Labour Party held five seats: Northcote (2 seats), Hamborough, Glebe, and Waxlow Manor. The Conservative Party held two seats: Dormers Wells and Norwood Green.

9. The 1961 General Census (published in spring 1963) showed that, for Ealing as a whole, Indo-Pakistani birthplace accounted for 2,216 persons or just 1.2 per cent of the population. The vast majority of these were concentrated in a handful of Southall wards, with Hamborough and Glebe ranking the highest.

10. It should be stressed that the July 1963 special meeting at Beaconsfield Road School was an *ad hoc*

initiative of its headmistress, Miss Webster. To a degree therefore, SDEE's and SBC's immediate involvement in the affair only came about as a result of Webster's initiative. Webster was in fact a founder member of SIFC and her aim had been to bring about parental discussion and awareness on the issue, and not to create a sense of alarm amongst white parents. Moreover, according to Grubb, she had been originally responsible for mooting the quota idea and for suggesting it to Boyle; see FitzGerald, 1986b.

11. Boyle specifically cited the case of Birmingham City Council case in his speech to the House of Commons. The resolution of the Southall problem in favour of racial quotas, he argued, would give other education authorities confidence to adopt similar quotas. Birmingham, he claimed, had already begun consulting his own Ministry as well as SDEE on the mechanics of the proposed one-third quota system.

12. Local government reorganisation was deliberately staggered over 1964-65. The first elections were held in spring 1964 to elect councillors to plan for the amalgamation; their terms of office as councillors, however, did not begin until spring 1965 when LBE itself was formally established.

13. For the first LBE elections in May 1964 Southall was assigned 12 seats in 4 wards: Glebe, Northcote, Waxlow Manor and Dormers Wells. The election result in these 4 wards was a massive victory for Labour: nine out of twelve seats. Labour carried all the seats in the former three wards whilst the Conservatives won all the seats in Dormers Wells.

14. A second set of local government elections also took place in spring 1964: the inaugural elections for the first Greater London Council. Four members were elected for the Greater Ealing division of the Greater London Council. Again, the new authority was not formally constituted until spring 1965, with its members having a similar transitional role as the first LBE members.

15. Borough-wide, the Labour group secured 34 out of 60 available seats in the LBE elections, with the Conservatives holding the remaining 26 seats.

16. SDEE's immigrant education sub-committee wrote directly to white parents of children at other mainly-white schools to seek their co-operation. The long-term educational and other benefits of integrated schooling were strongly emphasised in the letter. Mention was also made of the fact that the headmistress of the school had received an MBE award in recognition of her school's pioneering immigrant education work.

17. The first compulsory dispersal of Asian schoolchildren began at the start of the 1964-65 school year.

18. SDEE figures from August 1964 showed that immigrant-classified pupils numbered 700 in Southall's primary schools and 400 in secondary schools (excluding those in reception class programmes). SDEE's report was keen to stress that it had not lost the initiative, notwithstanding its own estimates which suggested that immigrant numbers were likely to expand sharply in the following year.

19. An innovative survey was set up by SDEE in February 1965, partially aimed at convincing new LBE councillors of the need to adopt dispersal alongside other immigrant education policies. Its purpose was to develop new aptitude and ability tests to check against the possibility of existing tests being culturally-biased against Asian schoolchildren. The survey was designed to show that SDEE's immigrant education policy went further than its short-term call for dispersal.

20. The February 1965 Education Committee (transitional) meeting passed a resolution calling on the full LBE Council to request additional funding from Whitehall. A 'special allocation' of £2,370 was specified by the Committee in respect of its planned reception class programme beginning in the autumn term, 1965. The aim of the resolution was to place pressure on the new LBE administration to take early responsibility for the problems of immigrant education and to begin lobbying the centre for new resources.

21. The most salient race relations issue during the first few years of LBE's tenure was the row over public housing. In 1965 six rebel Labour councillors voted with the Conservative opposition group for an amendment seeking a 15 year residency rule for non-UK-born applicants for LBE public housing. Five of the six rebels were subsequently expelled from the Labour Group and took up seats as Independent members until the May 1968 local elections. The expelled councillors' *ad hoc* leaders, Councillors Steele and Lamb, subsequently joined SRA and were successfully returned as SRA councillors in May 1968; see Gazette Series, 18 June 1965: 1; 9 July 1965: 1; and 17 May 1968: 1.

22. The SRA Secretary was appearing on the Independent Television programme "Dateline" screened on 8 November 1965. The programme also carried a short interview with the new headmistress of Beaconsfield Road School, Margaret Goodhall; see ITV, 1965.

23. The sub-committee's figures showed that by January 1968 no less than 22 LBE schools contained more than 30 per cent immigrant-classified children. Nine of these schools (including six of the highest concentrations) were in Southall: Featherstone Infants (32.5 per cent); George Tomlinson Secondary (34.5); Tudor Infants (37.0); Dormers Wells Secondary (39.8); Featherstone Secondary (45.8); and Tudor Junior (46.2).

24. The May 1968 local election results were disastrous for Labour and an overwhelming success for the Conservatives. Out of 60 seats, 53 were won by the Conservatives; Labour won just 5 seats, barely ahead of SRA's 2 seats. Two of Labour's 5 seats were in Southall wards (Glebe and Northcote), and remainder were in Northolt.

25. A minor row erupted in January 1969 when the new Conservative administration announced that it intended to use Bordeston Secondary School in Ealing as an immigrant language centre. Previously, LBE's own Education Department officers had described the premises as 'unfit and unsuitable for educational purposes' but it was now deemed appropriate for immigrant educational provision. An 800-signature petition organised by IWA was dispatched to the Minister of State at the Department of Education and Science, Edward Short, protesting against LBE's 'alienating proposal'.

26. An example of such mistrust came in mid-1969 when LBE was accused by IWA and EIFC of 'supplying damaging statistics' to Enoch Powell, MP. In June 1969 Powell delivered speeches in Wolverhampton and Greenford (in Ealing Borough) in which he gave details of the numbers of immigrant schoolchildren in selected local education authorities, including Ealing. These figures had been supplied to Powell with the permission of the Education Committee chairman and senior Education Department officers. Powell revealed that 17.3 per cent of children in LBE schools were classified as immigrants and that this was probably an under-estimation of the actual figure; see Gazette Series, 13 June 1969: 11.

27. In the run-up to the 1970 General Election, the strong anti-Labour swings recorded in the opinion polls suggested that even putatively safe Labour seats such as Southall might be at risk. Bidwell's reaction was to launch a campaign to attract Asian voters in his constituency. His sudden hostility towards bussing was presumably a part of this campaign, though perhaps not exclusively so.

28. In the event Bidwell secured re-election in the June 1970 poll with a 4,222 vote majority (reduced from 5,347 in March 1966).

29. Grubb emphasised that Hartles' forecast may have been based on unsound assumptions. Grubb argued that the demographic trends over the previous 2-3 years would not continue. Moreover, he argued, the 1971 bulge in the numbers of secondary school immigrant pupils had been caused by immigration rules that required immigrant parents to bring their children into the country before they reached 16 years of age.

30. An emergency meeting was held on 19 July 1972 between senior LBE ruling-group councillors, senior LBE education officials, and Department of Education and Science and Home Office

officials. The LBE side pressed the case for maximum central government aid for the proposed two new schools. These schools were scheduled to be ready by 1974-75 and, it was stressed to the Whitehall officials, they would not be subject to the 40 per cent quota.

31. ECRC's education sub-committee had previously voted 12:3 in favour of a similar motion sponsored by Grubb calling for the re-introduction of neighbourhood catchment areas.

32. In April 1972 it was revealed in the local and national press that Goold was also a leading member of the Monday Club and had been a past executive member of the British Campaign Against Immigration.

33. The Select Committee contained twelve members including Southall's Labour MP, Bidwell. It was constituted in November 1972 and its first investigative report on education was published in July 1973. The dispersal question occupied a single chapter of an eleven chapter report. The Select Committee received written and verbal evidence from Ealing witnesses during spring 1973 whilst in session at Ealing Town Hall; these sessions were all chaired by William Deedes, MP. For further details see H.C. 405 - I and III.

34. In December 1974, Elliott and Hartles wrote a joint letter to the Secretary of State for Education, Reg Prentice, urging his department to speed up approval of LBE's school expansion programme. The letter specifically referred to LBE's declared aim of trying to end dispersal within three years.

35. The Board's investigation was set up under Section 18 of the Race Relations Act 1968 to 'reach a proper conclusion on the facts of the local dispersal arrangements'. Maurice Kogan, an educational policy specialist at Brunel University, was appointed as an assessor to the enquiry in late-1974 and presented his report to the Board in July 1975. The published report left a number of matters unresolved, most crucially the issue of the educational impact of the policy on Asian schoolchildren. In particular, between pp. 24-9 Kogan argued that the programme was both discriminatory as well as beneficial to immigrant children. This conclusion appears to have been an *extraordinarily* ambiguous outcome for a study of what was an extremely heated and polarised local political issue; see Kogan, 1975.

36. A good example was Scope, an Asian community youth organisation which published its own findings on dispersal in September 1974. The report vehemently condemned dispersal as a policy of 'racial expediency'. Hartles, not surprisingly, replied on LBE's behalf, claiming that, Scope's conclusions were 'unsound' since they overlooked large aspects of LBE's educational provision for Asian schoolchildren; see Gazette Series, 6 September 1974: 1.

37. The Conservatives were returned to office in May 1978 capturing 41 out of 60 seats. Despite the strong Conservative swing, comparatively little of it was felt in Southall, where 14 out of 15 seats were won by Labour. The only seat Labour did not win was captured by an Independent, Councillor Gupta, who was elected in Northcote ward.

38. ECRC's criticism of LBE's plan to sell off a school to the Church of England was based on the view that it would create a selective, all-white school population in the school concerned. Few among Twyford's black school population were Anglicans, a fact which seemed to alert ECRC to the potentially discriminatory impact of the school's closure; see Messina, 1984 The episode was particularly interesting becuase it highlighted the extent to which ECRC leaders had become conscious of the indirect discriminatory consequences of the policies and prodecures of LBE.

39. As early as November 1978, Hartles had written on behalf of the Committee's Chairwoman, Councillor Lady Henniker-Heaton, to the executive committee of SGSS (a local Sikh *Gurdwara*). Hartles requested detailed statistics on the Sikh population in Ealing to help LBE evaluate the proposal. Grubb and ECRC strongly opposed the plan in motions successfully carried by the ECRC executive in February 1979. Moreover, in February 1980 the staff of Villiers High School were reported to be strongly against the *Gurdwara's* bid.

40. The cheque for £25,000 was immediately returned since it had been paid to LBE without a confirmed offer of sale for the school.

41. At this time Home Office S.11 rules did not require LBE to specify the composition of its annual S.11-funded expenditure. Thus, it is impossible to isolate the amounts spent on the dispersal programme from LBE's aggregate S.11 expenditure.

6 Race and local politics in Barnet Borough, 1956–86

Introduction

In this chapter I sketch a historical picture of race, local politics and public policy in Barnet Borough (in outer-north London).[1] My broad aim is similiar to that in Chapter 4: to provide a detailed overview of developments in this field over a twenty-one year period between 1965-86.

Barnet presents another example of the "non-politics" of race. That is, the issue of race is often conspicuous by its absence in public policy discussion and debate, both in the borough in general, and in the policy-making structures of the local authority in particular. However, while this process came under considerable strain in Ealing, leading to dramatic developments from the late-1970s onwards, no such wholesale reform resulted in Barnet. Race and the policy areas it touched upon most regularly were kept off the agenda of local politics and policy-making. Moreover, in contrast to Ealing, this process was not subject to an evenly balanced local two-party system.[2] Barnet presents us with an illustration of the impact of race in the policy process in a dominant one-party borough. This factor, in part, seemed to contribute to the ability of dominant policy actors - ie. successive Conservative adminstrations - to keep race off the local political agenda. Thus, in Barnet the important feature of the historical evolution of the race-public policy nexus has been the degree of continuity, rather than change, in the period since local government reform in the mid-1960s. In short, the local authority, the London Borough of Barnet (hereafter LBB) has been vastly more successful in marginalising not just race as an issue, but also all race-related policy-making. The question remains, however, whether this marginalisation was a consequence of the behaviour of the local authority in Barnet, or a result of the particular nature of other policy actors in the borough.

The story of race and local politics in Barnet is largely the story of the management of an awkward and volatile issue by consecutive Conservative administrations. LBB has been run by a single party throughout the period since 1965, and I will argue that *de facto* one-party systems - in this case presided over by Conservative Councils - react to race issues in a markedly different way from Councils in which administrations alternate between the two major parties.

But, it is not only in one-party local political systems that race is overlooked in the policy agenda. As Chapter 4 above showed, both parties shared a willingness to isolate race from the mainstream policy agenda. In Ealing it was only in the late-1970s that the parties began to noticeably diverge from this consensual approach. In particular, the Labour Party embarked on a bid to transform the hitherto de-politicised nature of race relations in the borough. The position in Barnet provides a sharp contrast. Successive Conservative administrations have been able to steer clear of the new era of highly racialised local politics, so common in neighbouring boroughs such as Ealing.

In addition, there are a number of factors relating to the community-based policy actors in Barnet that appear to have contributed to the way in which the RPE has developed. These factors will be explored further in the chapter, but it is important to note that there are crucial differences between the two boroughs. My argument has been that features of the ethnic minority communities serve to structure the overarching environment in which race-related public policy is either pursued or deflected in a particular borough. These factors combine with the nature of local party politics and the local authority administration to influence the RPE. Thus, by describing the RPE in these two boroughs, it is possible to identify significant variations and explain why race-related public policy developed differently in each borough.

The twenty-one year period of Conservative rule in Barnet is documented in three phases. Firstly, the period between 1965-71 when policy actors first became aware of racial tensions and conflicts. Secondly, the period between 1971-78 shows the emergence of a recognisable RPE. Finally, the period between 1978-86 in which a number of radical challenges to the liberal-inspired RPE were successfully rebuffed by the Conservative administration and its allies.

The emergence of race, 1965-71

A striking feature of local borough politics in so many parts of London during the mid-1960s was the alarmist way in which the slow trickle of black Commonweath immigrants was debated among local political actors. Nowhere was this more felt than in Barnet. Despite the tradition of large-scale Jewish settlement in the area, the arrival of significant numbers of Asians in particular during the 1960s quickly led to sharp political controversy in local politics.[3]

There are few references in the business of the local authority, LBB, to black immigrants much before 1967. For the first couple of years following the creation of the borough in 1965, immigration was, for the most part, a small but escalating issue of concern to the local press and a handful of more outspoken local politicians. That said, the local authority was by no means insulated from grassroots race relations developments. By the time LBB first became directly involved in a race-related public policy matter (1967), it was clear that its concern and actions pre-dated the immediate policy debate.

In the case of Barnet, very few early reliable estimates are available for the population sizes of the borough's various ethnic groups.[4] Certainly, the Jewish presence in the borough was long-established and was thought to be fairly stable in size (Alderman, 1983). Barnet, therefore, was already familiar with a plurality of faiths and, to some degree, cultural backgrounds. However, for a borough already used to cultural and religious heterogeneity, the gradual move towards racial diversity appeared to come as something of a shock. In the words of one commentator:

> For the most part, most people seemed to be quite used to the fact that Jews played an important part in the affairs of the borough. There was always a certain degree of resentment of this fact, but I wouldn't go as far as to label this out-and-out anti-semitism. Now, remembering that, the settlement of large numbers of Indians in the area somehow seemed to be more than many local

114

people and local leaders could accept. We had always been used to many different groups of people in the borough - particularly living around Golders Green and those parts closest to central London - but the appearance of Indians and their families in the suburban streets was something altogether new and, I must say, very hard for many people to understand or accept. (Interview: former Conservative councillor, LBB, 1985)

Issues of racial discrimination featured heavily in public debate at the time, both nationally as part of the "liberal hour" of reform, as well as locally in a political environment sensitive to white fears about black settlement. Although the evidence is scant on this point, it would appear that grassroots feeling against Asians was both widespread and deeply antagonistic. Allegations of discrimination in, *inter alia*, the local employment and housing markets was widespread. The local press, in particular, raised the thorny issue of discrimination, arguing for greater hospitality on the part of the local white community: 'A man that England needs' an editorial concluded, 'will be forced to leave because of prejudice... It seems that as the colour of the skin gets darker, so does the prejudice' (Times Series, 1 December 1967: 16).

Allegations of official discrimination

At a surprisingly early stage, LBB found itself caught up in the local debate over racial discrimination. In autumn 1967, a major row broke out in both the local and national press over claims that the Finance Committee chairman, Councillor Hills, had sought to operate a racially discriminatory council house sales policy (Times Series, 9 November 1967: 1). The allegation, although partially true, surprisingly resulted in a vote of full confidence in the chairman being passed by full Council, as well as a reaffirmation of LBB's policy not to discriminate on racial grounds.[5]

Less than a month later, the discrimination issue arose again. The General Purposes Committee of LBB resolved that its Grants sub-committee should question recipient local voluntary organisations on issues of racial discrimination in its mechanism for the distribution of grants (Times Series, 8 December 1967: 28). Such a proposal, in effect, amounted to an early ethnic monitoring policy. These events marked an important stage in the borough's approach to issues of direct racial discrimination and equal access to public funds. However, it is worthwhile remembering that the controversy was originally fuelled by a public outcry over alleged anti-Jewish discrimination by a local, LBB-subsidised, golf club.[6]

Inevitably, early race relations antagonisms were reflected in allegations about the effect of black immigrant settlement on local property prices. Needless to say, such a link was far from demonstrated. However, the claim that immigrants depressed the local private housing market was widely circulated and, for the most part, treated seriously by many politicians. This sort of public dispute first surfaced in those parts of the borough that either contained sizeable immigrant populations or those neighbouring on such areas. For example, wide press coverage was given to the 'immigrant problem' in West Hendon in spring 1968 (Times Series, 1 March 1968: 10). Similar stories followed concerning parts of Golders Green, Finchley Central and East Finchley (Times Series, 28 January 1968: 1 and 4 February 1968: 6). Several complaints over the issue of planning permission being given to various Asian religious and community centres, also received wide attention. Whilst the property prices debate appeared to resolve itself over the longer term, residents' objections to Asians' religious and community centres proved to be more intractable. The issue was to resurface periodically during the following two decades.[7]

In spring 1968 a major row broke out over residents' objections to the establishment of a Hindu temple in Golders Green (Times Series, 8 March 1968: 19).[8] The objectors' case was actively supported by a backbench Conservative councillor, who argued that LBB had secretly colluded with the management of the temple to deprive local residents of the right to object to the temple's presence. This episode, in many ways, was to set the scene for a long series of skirmishes between the borough's black and white communities and their supporters. Arguably, and as we shall see later in this chapter, these arguments were still as alive in the mid-1980s as they had been twenty years previously.

The local diet for race relations controversy was further fed by the periodic activities of far-right, anti-immigrant groups. Not surprisingly, many of these groups were associated in the press' and public's mind with neo-fascist ideology, and for that reason, found themselves under bitter attack from Jewish organisations and their supporters. The letters' columns of the local press were bursting with correspondence about the alleged anti-semitism of these far-right groups, as well as about the position of Jews in the concurrent immigration and discrimination debate. For instance, the pros and cons of the Rhodesian Unilateral Declaration of Independence was exhaustively debated in letters to the local press (Times Series, 3 November 1967: 12). More often than not, the avalanche of letters sought to discuss the issue using concepts such as the purity of racial groups and cross-national white kinship. Elsewhere, an ex-Mosleyite fascist group, the Union Movement (hereafter UM), was also active in the borough. Its self-styled primary aim was to try to 'warn white public opinion' of the 'impending flood' of Asians and others into Barnet (Times Series, 1 March 1968: 11 and 15 March 1968: 11). It is as well to remember that the bulk of its public activities took place against the explosive backdrop of the Kenyan-Asian crisis and the Powell affair of 1967-68. Doubtless, these national events served to exacerbate local tensions, focusing greater attention on groups such as UM than would otherwise have been the case.

In sum, it appeared that a sizeable groundswell of opinion existed in the borough which saw Asian immigration as a threat to the white community on grounds of racial exclusivity. It was argued by many that mutually exclusive races existed and their integration could not be achieved in Britain, let alone Barnet. It was against this background, therefore, that any future reforms or initiatives in local race relations would take place.

Liberalising moves in local race relations

The consolidating and expansionary moves embodied in the 1965 White Paper, *Immigration from the Commonwealth*, were, in large part, a response to the emergence of the community relations movement in numerous localities up and down the country (Cmnd. 2739). In Ealing, for example, the community relations movement can be dated from the mid-1960s at earliest. In the case of Barnet, in contrast, the evidence for such a movement before the early-1970s is conspicuous by its absence.

Press reports from the mid- and late-1960s suggest that a number of individuals and groups regularly voiced a liberal, enlightened style of argument in local public debate on race relations. Such race liberals frequently included *inter alia* members of the clergy, individual activists, the Liberal and Labour Parties, a handful of Liberal and Labour councillors, as well as an occasional Conservative councillor or two. However, any co-ordinated action by these liberally-inclined individuals failed to materialise. In February 1968 the local press ran a series of editorials suggesting the need for a co-ordinated voluntary effort to arrest racial tension (Times Series, 16 February 1968: 12). However, the narrow and strongly paternalistic tone of the editorial's recommendation meant that only a particular type of organisation was on the cards:

> What we must do is educate them into our way of life. Teach them our customs, our laws. It is only by doing so that we can make sure that the only difference between ourselves and the coloured immigrants...is a question of colour and nothing else. (Times Series, 16 February 1968: 12)

Kenyan-Asians, Powellism and the first immigration crisis

The growth of the immigrant presence in Barnet received greater and greater attention in the local media and public debate as the 1960s wore on. Starting from a position whereby black immigration barely commanded any attention at the time of the 1964 General and local elections, its impact increased steadily, climaxing in 1968 during the Kenyan-Asian episode. The issue was fiercely fought out in local borough politics and involved black and white individuals, mainstream political parties, elected councillors, far-right political groups, local MPs, the local press, and others. It is therefore worthwhile examining the 1968 local debate on immigration in some detail to assess how the various political actors lined up. Their respective positions on Asian immigration into Barnet held important clues as to how they would approach future debates on race-related issues and policy demands. These issues would include demands from black community interests (eg. the religious premises question) and, in due course, calls for some form of independent community relations agency in the borough.

The reactions of certain politicians to the Kenyan-Asian crisis are particularly telling. The borough's four Conservative MPs all voted in support of the Labour Government's restrictive legislation in response to the crisis (Times Series, 23 March 1968: 5).[9] The argument used to support this legislation centred on the duty of government to check the unrestricted flow of New Commonwealth immigrants into the country in general and, specifically, to areas such as Barnet. Whilst many local Labour politicians remained silent on the issue, one in particular - Tim Sims, vice-president of the Hendon South branch - adopted a high profile in support of the Government's restrictive measures. He argued that: 'The question we must ask ourselves before we allow immigrants in is have we enough houses and hospitals...and so on' (Times Series, 22 March 1968: 5). Amongst councillors from both main parties, there was broad support for the line taken by the centre. The main exception were the Liberals, both in the Council and in the constituencies, who persisted in their progressive, enlightened position on the issue. Their criticism went much further, to the point of a direct 'accusation of racialism' by a Young Liberal spokesman directed at both the Labour and Conservative Groups in the Council (Times Series, 15 March 1968: 11).

The broad consensus in favour of the restrictive legislation extended to the local press, who, citing the rhetoric of the "liberal hour", claimed that restrictive immigration and successful integration policies were in fact different sides of the same coin (Times Series, 22 March 1968: 5). The case was supported with references to Asian immigrants in the borough who backed the Government's actions. However, strong local criticisms of the legislation were not left unreported. For example, a well-respected local public figure, Rabbi Reverand Saul Amias, fiercely condemned the policy of slamming the immigration doors shut:

> We must protest not only when Jews are the suffering minority but also when there is an injustice to any people. The Jews should be shouting from the rooftops [and] we should see that we are in the vanguard of those who protest against this type of action. (Times Series, 29 March 1968: 14).

Meanwhile, the local press gave wide coverage to a controversial unsigned article that appeared in a local church magazine, claiming that:

> Coloured immigrants are not the cause of our employment, housing and education difficulties. The problems are not immigration problems. They are problems we already had but which we could not see. Nothing is solved by keeping Britain white. (Times Series, 5 April 1968: 10; Focus, 2 April 1968: 1)

Voices of protest were also heard from further afield. For example, local United Nations Association (hereafter UNA) groups were regularly engaged in criticism of central government policy. The Hendon UNA branch held a well-reported public meeting to discuss the issue with an invited speaker from the Race Relations Board. The occasion was used as a platform to argue the case for greatly extended race relations legislation - the second Race Relations Bill was due for parliamentary consideration at the time - to combat the discrimination faced by immigrants already settled in Britain (Times Series, 5 April 1968: 15).

The local debate served to structure the broad battlelines on race-related public policy in three ways. Firstly, the crisis helped to bring race relations onto the edge of the agenda for public policy debate. Secondly, it helped to crystallise the ways in which certain groups and individuals were prepared to explore, and possibly endorse, liberal, community relations-minded reforms, whilst others were not. Thirdly, certain aspects of the debate were to recur in the early-1970s during the Ugandan-Asian crisis. The first episode contributed to sketching the earliest map of the RPE, while the second proved to be the key to consolidating the RPE. In other words, the evolving relationship between race and public policy in Barnet is essentially a story of the period before a recognisable RPE, followed by the period thereafter. The main historic demarcation line therefore lies during the early-1970s at the time of the Ugandan-Asian episode and the subsequent establishment of a borough-wide community relations council.

The consolidation of race, 1971-78

The Ugandan-Asian episode is significant for three main reasons. Firstly, key RPE battlelines were drawn up during this period. Secondly, it represented a spell of intense activity by all policy actors, in which various liberal and other paradigms were proposed for dealing with an expected large-scale influx of immigrants into the borough. The successes and drawbacks experienced by these paradigms and their respective supporters also provide us with important sign-posts for the contextual setting of future race relations debates. Thirdly, the liberal consensus between the parties in the borough underwent a dramatic rise and fall during the early-1970s. The downfall of the consensus culminated in the 1972 immigration crisis. As in the demise of the "liberal hour" on the national stage, a similar sharp turnaround in values and assumptions can be seen in Barnet at this time.

At first, the response to the news of the Ugandan crisis united black and white community leaders in the borough. All expressed their concern over developments and condemned the actions of the Amin régime. The issue was seen as an example of widespread, organised discrimination against the Asian minority. Black and white, as well as Left and Right, condemned the worrying but distant situation in Uganda. However, the full impact of the crisis was not immediately apparent, and the prospect of mass Asian immigration to the borough was not anticipated (Times Series, 25 August 1972: 1). This picture changed dramatically however once permission had been given by the Home Secretary, Robert Carr, for their arrival in Britain.

The Ugandan-Asian crisis

Following Carr's August 1972 intervention, a furious burst of activity immediately took place in the borough. Numerous groups and individuals quickly began to organise themselves, either to give encouragement to the refugees' possible settlement in the borough, or to vehemently oppose it. It is difficult to know whether or not the opponents genuinely believed settlement could be averted; such a policy was beyond the scope of either national or local government to legally enforce. It is more likely that the opposition to refugee settlement represented a combination of two elements: firstly, a groundswell of anti-immigrant feeling, and secondly, an organised attempt to block the use of the local authority's resources to aid such settlement. However, the influx was recognised by most parties as unavoidable in the last instance.

A handful of Conservative backbench councillors were among the first to officially oppose the anticipated influx. The protests were lead in part by Councillor Alan Musgrave-Scott - an active member of the Monday Club - who wrote to the LBB Town Clerk in forceful terms:

Barnet has enough and should take as few Asians as possible. These Asians will not bring enough money out to enable them to buy homes. Action should be taken to bring pressure on the Government. (Times Series, 1 September 1972: 1)

He cited several reasons for Barnet's inability to cope with the threatened influx. These included recently published unemployment figures for August 1972 which showed a noticeable rise in joblessness, mostly concentrated in the Finchley and Hendon areas. In addition, LBB's waiting list for public housing was expanding. The refugees' arrival, he argued, would only swell the queue, since applicants required a residency qualification of five years in Greater London (with the most recent year of residency in Barnet). He also emphasised reports carried in the national press - emanating, it was claimed, from the Ugandan capital, Kampala - mentioning Hendon and Finchley as popular destinations for many Asian refugees.

The initial response of some other councillors was more positive. The chairwoman of LBB's Social Services Committee, Councillor Thrubun, held a well-publicised meeting at her home at which 'high level discussions' took place involving, *inter alia*, other senior councillors, the Social Services Director, the Citizens Advice Bureau, and others. (Times Series, 1 September 1972: 1). Senior LBB officers also chose to react with relative calm: 'We don't know of an influx. There are no panic stations' said a LBB press officer (Times Series, 1 September 1972: 1). The local press also gave prominence to the words of a leading local executive member of the Association of Asians in Great Britain:

> They [the refugees] intend to disperse. If some make Hendon or Finchley their first stopping place, it will be because they have friends or relatives there. But they intend to move on...one borough cannot absorb large numbers of doctors, lawyers and shopkeepers. (Times Series, 1 September 1972: 1)

The editorial line taken by the local press was similiarly cautious, yet characteristically liberal in sentiment. It argued that, in principle, Barnet had already successfully absorbed many immigrants and could do so again:

> There is no cause for panic - that was the message from the town hall this week, and we agree with that sentiment. The area covered by Barnet already has a cosmopolitan look and has provided a haven for immigrants for decades... The evidence is that we can happily absorb fresh immigrants. (Times Series, 1 September 1972: 1)

A week later, however, the press attacked LBB over its apparent silence on the growing crisis. The 'don't panic plea' of LBB was, argued the editorial, no longer sufficient. Moreover, examples of 'responsible action and forward planning' were cited from neighbouring boroughs such as Brent and Harrow, and the Conservative LBB administration were accused of being 'out of touch with reality' (Times Series, 8 September 1972: 1 and 12). Enormous pressure was being placed on LBB to take a decisive stand. The local press, in a subtle yet important change of tune, began highlighting local fears, arguing, for example, that 'preferential treatment should not be given to the newcomers' (Times Series, 15 September 1972: 1)

The issue was sharpened dramatically following the intervention of the Conservative MP for Hendon North, John Gorst. There were reports of Gorst's meeting with the Prime Minister, Edward Heath, at which the Government's policy to admit the refugees was strongly criticised (Times Series, 8 August 1972: 1).[10] His intervention undoubtedly gave a powerful lead to those who opposed a greater Asian presence in the borough. Indeed, Gorst's argument centred on the 'strength of feeling in [his] constituency against the decision' (Times Series, 8 September 1972: 1). In contrast, the Conservative MP for Hendon South, Peter Thomas, took a less negative line, stating Britain's moral and legal obligation to admit the refugees.[11] The issue, moreover, was given widespread coverage in letters to the local press. Opinion here appeared to divide roughly evenly, though there remained a strong sense of populist, and easily mobilised, feeling against the impending influx (Times Series, 15 September 1972: 4).

Much of the above had little to do directly with LBB's policy over the crisis. In the main, the public pronouncements of these various groups and individuals only shaped the climate in which the issue was discussed. The LBB administration certainly operated within that climate but, it must be said, also had to respond to other criteria. The most important of these, undoubtedly, was the sure knowledge that the issue of whether the refugees should be allowed to settle in the borough was not an issue at all. It was debated in an air of unreality, since LBB possessed no powers whatsoever to restrict their local settlement. Leaders of the LBB administration certainly recognised this important limitation (Interview: former Conservative councillor, LBB, 1986). Therefore, the locus of the Conservative administration's attention fell on the related, but conceptually distinct, question of its own role and responsibilities as a local authority in the face of the inevitable influx of significant numbers of Asian immigrants.

Illiberal reactions and counter-reactions

Late in September 1972 the Government-appointed Ugandan Resettlement Board (hereafter URB) solicited the views of LBB on its proposals to help absorb the refugees (Times Series, 29 September 1972: 13). Earlier that month LBB's General Purposes Committee had agreed not to take any particular line until more was known about the scale of the possible influx (LBB, 1972a). The initiative taken by URB meant that LBB was now compelled to state its official position, and the full Council met for that purpose on 4 October 1972 (LBB, 1972b).

Not surprisingly, the meeting was approached in a mood of confrontation from both sides. The outcome was a majority vote (by a large 31:16 margin) against any additional public housing being made available for use by URB for the refugees (Times Series, 6 October 1972: 1; LBB, 1972c).[12] The debate highlighted the wide rifts that had opened up as a result of the URB request, both between the Conservative and Labour benches, as well as within each parties' own ranks. Later, Hendon South Constituency Labour Party passed a motion condemning LBB's actions and called on it to make sufficient resources available in order to welcome the refugees to the borough (Times Series, 6 October 1972: 1). The local press also ran a forcefully-written editorial on the controversial Council vote:

> A borough that has welcomed refugees and immigrants over the years, has turned its back on even an immediate token gesture of help. The attitude seems to be that Asians who get here under their own steam and with their own money will be welcome. (Times Series, 6 October 1972: 1)

An interesting aspect of this key debate was the race-specific and non-race-specific references to the Asian refugees used by the various policy actors. LBB's Conservative Leader, Councillor Alan Fletcher, argued vehemently in favour of a policy of formal equality. According to such a position, new Asian arrivals were said to be entitled to the same access to, and level of, public service provision as all other Barnet citizens. Fletcher's position - later endorsed by a majority vote in Council - was offered as a conciliatory and progressive policy that 'must lead public opinion, but must not get too far in front' (Times Series, 6 October 1972: 15). It was projected and largely accepted as a middle line between those who opposed any right of settlement for the refugees in the borough (however abstractly conceived or impractical) and those who wanted a positive lead from LBB through the allocation of specific housing stock to the arriving refugees.

In complete opposition to the acceptance of any refugees, stood those such as Conservative backbench Councillor Archie Smith who exclaimed:

I appeal to all councillors in town halls up and down the country to say long, loudly and clearly that there is no room at our inn. (Times Series, 6 October 1972: 15)

A number of Conservative backbench councillors were at variance with Smith's hardline position. Councillor John Gordon-Lee, in particular, condemned his position for offering no practical help in a unique emergency. Elsewhere, Labour members such as Councillor Michael Freeman accused opponents of 'bigoted prejudice' and 'hiding behind the fears of a minority' (Times Series, 6 October 1972: 15). Other Labour members, however, were less prepared to take positive steps to house the refugees. Labour Alderman Arthur Paul pleaded that the authority simply could not please everyone and therefore should concentrate on the 'interests of native citizens' of Barnet (Times Series, 6 October 1972: 15).

In all, there was only one direct reference to issues of racial prejudice or discrimination during the debate when a Labour Councillor, Lorna Levy, sought to remind her colleagues that the issue revolved around 'colour prejudice'. Her remarks were badly received, especially by some Conservative councillors who accused her of offending their right to 'stand up for their constituents' (Times Series, 6 October 1972: 15). This short exchange apart, the debate was dominated by familiar arguments to do with finite local authority resources, the fear of refugees receiving priority in public service allocation, and criticism of laxity in successive central governments' immigration policies. The local political debate over the crisis seemed to follow the lines of previous immigration crises - such as in 1962 and 1968 - only with greater intensity and animosity.

Beyond the Council Chamber, the decision to deny the URB request was condemned by a number of Asian EMGs. For example, the Hindu Centre in Golders Green sent telegrams of protest to the Mayor and the Conservative and Labour Leaders of the Council, claiming that the decision would be remembered with 'disgust, disregard and dishonour' (Times Series, 13 October 1972: 1). Later, the organisation's General Secretary, Pratap Mehta, caused controversy following allegations that he had called on local Asians to vote Labour at the next local elections (Times Series, 20 October 1972: 1).[13] Despite considerable confusion over his remarks, he was quickly rounded on by Conservative councillors for trying to 'sell Socialist propaganda' over the issue (Times Series, 20 October 1972: 1). Mehta and the organisation he lead were instrumental in setting up another body to pressurise LBB for a positive response. The Suburban Asian Action Group (hereafter SAAG) was launched in early-November 1972 to 'go to the voters and [to] try to draw the correct picture of the whole situation by putting down facts and figures' (Times Series, 3 November 1972: 1). SAAG represented a direct attempt to escalate the climate of the policy debate by threatening to 'remind the voter...to keep in mind which councillor has done what, and what they should vote accordingly' (Times Series, 3 November 1972: 1).[14] The organisation styled itself as a direct campaigning body, independent in its criticisms of local racial injustice, and autonomous in its relations with LBB. As such, it constituted a rather bold and unique race pressure group in the local politics of the borough, particularly when contrasted with the more low-profile, borough-wide CRC established a year later.

Almost ten years after the turning point of SAAG's establishment, several other autonomous race pressure group bodies were to emerge at the fringes of the RPE in Barnet. For the time being however, SAAG stood largely alone, though tacitly supported by individual community relations activists, several Labour councillors, and others. Despite its short-term campaign of 1972-73, SAAG remained an essentially moderate organisation, committed to persuading LBB through mobilising grassroots public opinion. For these reasons, it was a conceptually different policy actor to the tiny handful of more radical ethnic organisations that were to appear in local politics a decade or so later.

Finally, Golders Green Community Relations Committee (hereafter GGCRC) issued a statement expressing 'shock and dismay' at the Council's decision (GGCRC, 1972). However, the Committee's response was, in large part, a meek one. Its statement on the affair went on to suggest that a number of LBB's vacant properties awaiting demolition might have been offered to temporarily house the refugees. It specifically failed to condemn the authority or the Conservative administration. This moderate response is perhaps best accounted for by the Committee's on-going concern with establishing itself as a permanent member of the local RPE. This concern, on occasion, meant that its ability to participate in local opinion formation was restricted for fear of offending an administration which it was lobbying to establish and fund a local borough-wide CRC (GGCRC, 1972; Times Series, 13 October 1972: 1).

A "non-decision" policy outcome

The crisis was heightened as a result of a second full Council meeting convened on 8 November 1972 to further discuss LBB's non-co-operation policy (LBB, 1972d). At this meeting the remarks of two Conservative councillors in particular caused grave offence to many other councillors. A number of walkouts resulted, in protest to, among other points, the alleged anti-semitic remarks of a leading Conservative backbench critic of URB.[15] The meeting was also told of figures released by URB of numbers of Ugandan-Asians already known to be residing in Barnet (269 families involving 722 individuals).[16] These details were described as 'staggering' by those opposed to LBB action, citing them as evidence of Barnet having already received 'more than its fair share' (Times Series, 10 November 1972: 1).

Once again, the LBB Leader, Councillor Fletcher, urged that the authority should not commit itself to providing any services for the refugees as this would 'encourage indiscriminate entry' (Times Series, 10 November 1972: 16). Meanwhile, the broader debate tended to veer off into accusations and counter-accusations of anti-semitism and racialism, splitting the Conservative ranks in particular. Not surprisingly, opinion divided sharply on the underlying central issue: the ethnic and racial transformation of parts of the borough. An amendment tabled by the Labour Leader, Councillor F.L. Tyler, calling for co-operation between URB and LBB, was defeated.[17] The Council decided instead to refer the matter - once again - back to its General Purposes Committee and to instruct its chief officers to apply for URB funding *in lieu* of refugee-related educational and other expenditure (LBB, 1972d).

The crisis had clearly split opinion in the borough very sharply. Although much of the public face of the debate tended to veer away from direct references to race or colour, beneath this, race relations remained highly strained. Issues of anti-semitism and fascism continued to seep into the local debate, further polarising the factions for and against the refugees' local settlement. The debate soon became only indirectly concerned with whether LBB should intervene directly, for example by allocating public housing to URB. Instead, it had moved onto the abstract, with leading individuals fighting over the compatibility of such ill-defined concepts as "Englishness" and "Jewishness" (Times Series, 19 January 1973: 1).

The central policy question around which the protagonists fought was that of public housing. By early-1973 this issue had further converged on the Labour Group's proposal to assign some priority to refugees on the authority's waiting list, versus the Conservative's opposition to such a proposal. This inter-party dissensus had the affect of obscuring internal divisions within the ruling Conservative Group - mainly about allegations of anti-semitism within its own ranks. Councillor Leslie Pym - who was later to lead the Conservative Group - presented evidence from his own *ad hoc* survey from the western part of the borough, claiming that over 80 per cent of the community were against Labour's proposal (Times Series, 2 February 1973: 2). Such evidence and the intended party political point behind it, also indirectly served to remove the question of LBB's "non-policy" from the public agenda. Thus, the main debating point shifted from LBB's failure to devise a housing policy or any other service-delivery policy to cope with the expected influx, and towards Labour's alleged 'queue-jumping' policy suggestion (Interview: Labour councillor, LBB, 1986a).

The Ugandan-Asian controversy was never fully resolved. There was no explicit LBB policy decision directed at assisting the refugees' local settlement in the borough.

Most importantly, no action was taken to provide public housing or give any form of priority in allocation. Councillor Fletcher's argument of treating the refugees equally alongside other Barnet citizens prevailed. In short, the episode demonstrated the triumph of "colourblindness" in LBB's approach to public policy on a major RPE issue. Moreover, the Conservative ruling-group's success in diverting attention towards the contrasting, colour conscious approach of their opponents, meant that the "colourblindness" approach was set to dominate LBB's participation in the local RPE for many years to come.

Developments in the local community relations movement

The community relations movement had not managed to get very far in Barnet during the 1960s. Despite a short period of intense activity around the time of the Kenyan-Asian crisis, the movement remained largely stalled and dependent on the voluntary efforts of a committed core. Further, a CRC spanning the entire borough had yet to get off the ground; in the meantime, GGCRC stood alone as the only viable community relations body in the borough. The movement had not managed to find or open any doors into local government support or sponsorship for its work, and as an entirely voluntary group, GGCRC remained essentially relegated to the periphery of the LBB-dominated RPE. The Ugandan-Asian crisis of 1972-73 served to add momentum to the community relations movement in the borough. It proved to be the first major race-related issue on which the CRC viewpoint was both loudly articulated as well as widely reported and received. GGCRC emerged as a reasonably cohesive policy actor whose views could no longer be ignored by other key policy actors, most notably the Conservative and Labour Groups on LBB Council. This development was to add a new slant to local race relations - and the RPE in particular- for the remainder of the 1970s. By the late-1970s, a borough-wide CRC had fully established itself and had begun to see itself - and be seen - as a regular and integral participant in race-related public policy discussion in Barnet.

The philosophy of "community relationsism" and the emergence of GGCRC as a central character in the borough's race relations during the early-1970s, resulted from three main factors. Firstly, as in the case of the late-1960s immigration row, the community relations movement had to concentrate its efforts to try to halt the erosion of liberal values in local race relations. The evidence for a "liberal hour" in Barnet's race relations is somewhat sketchy. Nonetheless, some of the themes of the national "liberal hour" had certainly filtered down to local borough level. In particular, the widely-recognised national need for voluntary, racial harmony-oriented bodies had percolated down to Barnet during the early-1970s.

It is arguable that LBB would eventually have come to recognise this important role by sponsoring - at least in part - the formation of a borough-wide CRC (Interview: Conservative councillor, LBB, 1986b). In the event, GGCRC cited its own public criticism of LBB's non-co-operation policy as a major reason why the authority did not promote the CRC cause. Even at this early stage - before a borough-wide CRC had emerged - LBB had begun to lay down the ground-rules for any future relationship. According to a Conservative backbench councillor at the time:

> The trouble seemed to be that the [Golders Green] Community Relations Committee took the view that it could tell us [the Council] what to do and how to behave. Quite simply, they were mistaken because that is not how we think local government should work. Our responsibilities lie to our ordinary constituents in the wards first and foremost...we are answerable to them and them alone. No pressure group with a vested interest...can then come along and tell us about our responsibilities to a group of people who have no connection with the area but who want to live here. We took the view that if they wanted to live here, then our responsibilities to them should match those we had to native citizens of the borough, and no more. (Interview: former Conservative councillor, LBB, 1985)

Secondly, GGCRC was keen to expand its base across the borough and was unafraid to ride on the back of the Ugandan-Asian controversy in order to do so. These tactics might have contributed to a sense of GGCRC merely empire-building. GGCRC's critics argued that the CRC was unable to advance a case for its expansion or recognition by LBB on its own merits, and thus turned to current issues such as the refugee crisis as a source of support. Moreover, the sense of unwanted interference by GGCRC in LBB affairs only served to weaken its case among the ruling-group (Interview: former Conservative councillor, LBB, 1985).

The public statement that GGCRC had issued in October 1972 criticising the "non-policy" stance of LBB also included a lengthy plea for a full-time officer to be appointed with LBB funds (Times Series, 13 October 1972: 1). Curiously, GGCRC claimed that by agreeing to fund such a visible post, LBB would be giving a sign of goodwill in local race relations. GGCRC thus gave the impression that it was trying hard to mitigate the negative impact of LBB's earlier decision not to assist the refugees. Either way, the ploy failed to convince many members of the LBB administration (Interview: BCRC executive member, 1985).

GGCRC however persisted in trying to forge a link between the local immigration controversy and the need for its expansion and funding from LBB resources. In February 1973, LBB's General Purposes Committee again refused to help establish a borough-wide CRC in conjunction with GGCRC (LBB, 1973). GGCRC's chairman, the Reverend Reg Trueman, whilst protesting against this decision, also emphasised that a proper CRC could greatly assist LBB with some of the problems it was facing following the 1972 influx. To neglect these problems, argued Trueman, was to store up trouble for the future, something which 'could be obviated if the borough had a community relations officer with a small permanent staff' (Times Series, 2 February 1973: 15). There was little to disguise the CRC's single-minded determination to secure LBB sponsorship.

Thirdly, the community relations ideal had gained considerable ascendancy in the borough. By the early-1970s and irrespective of LBB's luke-warm stance, the ideal was moving towards expansion in size and scope. According to the 1971 General Census 16.9 per cent of Barnet's population were born outside the UK (OPCS, 1973; Times Series, 13 April 1973: 8). A significant demographic movement was taking place in the borough. Furthermore, much of the New Commonwealth-born settlement of the early-1970s had not shown up in the 1971 figures. This basic change gave liberally-minded community relations activists a strong base from which to argue their case. At a February 1973 meeting convened by Camden CRC, the Chairman of the Race Relations Board, Sir Geoffrey Wilson, said (in relation to Barnet): 'An immigrant community relations council of some sort [would be] useful...though it depends on whether the size of the immigrant community warrants the cost' (Times Series, 2 February 1973: 15). The message clearly was that the immigrant ethnic minority population in Barnet now warranted such a move and that LBB should respond accordingly.

Barnet Community Relations Council (hereafter BCRC) was eventually established in September 1973 at a well-attended public meeting held at Hendon Town Hall (Times Series, 28 September 1973: 36; Interview: BCRC leader, 1985). Initially composed of 'a miscellaneous collection of citizens', BCRC was keen to stress its cross-ethnic, bridge-building role:

> We believe there are social needs in Barnet which might be better met if there were such a council to serve the *entire community*, not just the minorities. There would be opportunities for new residents to play a more positive role in our borough. (Times Series, 28 September 1973: 36 - emphasis added)

The inaugural meeting was presided over by the new CRC's acting Chairman, the Conservative MP for Hendon South, Peter Thomas, who pointed to the value of such an organisation to LBB:

The [community relations] council must recognise the need for, and must obtain the support of, the local authority. It would be in a unique position to serve a very useful role in public education by increasing mutual understanding on the part of the immigrant and host communities. (Times Series, 28 September 1973: 36)

BCRC's launch was generally accompanied by support from many other policy actors with an interest in local race relations. These included encouraging messages from, and representation on BCRC's executive for, the Mayor, Deputy Mayor, leaders of the major parties on LBB's Council, local Church leaders, leaders of selected EMGs, and others.[18] On the thorny issue of party politics, Thomas pointed out 'the council must be non-sectarian and non-party political' - a rather ironic remark given that the major parties were all represented on BCRC's executive (Times Series, 28 September 1973: 36). A decisive attempt, therefore, was made to steer BCRC towards a role of removing local race relations issues from the substance of local party competition.

BCRC's early development during its first five years was rather sporadic and modest. Insofar as it managed to attain a public profile, it was as a body concerned with public education, public meetings, seminar discussions, multi-cultural festivals, and similar activities. It was also associated with the remaining elements of a liberal and rather optimistic perspective on race relations. This viewpoint appeared to suggest that discrimination could be overcome through BCRC simply "being there" as the local race harmony body, without doing anything in particular, or ensuring that others such as the local authority did something (Interview: BCRC leader, 1985). Its low profile was perhaps reinforced by the absence of any further major local crises over immigration. The result was that the issue of Asian settlement - and immigration numbers in general - began to decline in salience in local politics. The attention of local policy actors, although periodically distracted by the far-right's attempts to resurrect the numbers question, slowly shifted to practical policies directed at the grassroots Asian immigrant community in the borough. This re-orientation was gradual and approached with great caution by all RPE participants, and by BCRC in particular.

The re-emergence of racial politics in the late-1970s

The sharper, more visible face of racial politics returned to the public domain in Barnet towards the end of the decade as a result of three inter-related factors. Firstly, the rise of organised, anti-immigrant political groups resulted in the race issue becoming more salient in local politicians' and policy-makers' minds. This development was seen across many parts of London including Barnet. The results of the 1977 Greater London Council elections were a dramatic illustration of the electoral rise of the far-right, largely on the back of the race and immigration issue (Husbands, 1983). Secondly, a small handful of radical, black EMGs emerged in response to the rise of the far-right (Messina, 1984). Their common aim was based on counter-attacking the far-right - often directly! - thus serving to sharply polarise local opinion. Messina (1984 and 1985b) has suggested that the impact of both extremes served to defuse the volatility of the race issue in the longer term. The evidence for this view is still somewhat sketchy and, in fact, the opposite result was apparent in the short-term. More significantly perhaps, the emergence of the far-right did appear to bring about a reaction among those on the Left, as well as, to some degree, those not previously politically active. In Barnet a small handful of black youth-oriented political groups emerged at this time, though on a more modest scale than elsewhere in London (eg. Ealing). Thirdly, the above developments, together with the decline of the inter-party consensus on race, placed tremendous pressure on BCRC. Its traditional "buffer" role was increasingly undermined, not least by the major political parties themselves, one of which (Labour) was edging towards a more polarised, radical posture on local race relations.

The stable RPE which had evolved since the mid-1960s, and had co-opted the local community relations movement during the early-1970s, was now undergoing a period of accelerated change. The result was the forging of a wider and more coherent RPE by the mid-1980s. However, despite significant changes during the enhanced racialisation of politics in Barnet in the late-1970s, the RPE continued to be dominated by the LBB Conservative adminstration. LBB's over-riding concern was two-fold. LBB wanted firstly to avoid the permanent racialisation of local politics and, secondly, to try to use the CRC as an agency to promote its own belief in "colourblind" local community relations.

During the period 1978-86, LBB's position of dominance was used to great effective to offset the further ascendancy of racial politics in Barnet. In other outer-London boroughs (including Ealing to the west), a new era of sharply divided public debate over race issues was unmistakable. LBB was determined to avoid racial politics taking hold in Barnet, and, most crucially, it was prepared to use all its available political tools to minimise the chances of such a situation. Its principal tool was the ability to try to mobilise bias in order to challenge the legitimacy of other policy actors who wished to debate race issues in open and direct terms.

The routinisation of race, 1978-86

The period 1978-86 contained a number of important grassroots developments in Barnet. During these years important changes took place in local race relations, contributing to the state of flux and confusion in aspects of the borough's RPE. How and why did these changes take place? In this section I describe change among EMGs, trends in BCRC, and the growing sharpness of local disputes such as that over police accountability.

The developing maturity of Asian EMGs

An important feature of this period was the emerging confidence and strength shown by the borough's various Asian EMGs. Although the numbers of these organisations did not markedly increase during the late-1970s and 1980s, the volume and scale of their bids for public monies rose noticeably.[19] The result of this development was the emergence of an important, if sometimes poorly organised, group of policy actors in the RPE in Barnet. Although many of these organisations had skirted at the edges of the RPE for many years previously, their cumulative impact in securing policy-makers' attention on their specific policy demands, is only apparent during the 1980s.

These policy demands consisted of repeated requests for LBB funding and other subsidies. The resources sought were often designated for use in various self-help community projects, and would usually be targetted at either the Social Services Committee or the General Purposes Committee. Project-aid to enable EMGs to carry out service-oriented duties dominated these organisations' bids for funding. A well-known example in Barnet was the Sangam Association of Asian Women (hereafter SAAW) who, beginning in 1978, had steadily increased the size of the resources it sought and was granted (LBB, 1978). Its initial funding was mostly out of Urban Aid monies provided jointly by LBB and the Department of the Environment.[20] This funding arrangement meant that EMG projects were in competition with the projects of non-ethnic, mainstream community organisations such as tenants' associations, under-fives' groups, sporting and cultural organisations, and so on.[21]

From 1982 onwards, LBB's General Purposes Committee appeared to initiate a small, *ad hoc* re-ordering of priorities in the allocation of Urban Aid monies. The Committee regularly included at least one EMG project-related bid in its major nominations for Urban Aid. The result was that some groups and projects were better received than others. Moreover, a few bids were occasionally solicited by the General Purposes Committee based on its loose perception of the needs of ethnic minorities in the borough. However, it is important to stress that at no point did LBB operate any aspect of public policy that specifically allocated resources for *race-related* forms of expenditure. The process of funding for EMGs began and steadfastly remained part of a broader budget process in which ethnic groups competed both with one another as well as with non-ethnic organisations.

The rationale behind LBB's policy towards such funding programmes was one which emphasised the need for limited public funding to promote independent, self-help activity. The aim was not to encourage long-term, self-sustaining funding relationships between LBB and these organisations. To take the example of a typical application by an Asian religious community organisation for Urban Aid sponsorship for the purchase of a community centre, LBB's General Purposes Committee noted in November 1980:

> The DOE Circular 21 stipulates that projects to be approved must benefit an area of special social need and demonstrate how the deprivation identified is to be alleviated. The Society [ie. the EMG applicant] needs a permanent centre for alleviating the hardship and problems of the Asian immigrant community and making them self-reliant. In particular, the Society intends to cater for the elderly;...provide language and other tuition in the English way of life for women; provide educational, social, vocational and civic advice to the disadvantaged; intensify its youth activities; provide educational facilities; and arrange playgroups for working mothers. This programme seems to indicate an attack on areas of possible deprivation within the meaning of the Circular. (LBB, 1980a and 1980b)

Such a bid from such an organisation went a long way towards meeting LBB's unofficial aim of using Urban Aid monies for community self-help purposes. In contrast, other groups seeking to obtain funds for broader purposes, not directly linked to projects providing services to the ethnic minority communities, were looked upon less favourably (Interview: Conservative councillor, LBB, 1986a). BCRC's successive bids for project-linked funding is a good case in point. Here, BCRC's funding relationship with LBB had always been in turmoil to a greater or lesser degree. Issues of BCRC's alleged involvement in local politics in particular had persistently resulted in rows between both sides. By common agreement, BCRC's annual bids for funding were looked upon in a very different light to those from 'ordinary' Asian EMGs (Interviews: Conservative councillor, LBB, 1986a; Conservative councillor, 1986b; Labour councillor, 1986a; BCRC leader, 1985).

In 1982-83, the absolute level of BCRC's funding from LBB totalled just £630. This amount represented a contribution towards BCRC's adminstrative expenses and was adjusted upwards only fractionally over the following few years. With BCRC's operating costs exceeding £8,000, the scale of LBB's commitment can be seen. As part of a general inventory of the borough's financial commitments to 'community relations-type work' carried out by the LBB Chief Executive in April 1982, BCRC's grant ranked fifth in a field of six specific grants (LBB, 1982a). Measured in these terms, LBB's commitment to so-called self-help projects dwarfed its tiny subsidy to BCRC.

Applications for relatively small sums were also judged by the same, unstated, criterion of not supporting what LBB saw as "political" bodies or projects. For example, the Hindu Cultural Society's (hereafter HCS) bid for £60,000 to help set up a community centre for social-welfare activity was sympathetically treated. In sharp contrast, a black Labour councillor's amendment to allocate a mere £200 to Barnet African Caribbean Association (hereafter BACA) towards the costs of an Afro-Caribbean youth festival was rejected outright (LBB, 1982b). The justification for LBB's rejection rested on a Conservative backbench councillor's second-hand information alleging that the BACA-sponsored festival included seminars on 'black consciousness and racism in the police force' (Times Series, 19 May 1982: 3).

The findings of the Chief Executive's 1982 inventory illustrate the priorities of LBB and are shown in Table 1 below:

Table 6.1

Financial assistance to community/race relations by LBB,
Chief Executive's report, April 1982

Name of organisation	Purpose of grant-aid	Grant approved for 1981-82 (£)
Barnet Community Relations Council	Administrative expenses	630
Barnet Home Tutor Scheme	Organiser's salary; administrative expenses	8,750
Sangam Association of Asian Women	Administrative expenses	20,250
Overseas Student Friendship Association	Administrative expenses	330
Hindu Cultural Society	Assist purchase of property	60,000
Total...		121,160

Source: LBB, 1982a: 2

LBB-EMG relations

Two issues tended to dominate LBB's relations with Asian ethnic organisations during the 1980s. The first concerned the time-worn, but now increasingly salient, question of these organisations' search for premises for community and/or religious centres. LBB became involved in this issue as a result of a decision taken in 1977 to give nominal backing to one such organisation's search for a home (HCS). The second concerned the on-going public row since 1982-83 over the use of public facilities (such as parks, schools, etc.) by EMGs for religious and other festivals. This issue centred on the dispute over HCS' use of a large public park in Finchley for its annual, autumnal *Dussehra* festival.

At the time of LBB's original involvement in the former issue, the number of organisations seeking suitable homes totalled only four.[22] The first and by-far best organised attempt to lobby LBB came from HCS, presided over by a putative conservative management committee. LBB's General Purposes Committee and then full Council approved HCS' bid for LBB sponsorship for Urban Aid monies (for £60,000). The 1977 grant took the form of a subsidy for the purchase of suitable premises, and was renewed annually for the following ten years because of HCS' failure to locate a suitable property.[23] By the mid-1980s pressure mounted from both HCS' membership as well as from LBB councillors and officers for HCS to speed up its search, since the Urban Aid grant would expire in 1986.

HCS' success in gaining LBB's support opened the way for a number of other organisations. HCS had shown that dividends resulted from the combination of a low political profile and a high self-help profile. The organisation's July 1980 application for Urban Aid funds included an extended tract highlighting what its executive - correctly - perceived as the profile most likely to win favour with LBB's ruling Conservative Group:

The Society [HCS] encourages its members to participate and play their role in the activities of the borough and other organisations. Some of our members are actively involved in the Barnet Community Relations Council, School Parent Teacher Associations, Action in Distress, Christian Aid, and Barnet Anglo-Asian Conservative Society. (HCS, 1980: 2)

By 1982 at least three other organisations were lobbying LBB for help over accommodation. One was BCRC, facing an end-of-lease eviction from its offices. The second was the Islamic Association of North London (hereafter IANL) - (LBB, 1984c; IANL, 1984). The third was Barnet Elderly Asians Group (hereafter BEAG).[24] The latter two were nominated for inclusion in LBB's bid for Urban Programme grant in 1983-84 (LBB, 1982c). Both of these organisations had based their strategy on that pioneered in Barnet by HCS: a self-help profile centred on small- and medium-scale project work, geared towards their own members, and not obviously likely to affect other ethnic communities or intrude into local party politics.

Meanwhile, BCRC's application for an LBB subsidy to relocate its offices remained on the backburner. LBB was not prepared to step in to sponsor BCRC's need for a new home. The application was viewed by the Conservative frontbench as a CRC exercise in self-sustenance, unconnected to outside project work, and likely to promote long-term "political" rather than self-help concerns. According to a Conservative member of the General Purposes Committee:

> As I see it, there is a fundamental difference between this Council agreeing to help the Asian communities find a home where they can meet for their own activities, and bailing out the Community Relations Council. I, and many in the Council, are not convinced of the benefit the Asian communities derive directly from the Community Relations Council. It seems that it [BCRC] wants the Council's money to subsidise its campaign of criticising the Council at every opportunity. The only people they are helping are themselves and I suspect that very few Asians in Barnet agree with them. It seems to me that very few people can make a fuss about the Asian organisations we are trying to help because they are concerned with providing services and help to enable their members to integrate into this society. In my opinion, it's not something you can criticise because it helps everyone, Asians and non-Asians, without continually attacking and undermining others as the community relations mob are always seeking to do. (Interview: Conservative councillor, LBB, 1986b)

Later, during 1985-86, the pace of applications for LBB assistance in finding suitable premises for local EMGs increased rapidly (LBB, 1984a; 1984b; 1984c; 1985c; 1986a).[25] In part, this increase reflected changes in the Asian (and other ethnic minority) communities, whose EMGs were now turning to adopt a role as the direct representatives of these communities in local politics. Asian EMGs were pressing and being pressed to become a part of the map of local ethnic politics, and, in doing so, to go down integrationist path already forged by the local Jewish community. Hindu temples and Islamic mosques, in short, were set to mimic the route previously established by local Jewish synagogues and community organisations.

The dispute over Asian EMGs' access to local public facilities such as parks and school halls was an altogether more complex one. In part it was related to the issue of permanent accommodation for these organisations, since many had been meeting in hired public halls and schools for many years. There was another side to this issue which focused specifically on the application by a handful of organisations to hold large-scale religious and cultural festivals in local public parks. The best documented example is seen in HCS' annual celebration of the religious and cultural festival of *Dussehra* in Finchley's Victoria Park since 1983. Initially, the park was allocated to HCS on a written - though ambiguously-worded - understanding that the festival was not 'religious in nature' (LBB, 1983a). A year later, shortly before the second annual festival, a Conservative member of LBB's Development and Estates Committee tabled a successful motion to allow a circus to be held in the park in September 1985 (LBB, 1984d; 1984e). As LBB had a long-standing policy of allowing only two public events in the park in any one year - a summer carnival being the other regular event - the motion meant that the HCS festival had, *de facto*, been banned.

The immediate impact was that the highly charged issue of the comparative willingness of Asians to integrate into Barnet society once again became the focus of public debate in the borough. This abstract concept was crudely measured by many in terms of the propensity of Asian EMGs' to hold religious festivals. The debate soon degenerated into a full-scale row over aspects of race, culture, religion, immigration, and so on, as so often seen in the borough during the 1960s and early-1970s. A small handful of Conservative backbench councillors determinedly held onto the view that the festival should be excluded for what they described as 'cultural reasons' (LBB, 1985b). The views of one Conservative councillor verged on intolerance of a higher order:

> As far as I am concerned, I am certain my constituents in this ward would be much happier with an example of traditional British culture... rather than a loud and unwanted display of a foreign culture. If they want to make a song and dance about their religion or culture, let them; but let them do it where the rest of us don't have to put up with it. (Interview: former Conservative councillor, LBB 1986a)

A meeting of LBB's General Purposes Committee to resolve the issue was preceded by sharp exchanges in the local press and elsewhere. HCS itself attempted to mobilise support by encouraging members to lodge complaints with the LBB Chief Executive. A 600-signature petition was submitted calling for a reversal of the controversial decision. In addition, the meeting considered the evidence of a handful of letters of complaint about the festival received by the Chief Executive. A Labour motion seized on LBB's objection to the alleged noise and inconvenience of the festival, arguing that a circus was sure to have similiar side-effects (LBB, 1984f; Interview: Labour councillor, LBB, 1986b). The issue was further clouded as a result of the disclosure that the park was subject to a covenant - originally laid down in 1899 - specifically precluding its use for 'religious and political meetings' (LBB, 1985a). The decision was referred by the Committee to full Council and narrowly reversed following a lengthy and acrimonious debate (LBB, 1985b).[26] A few months later in spring 1986 the Committee considered a joint proposal from the Chief Executive and the Director of Technical Services to carry out a comprehensive review of LBB's policy on granting permission to community groups for the use of parks and public spaces. The review recommended that HCS be given permission for continued use of Victoria Park on the understanding that it did not hold 'any form of religious ceremony' in the park (LBB, 1986b). The Society's executive body quickly responded with an assurance that future festivals would not be religious in nature. An administrative compromise had successfully defused a potentially explosive conflict.

Advances and retreats for BCRC

By the early-1980s the relationship between LBB and BCRC had stabilised following the battles over immigration during the early- and mid-1970s. BCRC had almost become accustomed to the low overall level of support and interest shown by LBB in its work. Leaders of BCRC were increasingly conscious of having fallen behind in the sense that neighbouring CRCs received much higher levels of subsidies from their local authorities, and, indeed, its scale of operation and overall work programme remained small by the standards of Brent, Haringey or even Harrow. BCRC was thus looking to expand in terms of its personnel and work programme by trying to push "community relations" further up the agenda of local politics and policy-making. As Table 2 below shows, BCRC's subsidies from LBB remained modest, limited to nominal contributions towards its annual adminstrative costs of over £12,000:

Table 6.2

*London Borough of Barnet non-project related grant to
Barnet Community Relations Council, 1979/80 -1983/84*

	1979/80	1980/81	1981/82	1982/83	1983/84
			£		
Amount of grant *	300	630	630	370	1,000

* Grant made by LBB General Purposes Committee and exclusively related to BCRC
administrative costs; does not include project-related grant, eg. for Barnet Housing Aid
Service.

Source: LBB, 1984a.

BCRC's persistent lobbying of LBB appeared to have paid some dividends when, in
early-1983, a bid for a greatly increased grant of £1,000 was approved (LBB, 1983a).
The level of grant was beginning to look less like loose change. In order to secure this
limited breakthrough, BCRC had persistently projected a profile of moderation,
stressing the range of functions it performed indirectly assisting the local authority.
These functions were directly placed alongside selected projects which had a strong
record of LBB funding, especially those aiming to promote the otherwise ill-defined
goal of racial harmony. Examples BCRC cited included its offshoot, Barnet Housing
Advisory Service (hereafter BHAS), and the English Language Barnet Home Tutor
Scheme (hereafter BHTS), both of which were partially funded through LBB Urban
Aid sponsorship. BCRC therefore argued that it was 'anomalous that the Borough has
so far not been willing to finance the...backup and co-ordination services needed by our
Executive Committee' (BCRC, 1982a).

At the same time, BCRC launched a campaign to try to give itself a higher profile in
local politics in the borough. An integral part of this campaign was a call for BCRC to
be given representation on LBB Council committees. BCRC's November 1982 annual
general meeting endorsed the proposal which was formally put to LBB in writing in
December 1982 (BCRC, 1982b). This initiative represented an important shift of
emphasis in BCRC's conception of its participation in the local RPE. However, LBB's
General Purposes Committee refused to accede to the proposal (LBB, 1983a). The
justification for LBB's refusal centred on the view that BCRC was trying to change the
unwritten rules of the local RPE:

> We don't have any objection to them giving their views, especially when asked
> by a particular committee, based on their specialist knowledge. But we cannot
> see the need for them to make an issue out of everything this Council does. Not
> everything is necessarily about race relations; in fact, the vast majority of the
> decisions we take have nothing whatsoever to do with race relations, and
> therefore do not concern [BCRC]... And where it occasionally comes into
> Council business, many of us try to make sure that colour plays no part in our
> decisions...we are determined to look upon Barnet's citizens as all the same.
> (Interview: Conservative councillor, LBB, 1986b)

Police accountability

Elsewhere, BCRC was becoming heavily involved in trying to influence the new
borough-wide police consultative body set up by LBB during 1983-84 (LBB, 1983c).
However, the LBB-sponsored body was far from the only institutional reform of local
policing over which LBB and BCRC fought. Indeed, the debate had a great deal to do

with alternative notions of, and proposals for, the accountability of the local police force.

During this period, no less than three different police "watchdog" bodies were in existence in the borough. Firstly, there was the LBB-sponsored Barnet Police Consultative Committee (hereafter BPCC), initially set up as an early response to the recommendations of the 1982 Scarman Report. This body only gave representation to BCRC alongside other local EMGs, emphasising the political dominance of the Committee's sponsor, LBB. Secondly, there was the BCRC-sponsored Barnet Police Liaison Group (hereafter BPLG), also set up in response to Scarman. This body essentially sought to provide a trilateral discussion platform - the police, the CRC and the local authority - for issues of local policing policy. Finally, there was the GLC-sponsored Barnet Police Monitoring Group (hereafter BPMG). Of the three, this body had by far the most radical profile, regularly seeking and receiving publicity for its critical stance towards local policing.

In the course of the local debate, BPMG was easily marginalised and dismissed in terms of its importance to the policing issue in Barnet. Its dismissal was the result of its own hard-line stance, based, as it was, on its own "independent" monitoring role, and its lack of machinery for regular discussions with the local authority, the CRC, or others. This aspect of BPMG contributed heavily to its isolation, most notably from BCRC which was conscious of the radical profile of the Monitoring Group. The Monitoring Group, according to a leading BCRC executive member, was 'nothing more than a group of committed activists speaking to themselves...they don't speak for the community and they aren't interested in trying to' (Interview: BCRC leader, 1986). It was precisely in this capacity that BCRC saw itself and its own police accountability proposal as being able to 'speak for the community'.

Consequently, BCRC's own project, the Liaison Group, was launched in order to provide a suitable arena for police-LBB-BCRC discussion which, unlike BPMG, could not be dismissed quite so easily. For a short spell, BCRC was able to forge ahead with the Liaison Group, although LBB participation remained luke warm at best. The real clash of interests and approaches to the whole issue of local policing policy arose very shortly afterwards when LBB began to take action to establish its own in-house body. The philosophical approach adopted by LBB was to view its own participation and that of local senior police commanders as *internal* interests; meanwhile, BCRC and other community organisations - including EMGs - were viewed as little more than *external* participants. The LBB-sponsored body, therefore, contrasted sharply with the sense of tripartism at the heart of the BCRC-sponsored body.

The constitution of LBB's Consultative Committee minimised BCRC's representational strength. BCRC was allocated 3 representatives, alongside 12 additional representatives from 11 local community organisations (LBB, 1983c). Although community participants such as BCRC, EMGs, and other community organisations, held slightly more seats than LBB and police interests, the direct BCRC input remained paltry, as did the formal input of specific EMGs. A leading BCRC executive member noted his organisation's resentment:

> There's no other way to look at it: the Council wanted to make sure that our influence would be as little as possible. They've always been suspicious of us...for many years, and the police thing was just one more example of that. As an organisation, we [BCRC] felt considerably weaker and more easily dominated in the Council's Consultative Committee than in our Liaison Group. But they were determined on being the sole legitimate body on the police issue and, with the help of the government and others, they were going to get their way. That said, I think we've managed to gain some ground in the Committee...like getting the chairmanship of the Committee as a non-Council appointment. (Interview: BCRC leader, 1986)

The outcome of the police consultation issue, like many other issues during this period, was that the relative weakness of BCRC in the local RPE was exposed once

132

more. Although part of the explanation for this weakness lies in LBB's domination of the RPE and local politics in general, it is also the result of the *type* of RPE that leading policy actors such LBB and BCRC were committed to. Both were essentially interested in non-radical, non-confrontational, race relations. However, in BCRC's attempts to bring about modest organisational change in the RPE, its actions were continuously perceived by LBB and others as confrontational. As a result, BCRC regularly came up against - and usually succumbed to - the veto of LBB leaders who were generally concerned to ensure minimal change in the RPE.

Conclusion

The issue of EMGs' and the CRC's access to public resources and facilities in Barnet covers similar terrain to the issue of educational dispersal in Ealing. Both issues demonstrate the ways in which race-related public policy demands were introduced with differing levels of success into the local policy-making environment on race. Previously, the RPEs of both boroughs were used to remove such race-specific policy demands from local politics. Such demands were instead channelled into intermediate buffer bodies like CRCs who sought to build a liberal, less race-specific, ethos in local RPEs. Such a liberal framework, though still important, had clearly begun to wane by the late-1970s. This process showed obvious signs of weakness and a growing inability to manage local race conflicts.

However, the main difference in the changing nature of the RPE between the two boroughs lay in the *types* of issues pursued by EMGs. Although these organisations sought to pursue increasingly race-specific policy demands, their strategies and motives differed considerably. In Ealing, the emphasis after 1976 moved to the demands of a new wave of comparatively militant Asian youth groups and movements (eg. SYM). This change was the direct result of the 1976 disorders coupled with the discrediting of older established Asian EMGs (eg. IWA). In Barnet, no such traumatic dislocations are apparent. Various established EMGs began to pursue policy demands that specifically benefitted their own memberships and leaderships. Moreover, these demands essentially consisted of policy goals and values that they had subscribed to for a considerable period. The significance of their behaviour in the 1980s lay in their enhanced individual and combined confidence to raise and pursue such demands. Thus, the apparent racialisation of aspects of the local RPE in Barnet was not so much race-specific (as in Ealing), but rather a noticeable shift towards the public discussion of policy demands long-held by EMGs.

This shift in the focus of the RPE in Barnet came about for two reasons. Firstly, several Asian EMGs had matured considerably since the mid-1960s and, by the mid-1980s, were pushing hard for recognition as key RPE participants. The unstable nature of LBB's relationship with BCRC also meant that LBB, as the dominant policy actor, was searching for new and more pliable allies to support its "colourblind" stance. Secondly and more significantly, the liberal policy framework had begun to buckle under the weight of misunderstanding and hostility - from LBB leaders in particular. An alternative, revised version of the framework, relying heavily on close liaison between LBB and selected Asian EMGs, had begun to gain ground. The long-term outcome of this movement away from an exclusively LBB-BCRC centred approach to the local RPE has been a sort of paralysis in Barnet's RPE. In this situation, neither BCRC nor any particular EMG, commanded strong or decisive voices in the RPE. Consequently, LBB continued to operate a "colourblind" RPE strategy with great success, unhindered by the threat - real or potential - of other policy actor's challenging its right or ability to do so.

Therefore, Barnet can be presented as an extreme case of the *mobilisation of bias* in the setting and manipulation of the local policy-making agenda. Bachrach and Baratz (1970) point to the way in which certain issues can be successfully manipulated by a quasi-élite group of agenda-setters within a city policy machine.[27] LBB is another example of such stage management of policy debate and substance. Key or fundamental policy issues almost never permeated into the local debate over race relations. Instead, policy actors were generally occupied with discussion of how existing policies and programmes could be modified or updated. The steering away from major issues is illustrated by the fact that BCRC remained on the sidelines of the RPE throughout this period; moreover, this complaint rarely, if ever, warranted the status of a legitimate RPE issue. Another illustration was the habitual discussion of RPE issues in non-race-specific terms.

Finally, Young (1985b: 288) has argued that race policy is debated and formulated within a 'culture of inexplicitness'. However, the empirical chapters of this study have demonstrated that the non-policy-making of the local authority leads not so much to a *culture* of inexplicitness as to a *law* of inexplicitness over local race-related policy debate. That is to say, in the case of Ealing (see Chapters 4 and 5 above), various policy actors often conspired to keep discussion about race related issues as inexplicit as possible, despite considerable community-based pressure to do otherwise (Saggar, 1991a). In Barnet, in contrast, key policy actors stuck to an agenda largely devoid of race, leaving others to demonstrate - if not forcibly assert - the need for any departures from this agreement. This distinction is most important to the understanding of the historical and ideological determinants of race policy in local politics and government. I shall return to this point in the remaining chapters.

Notes

1. During the mid-1960s, Barnet Borough had a population of approximately 300,000 persons, though it experienced a slight de-population trend during the period 1965-86. However, notwithstanding this small de-population, between the 1971 and 1981 General Censuses, Barnet's relative population size rose from seventh to second highest among the 32 boroughs of Greater London.

2. The Conservatives have been in office continuously in Barnet since its inception in 1965.

3. Barnet possesses one of the largest Jewish populations in London. Estimates of its size are difficult, but those offered by Alderman, 1983, appear as reliable as most. The Jewish concentration lies mainly in the western and southern parts of the borough, reaching a peak in the districts surrounding Golders Green (on the borders with Camden Borough).

4. Table 6.3 below reports actual numbers of Barnet residents according to the birthplace of their head of household as compared with the picture for outer-London boroughs in general (1981 General Census):

Table 6.3 *Numbers of usual residents in private households by birthplace of household, Barnet and outer-London boroughs, 1981 Census*

Birthplace of head of household

	United Kingdom	Irish Republic	NCWP	Rest of the world	Total
Barnet	201742	12774	36465	33338	284319
Outer-London boroughs	3289653	157372	488077	198221	4133323

Source: GLC, 1985

Early estimates of ethnic minority population sizes in Barnet are laden with difficulties. The 1971 General Census shows that almost 17 per cent of the population were born outside the UK. However, this figure tells us little about the numbers of black ethnic minorities among them. The 1981 General Census shows that some 12 per cent of the population live in households headed by someone born in the New Commonwealth or Pakistan (hereafter NCWP). More recent statistics from 1986, show that 20 per cent of live births in the borough were to mothers themselves born in the NCWP; see OPCS, 1987: 2.

5.   It had been alleged that Councillor Hills had personally sanctioned a policy of placing a red mark on applications from black individuals and families for local authority loans to buy their own homes. Hills made no attempt to cover-up the procedure but agreed to abandon it once it became publicly known - including coverage in the national press - during November 1967. The practice was universally condemned at a full Council meeting, though the Conservative Leader, Councillor Fletcher, claimed that the procedure had been misreported and did not reflect 'discrimination...on colour or religion in regard to our functions'; see Times Series, 9 November 1967: 1

6.   The golf club story was particularly significant since one of the club's infrequent patrons was the then Prime Minister, Harold Wilson.

7.   One of the early and recurring difficulties appeared to be the tendancy of some groups to lodge planning applications either without sufficient supporting evidence, or more damagingly, once a change of use had already commenced; see interview: former Conservative councillor, LBB, 1986a.

8.   The original controversy over planning permission for Asian religious and/or community centres occurred in early-1968. A small Hindu religious community, the *Shri Sai Baba* Centre, had located themselves in a two-storey converted house in Golders Green. Indeed, their case was featured in the local press, highlighting some of the problems faced by such groups in finding suitable premises; see Times Series, 1 March 1968: 5.

9.   In February 1968 the Labour Government secured the passage of the Commonwealth Immigrants Bill in a period of a few days. For a full account of the legislation, see Steel, 1969 and Deakin, 1970.

10.   Gorst had followed up his meeting with the Prime Minister with an exchange of public letters. The text of Gorst's reply from Heath was published in full in the local press. Its basic message, besides trying to assign blame on the previous Labour Government, was to state that the Government had little option but to admit the refugees; see Times Series, 22 September 1972: 1 and 11.

11.   The borough's third - and ultimately best-known - MP, Margaret Thatcher, did not state her position on the refugee crisis. Her lack of comment was mainly because of her frontbench portfolio in Heath's Cabinet (Education Secretary), though she happened to be in Australia throughout this period. Her agent, however, was prepared to disclose to the press that a large majority of her mail was strongly opposed to the imminent influx. The views of the borough's remaining MP, Reginald Maudling, did not receive any coverage, though he was also a member of the Heath Cabinet (Home Secretary).

12.   Earlier in the debate, the Labour Leader, Councillor Tyler, had tabled an amendment motion calling on LBB to place 30 houses at URB's disposal; this motion was also lost by a similar margin (35:14 votes).

13. Mehta had also taken the step of personally inviting two Labour councillors to attend a religious festival at the *Shri Sai Baba* Centre in Golders Green. It was at this meeting that Mehta made his bid to lobby the Asian vote for Labour. One of the invitees, Councillor Tyler, addressed the gathering: 'We do not regard the dispute as dead, and we shall continue our struggle to try to get more co-operation from the other parties to provide facilities for immigrants'; see Times Series, 20 October 1972: 1.

14. It is not clear from the available evidence, which, if any, other groups or individuals were linked to SAAG. The only name associated with the body was that of Mehta (also connected with the *Shri Sai Baba* Centre).

15. The controversial remarks were those of Councillor Musgrave-Scott. Labour Councillor Levy appeared to lead the spontaneous walk-out. She stated later to the press that 'some of his [Musgrave-Scott] views made Enoch Powell into a moderate'. Musgrave-Scott had earlier caused an uproar in the Council Chamber when he said: 'I try hard not to be a racialist'; see Times Series, 10 November 1972: 1.

16. In addition, the Town Clerk reported to the meeting that LBB was eligible to apply for grants (of up to 100 per cent) from URB towards the cost of providing educational and other facilities for the refugees.

17. An earlier motion tabled by Councillor Tyler had received near-unanimous support. His motion had welcomed the provision of URB grants and had called on LBB officers to investigate the matter further.

18. The inaugural BCRC meeting agreed to appoint its orginal working group as the steering committee to draft a constitution. A second meeting was convened in November 1973 to adopt the constitution and to appoint BCRC's first executive committee.

19. Despite the rise in bids for funding, there is nothing to suggest that additional monies were made available or targetted for EMG subsidies. Consequently, EMGs were forced to compete alongside other non-EMG bids, as well as against the longer standing funding relationships between LBB and a variety of Jewish community organisations.

20. The Urban Aid formula stipulated that LBB and the Department of the Environment would share expenditure along a 25:75 per cent ratio. This condition was laid down under the Department of the Environment's Urban Aid Circular No.18.

21. An example of an EMG application competing alongside various other projects was SAAW's 1978 bid for funding to establish an Asian women's centre in the western part of the borough.

22. These organisations were: the Hindu Cultural Society, the Brahmin Association of North London, the Oshwal Association, and the Greek Parents' School.

23. Urban Aid rules stated that a successful application for capital expenditure, although renewable annually, would eventually become time-expired after a period of 10 years. Thereafter, the local authority and/or the applicant group would have to submit a fresh bid, the merits of which would not necessarily be linked to any previous bids. In this context, HCS was naturally very concerned over the possibility of losing £60,000 capital grant originally earmarked for use to purchase a community centre in 1977. Eventually, HCS was able to locate suitable premises in late-1987, just months prior to disqualification under Urban Aid rules.

24. BEAG's 1982 application for project work funding was co-sponsored with Barnet Asian Women's Association. This co-bid was successful and was ranked near the top of LBB's order of priority in its submission for Urban Aid. Another EMG bid - from IANL - did not receive any priority in LBB's submission.

25. The main EMGs lobbying for LBB assistance in locating suitable premises were: IANL, the Brahmin Society of North London, the Oshwal Association, and the Greek Parents' School. Unlike their earlier applications, all of these organisations were now specifically aiming to win substantial LBB subsidies to help purchase vacant properties, with or without LBB's help in finding such properties.

26. Although the General Purposes Committees' decision was reversed by the full Council, the

motion stipulated that the decision to lift the ban would be subject to review following the 1985 festival. A similar number of complaints from local residents were received following the festival in 1985, but LBB's review conducted by senior officers chose not to recommend reversal of the decision once again; see LBB, 1986b.

27. Bachrach and Barataz's 1970 study was of city politics in Baltimore, Maryland.

7 The policy framework and the policy environment

Introduction

The study has shown how the liberal settlement led to a number of difficult and often unanticipated conflicts in local political systems. The evidence for these conflicts - not to mention their seeming intractability - litters the empirical chapters. Moreover, despite superficial contrasts, not dissimilar conflicts and choices were experienced by policy-makers and political élites in both boroughs. That said, we still require a more rigorous examination of the notion of conflict over race-related public policy.

This chapter explores the nature of conflict over race policy operating at two inter-related theoretical levels: one dealing with policy actors in the policy environment, and another dealing with the policy framework. The chapter then looks at how conflict at both levels affects the nature of the RPE. It argues that four major RPE-types encapsulate the most significant outcomes of the application of the liberal framework. A classification scheme is presented examining these RPE-types in roughly chronological order.

Conflict over race-related public policy

The language and substance of race policy discussed in this study frequently amounted to two very different things, both from one borough to another, as well as from one era to another. Much of the conflict over race policy documented in this study has been a symptom of wider conflict over the differing and evolving nature of the liberal policy framework. For instance, the various town hall-CRC rows illustrated in earlier chapters appeared to be composed of very different arguments in the two boroughs, and yet seemed the same. In other words, whilst the content of the arguments or conflicts over race policy varied enormously, the underlying "rules-of-the-game" have not. For that, responsibility rests primarily with the liberal framework.

The RPE involves conflict at two levels: the level of directly observable conflict between policy actors; and the less tangible level of conflict over rival interpretations of the conceptualisation of race in the policy framework. The former has a great deal in common with the sort of conflict over race in the policy process written about by many of the authors mentioned previously (Young and Connelly, 1981; Jacobs, 1986; Studlar, 1986; Messina, 1989). The latter stems from the distinction brought out in this study: the framework in which the policy process operates serves to shape both the nature of the process as well as the political conflicts that result. In order to explore the relationship between the levels of conflict, it is necessary to organise or group the variables mentioned previously. The purpose of this is to throw light on the nature of the inter-relationship between these factors. Analysis cannot be restricted to the direct interaction between policy actors in the RPE at a given moment under given circumstances. To do so, merely leaves us with a partial explanation of policy outcomes and decisions - and indeed non-outcomes and non-decisions. Most importantly, it ignores the related dimension of the policy process to do with the policy framework. Therefore, it is this framework that we are concerned with here, and the way in which it serves to shape the actual and potential behaviour of policy actors in the RPE.

The main policy actors in the RPE are made up of: EMGs, CRCs, local political party activists, local authority members, local authority (senior) officers, and various other local political élites. The RPE refers to three things: policy actors, policy programmes, and patterns of relationships. It is essentially concerned with describing the relationship that arises between the former category of interests on the one hand - ie. non-local authority interests - and the latter category of interests on the other - ie. local authority interests. The policy environment is, in itself, not intended as an explanation of the constraints presented by the policy framework. It is, rather, merely a description of the broad ground-rules or parameters of the policy framework.

How can conflict over race policy be characterised? The question can be approached from two levels. Firstly, we may answer with reference to the state of play or direct conflict between both major groups of policy actors. This conflict will, inevitably, ebb and flow from time to time, and from issue to issue. For example, a town hall administration may concede a CRC's bid for funding because of a combination of direct tangible factors. Such factors might include: its own manifesto commitment; the CRC's pliant, co-operative profile; the absence of controversial race issues dividing local individuals and groups; and so on. This approach, therefore, seeks to characterise the RPE by reference to what has happened, is happening, and likely to happen, within the context of the RPE itself, without reference to broader historical and ideological factors defining the RPE.

Secondly, we may describe the RPE in the context of the policy framework. That is, the conflict observed and measured in the RPE is, in itself, less important than the broad policy framework within which such conflict occurs. The "rules-of-the-game", in short, reveal as much - and possibly more - about why the issue of CRC subsidies is an issue in the first place. These two approaches are based on distinct, yet related, theoretical conceptualisations of the race-public policy relationship. The example of the issue of CRC funding has two related dimensions: on the one hand, the policy process through which funding was attained; and on the other, the fact that funding was an issue in the RPE at all.

Dimensions of the RPE

The study has shown how the power of initiative, legitimation and agenda-setting within the RPE has largely rested with one group of policy actors. The dominance of local authorities has usually occurred in an otherwise diffuse and poorly co-ordinated organisational setting, committed to a culture of non- or low race-specificity. The reasons for this outcome will be considered below.

The study has been interested in characterising the conflict in the RPE between the two main categories of policy actors: those inside the town hall and those outside. The empirical evidence presented from two London boroughs has shown that, in general terms, local authority interests (members and officers) have usually successfully dominated agenda-setting. Moreover, this group of policy actors has successfully controlled the legitimation of non-local authority interests (CRCs and EMGs) and their demands in the RPE. By control and manipulation of the agenda and the legitimation process, town hall interests have managed to secure and defend a position of dominance within the RPE. This situation has come about via the terms and application of the liberal settlement. Therefore the significance for the race-public policy nexus is not so much the *extent* of the local authority's dominance, but rather, the more fundamental question of *why* it is dominant to begin with (Bachrach and Baratz, 1970; Dearlove, 1973; Saunders, 1975).

Dominance within the RPE is an important feature drawn from the liberal policy framework. The framework tried to establish a core constellation of policy actors to replace the centre's frontline position of vulnerability on the race issue. In fact, by assigning greatest prominence to town halls - from the 1965 White Paper and the S.11 programme through to S.71 of the 1976 legislation - central government's own weak position in relation to race conflicts was underscored. In an attempt to deflect attention away from the national stage, liberal reforms merely handed over key responsibilities to a tier of policy-makers, who, in many ways, were less well equipped to deal with the problems of local race relations.

There are two main lines along which variance occurs in the RPE. These dimensions are: the structural coherence of the policy environment, and the conceptualisation of race. Each represents key aspects of both the interaction of policy actors within the RPE, as well as the all-pervading influence of the policy framework upon such interaction.

The first dimension represents a characterisation of the continuity and stability of relations between policy actor relations in the RPE. It attempts to measure the *structural coherence* or fabric of the RPE, and may vary on a continuum from a highly-developed network at one end, to a diffused and fragmented state at the other. In other words, we are concerned with the constellation of policy actor interests (Heclo, 1978; Rhodes, 1985 and 1986). This constellation will exhibit either greater or lesser coherence in terms of the strength and stability of the linkages between its participants. Of course, a developed, coherent constellation will not necessarily lead to a particular set of policy outcomes.

The evidence of the study shows that race policy environments have, in general, tended to be more fragmented than developed. Occasional examples of tangible, cross-policy actor linkages in the two boroughs have rarely been more than temporary, *ad hoc* phenomena. Development of such linkages has often come about in response to earlier breakdowns of communication between policy actors. A good example would be the initiatives taken by the local authority in Ealing to build links with alienated EMGs in the aftermath of the 1979 and 1981 Southall disturbances.[1] However, subsequent RPE crises, usually (but not always) to do with local immigration scares, have often led to the RPE's short-term fragmentation. An example would be the rapid undermining of the case for an early public subsidy being granted to Barnet's fledgling CRC in the wake of the 1972-73 row over Ugandan-Asians. Although CRCs and town hall administrations have built productive working relationships with one another from time to time, a continual feature of the evolution of the RPE has been the extraordinary fragility of such relationships. In both Barnet and Ealing, the slightest breeze inspired by anti-immigrant sentiment, invariably had the impact of a destructive gale upon local town hall-CRC relations. Any appearance of a local RPE based on a coherent and stable constellation of interests, disguised the underlying picture of an *ad hoc*, asymmetric relationship. Such a relationship merely reflected a short-run calm, only temporarily free of crisis and division.

The second dimension focuses on the *conceptualisation of race* in the RPE, ranging from the narrow, non-race-specific at one end, to the broad race-specific at the other.

The conceptualisation embodied in the liberal policy framework rested on a narrow, non-race-specific perspective. The implication of this crucial ground-rule was that, not only were policy actors such as CRCs and EMGs rewarded for their co-operation in trying to keep local politics and race relations on separate and parallel paths, but they were equally punished whenever they attempted to make these paths converge. The de-politicisation of race that Messina (1984) writes of, in fact, alludes to only one side of the coin. The other side - discussed in this study - recognises the serious and far-reaching sanctions potentially placed on policy actors threatening to challenge the prevailing conceptualisation of race.[2] The continual and routinised application of the narrow conceptualisation of race embodied in the liberal framework, will mitigate against explicitness in race policy debate. Thus, the liberal policy framework helps us to understand the important *historical* and *ideological* origins of the 'culture of inexplicitness' that 'renders...race issues and race policy initiatives undiscussable' (Young, 1985b: 286).

Conceptualising race and mobilising bias

It is not just direct RPE conflict which leads many policy actors to co-operate with, and be absorbed into, the agreement to de-politicise race. What is equally important is the potential threat of non-legitimation, coupled with the obvious absence of an alternative organisational arena beyond the prevailing RPE. This reality leads all but a handful of policy actors to abandon strategies that challenge the prevailing, narrow conceptualisation of race - virtually *before* they have seriously examined them! For just about all would-be challengers, the decision to participate within the RPE's terms of reference of a narrow conceptualisation of race, is more or less made for them. The liberal policy framework makes it hard for even the most radical EMG to avoid concluding that, by challenging and/or rejecting the existing narrow conceptualisation, the opportunities and likelihood of affecting policy outcomes in the RPE are extremely bleak. Indeed, the liberal policy framework places a pre-requisite, implicit acceptance of non- or minimal race-specificity on EMGs and CRCs, as one of the "rules-of-the-game" in order for them to participate as legitimate policy actors. Therefore, failure to abide by this implicit rule results in non-legitimation in the RPE tantamount to non-participation. The policy actor in question then effectively forfeits the chance of affecting the policy outcomes of the prevailing RPE.

The first dimension can be used to provide an understanding of the organisational structure of the RPE, and the power relations therein. It examines the structural, historical and ideological effect of the policy framework on relations between the policy actors; the empirical evidence shows that, in the main, town hall interests have been in the driving seat. It also looks at how the RPE is organised; the empirical evidence here has shown that, generally speaking, it has been poorly and ineffectively organised. Meanwhile, the second dimension also contains important clues regarding RPE power relations. The contextual setting of the RPE within the liberal framework has enabled dominant policy actors to utilise the prevailing narrow conceptualisation of race, in order to mobilise bias to undermine or de-legitimise other policy actors viewed as threats. The ability to mobilise bias via the narrow conceptualisation of race is a reflection of RPE power relations within the liberal policy framework. This power may be used in order to defend dominant status interests within the first dimension. Alternatively, it may be used to head off the development of a more coherent, and possibly more threatening, organisational network within the same dimension. The empirical chapters have shown considerable evidence of the mobilisation of bias by dominant policy actors, who have penalised other policy actors for trying to introduce much broader conceptualisations of race into the RPE. It is often easy to disarm rivals or challengers by claiming that they do not support the legitimate ground-rules of the existing policy framework. By arguing that others are not following the ground-rules, the dominant policy actor not only makes the rules, but also exercises political power by constraining the options and responses of others.

Classifying race policy environments

Following on from the above discussion of the dimensions of RPEs, a typology of several kinds of policy environment can be set out. Four types of RPE have particular resonance with the main themes and empirical findings of this study.

A typology of RPEs

Figure 1 below sets out a graphical representation of the interaction of these two main variables. Using two dichotomised variables, some four cells are apparent. Each constitutes characterisations of different types of RPE. Certain RPE-types will be more preoccupied with certain policy themes and outcomes than others. The locus of RPE developments in a particular borough during a particular period may be in two (or even three) overlapping cells, ie. the cells are not mutually exclusive. Four RPE-types in the* figure stand out and are discussed in detail below. Viewed together, they represent the sequence of the RPE's chronological development over the course of the past twenty-five years.

```
                          Structural
                          coherence

                  Fragmented              Developed
        ┌─────────────────────┬─────────────────────┐
        │                     │                     │
Narrow  │     Diffusion       │     Paternalism     │
        │                     │                     │
Conceptualisation            │                     │
of race │─────────────────────┼─────────────────────│
        │                     │                     │
Broad   │    Frustration      │     Radicalism      │
        │                     │                     │
        └─────────────────────┴─────────────────────┘
```

Figure 7.1 *Relationship between main RPE variables in the liberal policy framework*

Perceptions of what race policy is supposed to be, and the expectations the policy sphere generates, have evolved enormously over the period examined (Banton, 1985; Saggar, 1991b). This typology helps to explain the nature of, and reasons for, this evolution. In addition, by characterising RPE developments - either in an *ad hoc* manner, or more systematically across a range of race-related issues - the scheme allows us to theoretically link conflict over race and public policy at the levels of the policy environment and the policy framework, as well as to explain each in terms of the other.

Diffusion

The fusion of a fragmented organisational structure and a narrow conceptualisation will lead to a situation that may be labelled as diffusion. This cell signifies the essence of the RPE outlined by the application of the liberal policy framework in the period leading up to the liberal settlement in the mid- to late-1960s. Race was conceptualised during this early period in an unmistakably narrow sense. Public discussion of the so-called

143

"race problem" was given over almost entirely to trying to place the issue onto the policy agenda (Rose, 1987). Previously, race-related public policy discussion was minimal and diffuse. The accelerated discussion and activity of this era concentrated on trying to build a consensus in favour of the policy goal of racial harmony. As Hill and Issacharoff pointedly reminded us in the wake of the "liberal hour" (1971), this particular policy goal may not have necessarily been addressing any of the issues pertaining to racial discrimination and inequality. Thus, the liberal policy framework merely served to constrict the contextual setting of public policy debate to a narrow conceptualisation of race focused on the goal of racial harmony. Questions of narrow versus broad conceptualisations of race did not feature in great measure in the discussions establishing the liberal policy framework. It was later, in the light of implementation and evaluation of the policy outcomes of the RPE, that alternative, broader conceptualisations emerged - usually as part of the demands of alienated and excluded policy actors.

However, the durability of the original consensus over the narrow conceptualisation of race varied from borough to borough. In the case of Ealing, we saw that the variable only really emerged as a second dimension of the RPE in the early-1970s. Virtually all policy actors remained committed to a narrow conceptualisation as a sole, legitimate option in the period until - and arguably beyond - the establishment of various protest groups following the 1976 Southall disturbances. In attempting to develop a basic organisational structure for the embryonic RPE, their energies were focused upon the first dimension. In Barnet's case, evidence for variation in the conceptualisation of race is spectacularly absent for much of the period studied. Only in very recent times have there been signs of discussion and conflict over this variable among different policy actors. However, the introduction of conflict around the conceptualisation of race has usually led to the effective delegitimisation of new, radical policy actors. Dominant town hall-centred policy actors have moved to exclude rival policy actors committed to a broadening of this variable. In doing so, the largely predetermined, narrow conceptualisation of race was established as one of the key ground-rules for legitimate RPE participation.

Paternalism

A situation whereby the RPE is relatively fragmented and centred on a narrow conceptualisation of race will be recognised as a familiar paternalistic theme in the application of the traditional liberal policy framework. Such a theme was widespread in both of the local borough case studies. A RPE that has neither organisational substance nor grassroots pressures to challenge existing narrow conceptualisations of race, will be easily dominated by the local authority. In both boroughs, dominant policy actors were committed either to keeping race issues off the local policy-making agenda altogether, or else to restricting interaction between policy actors to matters of detail rather than substance. "Colourblindness", in other words, evolved as the central ethos of the RPE for the overwhelming bulk of the period analysed (Rath and Saggar, 1990).

The paternalistic RPE-type evolved because the liberal policy framework neither stipulated a suitable machinery for policy development and implementation, nor legitimised discussion of basic questions pertaining to racial disadvantage and inequality. The result was that crucial race policy issues effectively stayed out of the RPE, having been tacitly ruled as "off limits" by the terms of the policy framework. Not only were EMGs and CRCs subject to an exclusion handicap, but their very participation in the RPE hung upon their agreement to only seek to marginally influence the detail of previously determined policy. Opportunities for RPE participation were provided to those policy actors who had previously demonstrated their principal concerns as lying with, typically, the social-welfare needs of immigrants. For example, groups interested in non-English-speaking immigrants' language needs, mother-and-toddler groups, the elderly, the under-fives, and so on, stood some chance of recognition and legitimation of their RPE policy demands. In contrast, recognition was generally not accorded to those groups aiming to promote policy debate on race-specific issues, eg. the involvement of the CRC in Ealing in the protest campaign following the 1979 Southall disturbances.

Paternalism chronologically moves on from diffusion. Empirical evidence showed that in Barnet paternalism shrouded the terms of the tacit understanding within which the Conservative-ruled administration was prepared to "do business" with any and all policy actors in the RPE. There was little or no question over whether the local authority should share key responsibilities in the RPE. The RPE in Barnet has been very firmly lodged in such a paternalistic mould, making only occasional, tactical movements into surrounding typological cells in more recent times. The chances of the local RPE undergoing a massive transformation of character, thereby implicitly revising the terms of the underlying policy framework, seemed as distant in the 1980s as they did in the 1960s. The situation in Ealing has also tended to be dominated by similar paternalistic themes. However, grassroots developments beginning in the mid-1970s meant that paternalism was suddenly and dramatically superseded by frustration as the major theme of the RPE.

Frustration

A third position of significance in the scheme may be described as frustration, and results from a fragmented organisational structure in which there is a broad conceptualisation of race. The preponderance of race-specific political demands from many new policy actors are not balanced nor easily absorbed by other characteristics of the RPE. Consequently, these policy actors and their demands are excluded from the legitimate areas of concern of the RPE. Frustration - potentially explosive if left unchecked - will be the inevitable product. In practice, however, many town hall administrations will in due course acknowledge the very real dangers of alienation that are likely to result. Piecemeal reorganisation of aspects of the RPE will usually follow. If left unchecked, the obvious frustration of excluded interests can only be expected to escalate to higher levels (Rath and Saggar, 1990). The eventual, though remote, outcome will involve these frustrated groups turning to question and undermine the whole framework of local race policy. The empirical evidence presented in this study has shown that the liberal policy framework has served to shape a RPE which, despite obvious constraints, has nonetheless been *amply* flexible in terms of absorbing and deflecting major challenges to that framework.

The picture in Ealing between the mid-1970s and early-1980s matched this profile. The tensions created by the local authority's "colourblind" domination of the RPE suddenly and clearly became apparent. The 1976 Chaggar episode demonstrated that the existing RPE faced a very serious crisis over the alienation of Asian youth. An important split amongst Southall's EMGs took place over the protests and disturbances that followed. Generational factors, more than anything else, divided EMGs over their future participation and tactics in the prevailing, paternalistically-oriented RPE. Established groups such as IWA argued the case for continued RPE co-operation, without prior substantial reconsideration of the narrow conceptualisation of race embodied in the RPE. The local authority responded with limited conciliatory initiatives but had no intention of allowing explicitly race-specific issues onto the local policy agenda. The initiatives it did undertake sought only to nurture a consultative dialogue with moderate CRC and EMG elements, in the hope of establishing a loosely-corporatist RPE organisational structure. A new generation of Asian and Afro-Caribbean youth organisations rejected the local authority's conciliatory moves and instead articulated the case for non-co-operation. The efforts of black EMGs, argued these radical groups, should be turned to their long-neglected, race-specific interests. These policy actors' participation in the RPE would depend upon the recognition of a broader conceptualisation of race by the local authority. The narrow conceptualisation of race of the existing RPE was, therefore, under challenge. The town hall's response to the challenge could have taken one of two forms: selective reform of the organisational structure of the RPE (as it did); or permit further questioning and undermining of the liberal policy framework (which did not happen). The result was to temporarily deflect challengers' attentions away from the traditional policy framework and towards the reformed policy environment.

During the late-1970s and early-1980s, the local authority began to direct limited palliative measures towards youth provision in Southall. In many ways, this seemed too little, too late. For one thing, it did little to arrest the growing tide of race-specific radicalism amongst black youth movements in the borough. For another, the sour-tasting aftermath of the town hall's role in the events surrounding the 1979 Southall disturbances, quickly led to the alienation of moderate bodies such as IWA and ECRC. The loss of co-operation and legitimacy within the prevailing RPE threatened to plunge the RPE into crisis. However, the short-term rediscovery of black youth and community issues in the RPE plugged the gap, but only just.

That said, the key source of tension still remained: namely, the sharply contrasting conceptualisations of race held by town hall interests and their allies on the one hand, and the new generation of radical black youth movements on the other. Herein lay the seeds of potential conflict, threatening to undermine the legitimacy of not merely the RPE, but the prevailing liberal policy framework as well. Moreover, it has been suggested by some radical commentators (Sivanandan, 1976 and 1982; Ben-Tovim and Gabriel, 1982; Miles and Phizacklea, 1984) that, but for these limited concessions, the longer term impact of grassroots developments during the mid- to late-1970s would have been considerably more volatile. The successful management of race issues would have become increasingly difficult to maintain and defend within the paternalistic RPE.

The revised RPE was, however, highly fragile, and its departure from the earlier paternalistically-oriented RPE was little more than skin deep. Both the 1979 and 1981 Southall disturbances as well as other local conflicts - such as the row over grant-aided schools - served to highlight the relative weakness of non-town hall policy actors. Furthermore, these conflicts also illustrated the damaging consequences of the Conservative administration's steadfast refusal to re-examine the narrow conceptualisation of race centrally embodied in its own pursuit of "colourblindness". The "colourblind" strategy of the town hall was seemingly at odds with increasingly race-specific conflicts witnessed throughout the borough during this period. For example, the local authority's unbudging commitment to an abstracted notion of "free speech" over the National Front's April 1979 election meeting, resulted in the most damaging crisis of all. This crisis perfectly illustrated the wide gulf between the Conservative administration's narrow conceptualisation of race, and the broader conceptualisation now advanced by IWA, ECRC and others. The former saw the issue in terms of philosophical abstractions - ie. "free speech" - whilst the latter highlighted the adverse, race-specific consequences for Southall and its black citizens. The resultant conflict was as dramatic as any witnessed, reflecting not just the sharp mismatch in both sides' conceptualisations of race, but also their respective failures to recognise the potentially-explosive nature of this mismatch.

"Colourblindness", in short, became the main bone of contention between town hall and non-town hall policy actors. The Conservative administration's steadfast refusal to accept the racialised impact of their decision - ie. to permit the National Front meeting in Southall - reflected a philosophical position which did not recognise race-specificity in the consequences of policy decisions in general. Its critics argued that the decision reflected a philosophical and political unwillingness to protect the borough's black immigrant quarter from overt anti-immigrant sentiment. The local authority, they claimed, was even "colourblind" to the fact that it presided over a multi-racial borough. The defining characteristic of the RPE had clearly shifted from paternalism to frustration.

Radicalism

Finally, a fourth interesting and increasingly topical possibility in the scheme is an organisationally well-developed infrastructure which is based on a broad conceptualisation of race. This combination can be characterised as radicalism. The local authority, whilst still dominant, no longer commands a monopoly of power to legitimise the participation of other policy actors. Through a gradual process of strengthening links between both sets of policy actors, there is an eventual quasi-incorporation of both interests into a single broad interest. Thus, domination of the RPE is not specific to town hall or non-town hall interests, but involves a sustained interlocking of both interests. Of course, these interests are not precluded from acting in unison to regulate the entry of additional policy actors and interests into the RPE. But, given the other features of a radicalised RPE, it will not be for the same reasons that town hall interests have dominated and defended the paternalistic RPE for so long. Besides fusing different interests in order to co-dominate the RPE, the organisational structure of the RPE exhibits a high degree of cohesion (Rhodes, 1985 and 1988). A quasi-incorporation of one set of interests into another occurs when race is bureaucratised, particularly by left-wing Labour administrations. All policy actors appear strongly committed to the policy framework and are therefore mainly concerned with matters of detail between alternative policy options.

The conceptualisation of race variable is the key to this potential RPE-type. The acceptance of a broad conceptualisation of race at a stroke legitimises a whole host of policy actors, platforms and demands, traditionally excluded from the local RPE. The evidence from the two boroughs showed how moves towards introducing a broader conceptualisation of race into the policy process were invariably stifled, either by the paternalism of town hall domination of the RPE, or the frustration of a fragmentary RPE - or a combination of both. Once agreement is reached to broaden this variable, race-specific policy demands - as well as the policy actors responsible for them - are no longer barred from legitimate RPE participation. A narrow conceptualisation of race is no longer an inextricable feature of the RPE. The result is that a subtle, yet important, alteration in the application of the liberal policy framework is apparent. It may be at the level of the framework's abstract conception of the race-public policy nexus - in which case the impact is likely to be rather indirect. Alternatively, it can take place at the more meaningful level of the changing role of race and ethnic issues in local government policy practice - arguably a more direct impact.

The conceptualisation of race in the RPE has evolved rapidly in recent years. In Ealing in particular, this variable has broadened considerably from the late-1970s onwards. Recent research has shown that new, positive notions of ethnicity have been incorporated into the race policy and practice of local government (Young, 1984; Jenkins and Solomos, 1987; Saggar, 1987b and 1991a). The broadening of the conceptualisation of race to recognise the importance of the so-called "ethnic dimension" is pivotal, and will inevitably affect - and restrict - what can be achieved by even the most radical of policy actors. As Young and Connelly (1981: 162) argue:

> A disposition to be explicit about race is a prerequisite of the development of policies relating to discrimination, disadvantage and diversity. These dispositions are crucial. Where the ethnic dimension is disavowed, policy entrepreneurs have either to 'do good by stealth' or to place their faith in the (necessarily limited) development of practice.

It is precisely the question about the basic legitimacy of issues of race and ethnicity in the policy-making process of town halls to which this variable boils down. Without the attachment of such legitimacy to these issues, it is hard to see how town halls are supposed to tackle directly the problems of racial inequality and disadvantage. The capacity of policy-makers in the local RPE to move in this direction will also depend upon what Young (1985b: 300) describes as the 'appreciative context' of shared values between central and local government. The policy framework based upon the relationship between town halls and local policy actors on one hand and Westminster and Whitehall on the other, is, after all, a major aspect of the argument of this study (see also Chapter 3 above). The importance of the central-local axis in relation to the broad underlying aims and values of race policy, serves to further underline the far-reaching shroud of "colourblindness" that covers British public policy - a shroud which Kirp (1979) suggests is all too characteristic of the cultural environment of British politics and government.

Conclusion

The policy environment and the policy framework are closely and inextricably linked to one another. The empirical chapters have mainly focused upon race policy conflict at the level of the policy environment. Direct observable conflict over a given issue or event has preoccupied the energies of policy actors in the RPE in both boroughs. However, behind, and interspersed within, the policy environment-centred conflict, there has been a broader conflict over the legitimacy of the liberal policy framework. This chapter has argued that race policy conflict often involves debate and disagreement at the level of the policy environment and the policy framework, at one and the same time.

Having established the historical and ideological influence of the policy framework upon the policy environment, it can be seen that the former affects the latter in different ways at different times. Utilising two independent variables, four main of types of policy environment are distinguishable in the chronological evolution of local race policy conflict: diffusion, paternalism, frustration, and radicalism.

The empirical evidence has shown that local race policy has varied enormously, both between different local borough settings, as well as across different historical periods. The unifying theme within this picture of diversity has been the differential local impact of the liberal policy framework. The central thesis of this study has been that race policy debates and conflicts cannot be *fully* understood without reference to the influence of the framework for such policy. As with the proverbial elephant, race policy may be easier to recognise than describe. Moreover, it may not be one animal, but many. However, through this study, we may begin to theorise as to what defines it, and what does not. Therefore, we should at least be in a position to theoretically define race-related public policy, in terms of its origins, substance, experience, and so on. On this basis, the animal may be no easier to describe, but we can at least be confident of being able to recognise it when we see it - in all its heterogeneous and complex forms.

Notes

1. In 1982 the Conservative administration launched a major new initiative in community consultation and participation in local borough decision-making: Unified Communty Action (hereafter UCA). Three UCA branches were established covering the western, central and eastern parts of the borough (later expanded to four branches). Its principal aim was to foster direct relations and dialogue between LBE and various community organisations in the borough. A wide variety of community organisations were invited to participate in UCA, many of whom responded. UCA reports to the Town Clerk and Chief Executive's Department, and has been projected as a high profile attempt by LBE to maintain a working dialogue with the borough's community organisations. Critics, it must be said, have suggested that UCA offered LBE a convenient alternative mechanism to retain links with EMGs at a time when LBE-ECRC relations had effectively broken down (1980-84). This view of the UCA initiative was articulated to the author by a number of interviewees during fieldwork research. For a fuller and informative discussion of the UCA initiative, see FitzGerald 1986a.

2. The conceptualisation of race, it should be noted, constitutes both an independent *and* dependent variable. In this context we are mainly concerned with its status as an independent variable, shaping and explaining the RPE. The RPE has been conceived within a liberal policy framework, a defining feature of which is its narrow conceptualisation of race. As the liberal policy framework is a major independent variable, the conceptualisation of race also assumes the same status. However, the policy framework can occasionally be thought of as a dependent variable, insofar as

the local RPE was part of the broader policy framework. This point has only minor significance for the study, but we should be aware of the variable's potential dual status.

8 Conclusion

Introduction

Chapter 3 above outlined the terms of the liberal policy framework and argued that it placed an emphasis upon ill-defined conceptions of ethnic pluralism and racial harmony. The framework has a number of further significant limitations for the development of local race policy.

The Home Secretary's 1966 speech to NCCI referred at length to the policy goals of the liberal framework. Racial harmony was viewed in the context of 'cultural diversity', with integration, rather than assimilation, as its longer term aim (Jenkins, 1966). However, beyond this simple distinction, relatively little consideration was given - either at the time or since - to the application of this policy framework to actual, tangible political processes. Moreover, its application in the world of local government policy-making has come to be an ineffective and random process. Local authorities have found themselves edged into the frontline of race policy whilst lacking a clear orienting framework. Any coherent policy framework that existed was largely redundant by the late-1970s at the latest.

Much of the study thus far has been devoted to describing and accounting for the conflicts and tensions that resulted from the framework's application at the local borough level. This chapter compares the original framework established in the 1960s with the reality of actual public policy in the period since. Some obvious and some not so obvious difficulties have arisen in the application of the general policy framework to specific local political issues and choices. This chapter discusses two things. Firstly, it examines the different outcomes of the application of the liberal policy framework in the two boroughs studied. In what ways did the policy framework "succeed" and in what ways did it "fail"? Secondly, it presents an evaluation of the role of local authorities in handling race policy issues within the liberal policy framework. On the basis of the evidence presented in earlier chapters, how effective has the machinery of local government been in managing race-related public policy conflicts?

Successes and failures of the policy framework

The original liberal framework for race-related public policy was an important determining factor in setting the agenda for the local policy process. In doing so, the nature of the conflict over race-related public policy was defined, and to some extent constrained, by the broader liberal settlement. The framework had important implications in terms of what was fought over and what was achievable within the local RPE.

The liberal settlement recapitulated

The main features of the liberal policy framework were reviewed in an historical context in Chapter 3. Major political forces behind the wind of liberal reform included the pre-existing two-party consensus, the electoral sensitivity of both major parties, and the immediate need to dampen racial tension. However, the liberal coalition led by Roy Jenkins, NCCI and others, found itself continually constrained by party political pressures on the race issue. Neither Jenkins nor his supporters at the local level could go any faster than was permissible by the Labour Party's obvious defensiveness on race and immigration. In the end, the coalition was constrained on all sides by the advancing wave of race populists following the 1968 Kenyan-Asian crisis.

In terms of the mechanics of race-related public policy, the liberal policy framework avoided specifics. Indeed, much of the emphasis often rested on the delegation of responsibility for the issue downwards into the arena of local politics. Anti-discrimination legislation and the establishment of national race "watchdog" bodies constituted the other main pillars of the settlement. However, the centre was reluctant to take up full responsibility for either policy machinery or implementation. It stopped short at commissioning inquiries into areas such as the utility of legal redress mechanisms and the potential of local voluntary bodies. On the latter, the voluntary, non-statutory efforts of the community relations movement came to the fore.

The importance of involving local authorities in the attempt to subdue explicit racial conflict was increasingly recognised as the liberal framework proceeded into the 1970s. CRCs, whilst useful as committed believers in the liberal settlement, could not be relied on to co-ordinate the construction of the RPE. Maurice Foley's 1965 report to the Prime Minister made it quite clear that, if the triad of "localism", "community relationsism" and "harmonyism" were to be the way forward, then additional support would have to be provided by local authorities. This early footnote to the policy framework quickly grew in importance. By the time of the second Race Relations Act (1968), local authorities were firmly part of the policy framework's conception of the RPE. The third Act (1976) - and S.71 in particular - legitimated their dominance within the RPE.

Finally, perhaps the most important and lasting feature of the liberal framework was the premimum placed on the broad policy goal of racial harmony. This policy goal encapsulated a number of things, but often appeared to be a cover for the 'culture of inexplicitness' that characterised discussions over race-related public policy (Young, 1985b: 286). By focusing on racial harmony, policy-makers often constrained discussion of racial equality matters (Hill and Issacharoff, 1971). In recent years, the RPE has come under considerable pressure to find a place for racial equality-oriented issues on the legitimate policy agenda (Saggar, 1991a). However, some two-and-a-half decades after the establishment of the liberal settlement, the notion of racial equality continues to occupy an ambiguous place in the framework of public policy (see also Chapter 7 above).

It is against this backdrop that race-related public policy has been debated and fought over in local politics since the 1960s. Chapters 4, 5 and 6 above empirically illustrate these points in relation to two London boroughs. How have race-related public policy issues been dealt with in one borough compared with the other? In order to tackle this question, we first need to consider the distinction between explanatory factors that vary within a given borough, against those that vary across both.

In the case of some race-related public policy issues, the outcomes have been successfully determined by the parameters of the local RPE. However, in the case of other race issues, considerable variance can be seen, at least at the level of direct RPE conflict. The increased saliency and volatility of certain local issues, can occasionally trigger the participation of radical EMGs, resulting in a very different type of policy debate (although these EMGs' involvement does not necessarily affect policy outcomes). A major finding of the study is the variation between the experiences of the Boroughs of Ealing and Barnet. This contrast operates at a number of levels. For instance, the race issue appears to have been much more successfully routinised and absorbed into the existing town hall policy-making processes in Barnet. This routinisation was only partially and temporarily accomplished in Ealing, usually lasting no longer than the span of a single town hall administration.

Why does race become politicised at certain times under certain circumstances, and why does it become successfully routinised and de-politicised at other times under other circumstances? It is useful to try to isolate some of the key variables identified in the study as explanations for this phenomenon. Some variables focus on the way in which race issues are dealt with by local political systems; other variables, in contrast, focus on the deliberate, conscious actions of different policy actors in the RPE (Newton, 1976). Therefore, one set of variables is concerned with the characteristics or routinised biases of the policy process, whilst the other is concerned with the behaviour of defenders of, and challengers to, the local political system (Dearlove, 1973; Saunders, 1975).

We can usefully distinguish between: *inter*-local borough factors (that generally or usually vary across the two boroughs), and *intra*-local borough factors (peculiar to a given local borough). The former includes factors relating to local dispositions towards the liberal policy framework. They cover aspects of: local historical immigration legacies (notably amongst white migrant groups such as Jews or Poles); contrasting ethnic communities (such as socio-religious differences); party control (two-party competition versus dominant party control); and so on. The latter includes factors relating to local events and issues, party control, EMG-types, CRC strategies, and so on. The routinisation of race issues occurs at both levels. However, our primary interest rests with the way in which dominant, agenda-setting policy actors are able to operate within the terms of the liberal policy framework in order to successfully defuse race issues and pressures. It is the former set of factors - the local application of the policy framework - that best explains the routinisation and de-politicisation processes.

Two crucial findings of the study can be underlined here. Firstly, success from the point of view of the local authority administration often leads to failure in the eyes of other policy actors, eg. certain EMGs. The successes have been associated with policy routinisation and the removal of race issues from party competition. However, these successes have indirectly resulted in a whole host of new pressures that have often been difficult to manage within the existing RPE. These pressures, unless remedied, lead to frustration by many EMGs, which often translates into a sense of failure of the policy framework. The demarction line between policy successes and policy failures has become confusing in the face of differing and often conflicting perceptions of the liberal policy framework. Secondly, by presenting evidence of such variation, it is clear that no single, coherent, public policy on race has operated at local level in Britain in the period since the "liberal hour". From the experiences of the two case studies, both the perception and substance of race policy came to mean altogether different things from one borough to the next. Race-related public policy has become a little like the proverbial elephant: hard to describe, but impossible to mistake!

The routinisation of race

How and why is race-related public policy successfully incorporated and routinised into the prevailing town hall policy process and practices? This question provides us with a good handle with which to evaluate the application of the liberal policy framework. Certainly, its success or failure can be assessed from two angles. To the extent that explicit race issues and demands were effectively routinised by town halls, the established policy framework within which they were acting can be judged a success. However, as the empirical chapters showed, the prolonged and insensitive routinisation of race, contributed heavily to new race-related conflicts. Thus, the original problems and conflicts of the 1960s were not so much resolved by the liberal policy framework, as superseded by new, self-induced problems and conflicts.

Clearly, some local authorities have proved more adept at routinising race issues than others; moreover, certain policy issues have lent themselves more to such routinisation than others. The evidence presented in this study shows that, in general, issues of race and ethnicity were usually more effectively routinised in Barnet than in Ealing. In short, the RPE dominated by LBB was regulated and manipulated with greater sophistication than that dominated by LBE. Consequently, not only the consensual short-term goal of *de-politicising* local race relations, but also the converse goal of effectively *de-racialising* local public policy debate, was more successful in Barnet than in Ealing. A large part of the explanation for this outcome has been the differential local impact of the liberal policy framework. That is to say, certain aspects of the local political environment in Barnet - such as stable one-party rule - lent themselves more to the successful application of the liberal paradigm, than was the case in Ealing.

In Barnet, the local authority was spectacularly successful in insulating itself from calls for policy reforms. By arguing its case from a "colourblind" perspective, LBB managed to defuse its critics. Defusion was reinforced by the critics' inability to point to any direct evidence of the discriminatory impact of LBB's approach. Conversely in Ealing, LBE's position was undermined when it became clear that "colourblindness" resulted in certain deeply-resented discriminatory policies - for example, bussing and the general sense of neglect of Southall. Consequently, by the mid- to late-1970s, LBE was in such an invidious position within the RPE, that options of trying to routinise race were no longer seriously open to the town hall. The lesson, for many, seemed to be that the terms of the liberal policy framework had been applied too rigidly in the RPE, without adequate regard to the rapidly changing context of local race relations.

The routinisation of race within local authority policy processes is one of the consequences of the effective application of the liberal policy framework in the local RPE. What is involved in its successful, routinised application? The empirical chapters showed that routinisation was affected by the dominant policy actor - the town hall administration - identifying legitimate policy actors, methods and goals. These included, *inter alia:* regulating the participation of moderate elements amongst CRCs and EMGs; giving weight to those groups which only sought to build a loose consultative dialogue with the town hall; and ruling explicitly race-specific demands as "out-of-bounds".

Dearlove's (1973) study of town hall-pressure group relations in the Royal Borough of Kensington and Chelsea distinguished between "helpful" and "unhelpful" groups. This characterisation referred to the extent of shared interests between policy actors within and outside government. Similarly, the successful application of the liberal policy framework results in a community of shared policy preferences; it extends further, however, to a common sense of what is the legitimate scope of the local RPE, and what is not. The "insiders" in this relationship are responsible for maintaining and defending the status quo in terms of the areas of legitimate discussion of the RPE. The bias towards preserving the status quo means that these policy actors not only remain committed to the aims and values of the liberal setttlement, but also continue to see the benefits of doing so (Saunders, 1975: 36-41).

The liberal settlement emphatically opposed the discussion and formulation of race-specific public policy. This central value was shared by politicans from both parties during the period of the consensus on the race issue (Messina, 1984 and 1989; Saggar, 1991b). Despite the decline of the consensus, the empirical chapters revealed that many Labour and Conservative local politicians continued to defend the inexplicitness of race policy discussion, penalising those seen to be challenging this key aspect of the status quo. A number of community relations activists were viewed in such terms and excluded from legitimate status in the RPE. The result was that, as the application of the liberal framework progressed through the 1960s and 1970s, an ever greater proportion of RPE debate was devoted to major conflict over the aims and values of the framework. Race policy discussion consequently became less about detailed aspects of race policy, and more about what constituted race policy and what did not.

Routinising race issues became increasingly difficult - even in Barnet - simply because the areas of local government public policy under threat of becoming integral aspects of the RPE were much wider than before. The greater effort involved in routinising race notwithstanding, it still remained in the interests of dominant policy actors to try to exclude radical, race-specificity from the RPE. One of the primary methods of doing so in both boroughs was the selective incorporation of CRC and EMG leaderships into the mainstream policy-making process. The purpose of this exercise was to bring these challengers within the system and to hopefully broaden the community of shared values, if not shared policy preferences. The empirical chapters suggested that the results were more successful in Barnet than Ealing. The RPE was forced to recognise certain new grassroots pressures and to shift its focus - albeit modestly - in response. The traditional paternalism of the 1960s and 1970s was replaced with a more progressively-oriented ethos during the 1980s (see also Chapter 7 above).

Exclusion and incorporation

Dominant policy actors within the RPE will tend to exclude and de-legitimise unwanted interests, strategies and demands by defining them as not committed to the liberal framework. These "gatekeepers" act in the role of routinely defending the legitimacy of the liberal and paternalistic values of the existing RPE. They will occasionally venture further and brand certain interests as extremist and threatening, and as seeking to fundamentally challenge, rather than reform, the framework. These interests, of course, may be branded as such as a result of their frustration and impatience with the system. As Saunders (1975: 37) writes:

> Opponents of the status quo, representing interests which decision-makers do not identify, may be routinely "excluded" from participation in the political process by virtue of the strategies they are obliged to adopt.

But, by and large, such formal exclusion is generally avoided on the grounds that its consequences are often to exacerbate already tense relations between the town hall and its critics. By pressing for the exclusion of these hostile policy actors, or by provoking their self-imposed withdrawal from RPE participation, the town hall usually only ends up storing further problems for itself within the RPE, eg. the post-April 1979 crisis in relations between LBE and EMGs in Ealing. Exclusion will ordinarily only serve to place added pressure on the credibility and resilience of the RPE itself. Such an attempt was dramatically illustrated in the case of Ealing, where the effective exclusion of the CRC and certain EMGs in the late-1970s and early-1980s, only undermined the credibility of the RPE. The crisis in their relations served as a spur to the town hall to try to revive CRC and EMG participation a few years later. In other words, the legitimacy of the liberal policy framework for the settlement of local race conflict, proved to be of greater significance than the short-term conflict within the RPE itself.

Groups excluded from the RPE will, over time, get used to their position of exclusion and relative deprivation from the spoils of participation in the RPE. The only longer term chances of dramatic change within the RPE will come about through exogeneous, uncontrolled events - such as riots and other forms of illegitimate protest - or through the build up of local frustrations and evidence of discrimination. Both these routes, of course, are inter-related, since EMG frustration - like many forms of social alienation can precipitate disturbances if left unchecked or unappeased.

Herein lies the potential seedcorn for the transformation of not just the terms of the

RPE, but aspects of the underlying liberal policy framework as well. On a miniscule number of occasions, evidence for such a potential transformation could be seen in Ealing. However, the potential was not fully realised and the liberal framework - though not the RPE - remained intact. Therefore, a further testimony to the effective routinisation of race is seen in the fact that no serious or enduring challenge to the liberal paradigm was launched, let alone succeeded, in either borough. For supporters of the paradigm, perhaps no greater compliment could be paid to their approach to race and public policy.

Those groups and demands threatened with exclusion (or threatening to exclude themselves) will usually face a choice. On one hand, they can attempt to mount a challenge against the terms of RPE participation leading to their exclusion. Such a challenge will usually be from a position of existing formal exclusion. The challenge is tantamount to a threat made against the status of dominant policy actor(s), and as such, is easily rebuffed as a threat to the overall policy framework. If the group is already formally excluded from the legitimate RPE, this route will be a likely choice since the group will have few other options and little to lose. Further, this route is especially likely if, as in the case of Ealing in the aftermath of April 1979, many groups felt that their fundamental interests were under serious threat. The right of self-defence for Southall as a multi-racial community was commonly seen by the CRC, EMGs and others as one such fundamental interest. Thus, ECRC, IWA and SYM launched a direct challenge against not just the Conservative LBE administration's race relations strategy, but the legitimacy of the RPE in general. The bluntness of the challenge was partly because the formal, self-imposed exclusion of the groups gave them no other choice, and partly because LBE's actions were perceived to have struck so directly at the heart of the interests of Southall's black citizens.

On the other hand, many groups can usually be persuaded *not* to deliberately exclude themselves. Whilst criticism of prevailing local authority policies cannot always be deflected, these groups can be induced not to mount challenges to the legitimacy of the RPE, challenges which are bound in the long run to be damaging to dominant town hall interests. Such persuasion will, naturally, be reinforced by an unwillingness on the part of CRCs and EMGs to withdraw from the RPE unless forced to over deeply-held convictions. Instead, these groups are persuaded - and quite often persuade themselves! - to climb down over most non-principled issues. For example, the CRC leaderships in both boroughs showed a general reluctance to question the legitimacy of the RPE. Their self-persuasion to avoid major conflicts over the legitimacy of the RPE, in fact, tended to be the rule rather than the exception. Exceptions to this rule usually came about as a result of internal crises of identity within CRCs, or as a result of particular forms of provocation from local authority administrations.

The logic of trying to win concessions from within the existing framework is powerful. As events in Ealing between 1976-79 illustrated, despite the sharp deterioration in LBE-EMG relations, this logic was resurrected by the town hall and their moderate allies in the RPE. Put another way, LBE was able to successfully argue that whatever had gone wrong in the borough's race-related public policy, was a matter to do with detailed policy formulated within the RPE, and not a crisis over the policy framework. ECRC and IWA, in the main, accepted this position and quickly climbed down. The newly-created radical SYM, in contrast, did not. A form of political fatalism seemed to shroud the calculations of many of these moderate groups' actions and reactions within the RPE at this time (1976-79). In tactically agreeing to go along with the town hall's defence of its record prior to the Southall disturbances of June 1976, these groups implicitly focused their attention on the policy *environment* rather than the policy *framework*. The town hall had managed to deflect attention away from the conceptual framework and towards the bureaucratic process. It felt relatively sanguine about introducing limited, palliative, institutional and other reforms in relation to the latter, whilst remaining consciously defensive in relation to the former.

Ethnic diversity and local government public policy

The application of the liberal policy framework can be evaluated at two inter-related levels. To begin with, we can assess its general successes and failures - as done in the previous section of the chapter. Additionally, we can focus on the strong central role played by the main policy actor, local government - covered in this section. A handful of researchers have begun to turn their attention to an evaluative policy analysis of local authorities. For example, Young and Connelly's (1981: 3) timely study reports that:

> The potential role of local authorities is seen today as even more important than in 1976. It is now widely understood that they could play a central role in any strategy for achieving 'equality of opportunity and good relations between persons of different racial groups'.

This section aims to provide a critical evaluation of the performance of local government in responding to the challenge of a multi-racial community. What has been the record? And, how have recent developments affected future prospects for the liberal policy framework?

Town halls and the liberal policy framework

The liberal policy framework emphasised the role of town halls in the RPE. The framework included certain important in-built biases however. One of the most significant was the question of legitimate RPE participation, allowing local authorities to set the pace and dictate much of the agenda. This bias was reinforced by another: the extension of the dominance of local authorities during the 1960s and 1970s. The centrality of their role was hinted at in the 1965 White Paper, established through the first two Race Relations Acts, and finally confirmed beyond question by the 1976 legislation. Although tentative at first, the pre-eminent position of local authorities in the local policy process soon became a central feature of the RPE. How has the dominant position of local authorities, largely defined by the liberal policy framework, affected RPE developments?

The terms of the liberal policy framework made the implicit assumption that local authorities were suitably organised to handle race issues and pressures. On a number of accounts, simplistic assumptions were made in the analysis of race and public policy. For instance, it was thought that local authorities' institutional and organisational capacity would enable a speedy and effective response to the challenges of a multi-racial community. It was less clear whether they would provide an equal response to the challenges of racial discrimination and disadvantage at the local borough level. Foley's 1965 fact-finding report to the Prime Minister and the White Paper of the same year made it quite clear that, whilst voluntary community relations agencies occupied an important role, their organisational resources would have to be supplemented by town halls. Furthermore, the demands that would be faced by the embryonic RPE were thought to be broadly analogous to those faced daily by local authorities in other mainstream areas of responsibility, such as education or housing (Cmnd. 2739; H.C. Standing Committee B, 1965).

In making these assumptions about the suitability of local authorities, a number of crucial distinctions were inadequately or poorly *conceptualised* within the liberal policy framework. Four in particular stand out. Firstly, the institutionalisation of race was based on formal mechanisms which were usually confined to tackling overt forms of discrimination in, say, the local authority's housing or education service. The rationale quite clearly lay in not wanting to attract the penalties of anti-discrimination legislation, as in the case of LBE's eventual *volte-face* on bussing in the face of threatened prosecution. The rationale did not, therefore, lie in any deliberate political attempt to either recognise or eliminate indirect, routinised forms of discrimination in mainstream service delivery. On the bussing example, it was noticeable that the local education authority persistently refused to accept the policy's obvious differential affect on different ethnic communities. Therefore, the RPE was able to deal with grievances of direct discrimination as "legitimate" areas of concern, but not with allegations of indirect discrimination which were labelled as "illegitimate" concerns.

Secondly, it is not certain whether existing service delivery structures and policy-making processes were able to cope with the new and unique pressures associated with the introduction of race-related public policy issues. The town hall bureaucracy lacked a proper definition of its role and jurisdiction. It is one thing to establish a personnel with the objective of rooting out town hall discrimination. It is quite another for that personnel to be permitted to challenge - let alone reform - mainstream service delivery routines and practices which indirectly or unintentionally discriminate.

Thirdly, the functional structure of local authorities were a poor match for the requirements of race issues. Race is a multi-functional "problem"; different local authority service delivery departments, in contrast, only have single functions. The requirements of race issues cut across the traditional service delivery boundaries of local authorities (Saggar, 1990b). The liberal policy framework clearly failed to recognise this crucial distinction. Banton (1985: 75) has commented at a more general level on the mismatch between race pressures and policy-making processes in Britain:

> Racial relations have presented a greater difficulty because their features do not fit the structure of public administration. Some of the problems...might be seen from the ministries of employment and housing...but there are also those associated with education, health, social services, the police and so on, each [with] its own division of responsibility between central and local government.

Fourthly, the construction of a stable and effective RPE rested very heavily on harmony in town hall-CRC relations. This dependency, in the end, was often excessive, in that even nebulous racial harmony goals were often rendered unattainable without prior harmony in the town hall-CRC nexus (Gay and Young, 1988; CRE, 1989). CRCs, it would appear, made for a very unusual and ineffective client group in terms of local government public service delivery. Local authority administrations might be expected to be on good terms and be "doing business" with their local CRC at one moment, and at another moment, be openly at odds with one another. Rarely was there much evidence in the study's empirical chapters of town halls working with CRCs in a stable client group relationship, as exists and is found in other local government policy sectors, such as education or housing. Moreover, unlike the case of education, local authorities found that they were not dealing with recognised professional client groups, eg. teachers' associations and parents' bodies. Instead, a poorly organised set of interests, weakened by diffusion and periodic internal divisions, was all that existed in the race relations sphere, eg. CRCs and EMGs.

Hiro (1971) contends that the 1960s' attempt to try to de-politicise race was ultimately flawed. The strategy, he suggests, was centred on nothing more than the enthusiasm of the community relations movement and local authorities to be seen to be to be "doing something". Race issues, he argues, were, and would continue to remain, "political". Hiro claims that the chief locomotive of RPE reform ought to have been local authorities. However, the locomotive gathered only minimal steam, and even then only in relation to the routinisation of race issues. The early "liberal hour" focus on conciliation and voluntary efforts, working through CRCs and others, was therefore little more than a politically-calculated diversion.

Local authorities' poor organisational handling of race demands and pressures has become increasingly clear in recent times (LWT, 1980). The liberal framework seemed to create a number of false expectations amongst various policy actors that these demands and pressures could be successfully absorbed. Fundamental questions about the absence of a suitable organisational machinery were effectively by-passed in the formulation of the RPE following the liberal settlement. The policy framework may have agreed upon widely supported goals of public policy, but its choice of town halls as principal policy instruments was rather less suitable. Writing in the mid-1980s, Banton (1985: ix) postulates that one of the main reasons for the disappointment with

158

race policy was uncertainty over not just policy goals but policy tools as well:

> There may be widespread sympathy with Roy Jenkins' formulation of the goal for racial relations policies as 'equal opportunity accompanied by cultural diversity, in an atmosphere of mutual tolerance' but, very naturally at this stage of events, there is a...lack of certainty about the best *means* to the end, and therefore any discussion of the issue more readily becomes an exchange of broader political opinions. (Emphasis added)

Banton, however, perhaps under-estimates the extent to which an actual policy machinery was drawn up and incorporated into the RPE. The policy framework in fact specified a reasonably coherent machinery centred on local authority policy-makers (Katznelson, 1973; Saggar, 1991a). Moreover, the RPE was not left as vaguely mapped out as Banton suggests. Rather, the policy framework created a set of parameters within which the RPE would formulate its own localised terms of reference. Its inherent weak link, however, was to be found in its failure to address a series of fundamental questions. Chief among these questions was the the suitability and adaptability of the town hall policy machinery.

The suitability of town halls

Even if local authorities had been able to provide an appropriate institutional setting for pursuing race-related public policy, it is not clear whether the political will existed to acknowledge the legitimate place of race on the local policy agenda. Young and Connelly (1981: 13) note that:

> Local authority services seem unlikely to take explicit account of race where the ethnic dimension has failed to secure a place on the policy agenda of the authority. The creation of corporate "race relations" machinery may indicate that the significance of the ethnic dimension has been recognised.

The flip-side of this observation, however, is that such recognition has, to date, taken place almost entirely in boroughs run by left-wing Labour administrations. The liberal framework-inspired RPE resulted in a highly constrained and ineffective organisational machinery being given responsibility for race issues at local borough level. And yet, the evidence from these left-run boroughs in recent years has demonstrated that the formal incorporation and legitimation of race can be attained (Ouseley, 1984). Its legitimation, however, has only been possible through a combination of three factors: concerted local grassroots pressures during the late-1970s; the political impact of public disturbances during the early-1980s; and the recent radicalisation of various urban Labour Parties (Jacobs, 1986; Saggar, 1987b).

The conceptions and expectations of the role of local government were pitched at a high level relatively early in the day. The evidence is scattered throughout the "liberal hour". Jenkins' public speeches, Foley's initial report to the Prime Minister, the early NCCI reports, and a whole host of other material, all pointed the way towards bringing local government into the centre of the developing RPE. On the evidence presented in Chapter 3, it is arguable that those national policy actors responsible for formulating the first draft of the liberal policy framework were merely in search of useful allies. The "liberal hour", it was felt, would come to very little unless the "big guns" of British local government were drafted into the exercise at hand. Town halls were perhaps not so much *useful allies*, as *usefully placed* in the frontline of local race policy.

The liberal policy framework assumed that race policy could be organised and delivered via existing mainstream local government service delivery processes. Policy-makers were engaged in a process which did not so much poorly describe something they could identify, but rather, poorly described something they assumed they could identify (LWT, 1980). A number of inter-related and hollow assumptions were therefore all laid upon one another. Disappointment with public policy on race has been one of the obvious and most widely perceived consequences (Banton, 1985 and 1987). Indeed, the pace of race policy initiatives amongst a number of radical Labour-run town halls in recent years has, to some extent, been a reflection of past disappointments (Lansley *et al.*, 1989).

Town hall race bureaucracies

An interesting literature has emerged in recent years documenting and explaining the effective incorporation of black, grassroots political activism into town hall bureaucracies (Ouseley 1981; Benyon, 1984; Jacobs, 1986). In addition, the adoption of various equal opportunities initiatives by certain local authorities in the wake of the 1980-81 and 1985 disorders have been noted by researchers (Ben-Tovim *et al.*, 1986; Jenkins and Solomos, 1987). This literature is useful in helping to understand the ways in which RPE developments have accelerated at certain times, whilst remaining stagnant at others. A few policy analysts have turned to evaluating these important bureaucratic developments (Young and Connelly, 1981; Young, 1984). As we have already noted, the policy analysts' investigations must be prefaced with a general examination of the suitability and adaptability of town hall policy-making processes to the race-related public policy pressures placed on them.

Evidence presented in earlier chapters suggested that numerous practical and other difficulties were encountered by local authorities facing such policy demands and responsibilities. The limited number of effective policy instruments ranks high among them. For instance, with the exception of the partially-targetted S.11 funding programme, few policies and programmes were available to local authorities in this field. Moreover, as Young (1985b) reminds us, the vast majority of policy instruments available to both central and local decision-makers in this field are geographically-oriented, rather than (racial or ethnic) group-oriented.

By the time of the Race Relations Act 1976, local authorities were being called upon to perform a more precise and important role. Section 71 of the Act required that:

> Local authorities should make appropriate arrangements to...(a) eliminate unlawful racial discrimination; and (b) promote equality of opportunity and good relations between people of different racial groups.

The real significance of S.71 lay in its ambiguity and absence of sanctions or inducements to encourage its implementation. Not surprisingly, most local authorities have presented the case that their policies are compliant with S.71. Both of the local authorities studied have frequently cited this piece of legislation as vindication of their RPE strategies. This line of defence has been cited irrespective of whether they have been pursuing a *radical-progressive* strategic approach leading to policy-innovation or a *conservative-paternalistic* line of policy-maintenance (see also Chapter 7 above).

The advent of town hall race departments and bureaucracies has been a comparatively recent phenomenon. For the most part, the liberal policy framework pressed for a RPE which would avoid the wholesale incorporation of large, highly-motivated race bureaucracies into town halls. The emphasis instead lay in a RPE based on loose dialogue, voluntary initiatives, and arms-length relations amongst policy actors. As a result, the real source of frustration did not lie so much in Banton's (1985: xi) broad brush observations regarding the administrative structure (see pp.158-9 above). Rather, the difficulty lay in the political unwillingness of local authorities to establish an appropriate machinery to handle complex, multi-faceted and multi-functional race issues and pressures.

Therefore, it can be argued that local authorities have always been in need of a formal, clearly-established race bureaucracy within the town hall. Moreover, there has been a strong need for a clearly-defined client group. A client group, in this case, would presumably have included local ethnic minority communities, represented either by their EMGs or the CRC. The liberal framework-inspired RPE however, mitigated against the establishment of a strong working relationship between a race bureaucracy inside the town hall, and a client group outside. Consequently, only the loosest - and weakest! - constellation of interests emerged within the RPE during the 1970s and 1980s. This organisational weakness has served to perpetuate the lack of coherence in race policy formulation and implementation. Thus, a highly diffuse, paternalistically-oriented RPE characterises local race policy in Barnet (up to the present), and in Ealing (until the early-1980s).

"Colourblindness" as a race policy

A central feature of the liberal settlement was the nominal commitment to outlaw overt and intentional forms of discrimination. Public bodies such as local authorities were called upon to execute their traditional service delivery responsibilities with regard to this commitment. Moreover, by staying firmly within the bounds of this commitment, local authorities were not only steering clear of formal anti-discrimination legislation, but were also successfully maintaining their domination within the RPE.

For much of this period, town halls sought to maintain a strategy of "colourblindness" in public policy. This strategy can be defined as the deliberate, conscious attempt to avoid race-specific public policy discussion. It also involved the deliberate diversion of policy debate away from detailed discussion of "who-gets-what" themes, and towards a generalised endorsement of non-discrimination goals. Formal equality, rather than the *distributional* outcome of policy, was the key orientation of "colourblindness". By operating such a strategy, powerful bias was being mobilised against the introduction of race-specific discussion, as well as against those local groups that had styled their own lobbying strategies around race-specific demands. Further, the "colourblind" strategy distinguished between the contrasting demands made by a given policy actor. For example, ECRC and BCRC were continually attacked - and weakened - by successive administrations in both boroughs for their alleged obsession with race. In contrast, these groups' proposals to foster self-help-type projects were treated as constructive and responsible contributions to the RPE.

The prevailing liberal policy framework maximised the chances of maintaining a "colourblind" strategy, and local authorities often found themselves engaged in the routine defence of the framework. Furthermore, selective town hall concessions within the RPE can often be interpreted as an attempt to defend and buttress the traditional liberal paradigm. According to one group of radical commentators, continued manipulation of the policy framework, equating "colourblindness" with legitimacy, will serve as a powerful bulwark against any introduction of an ethnic dimension into public policy:

> The forces of resistance to racial equality within local government can be formidable...the most common of these in our experience is characterised by a refusal to acknowledge racism and relatedly to pursue any of the steps necessary to redress it. (Ben-Tovim *et al.*, 1986: 127)

The "colourblind" strategic approach dominated most of the period studied. However, as pressure mounted in the 1970s, the unavoidable contradictions of narrow "colourblindness" became apparent. On the bussing issue in Ealing for example, the local authority's "colourblind" profile in the RPE came under increasing strain. "Colourblindness", it was vehemently alleged, resulted in differential local public service delivery - discrimination by other words! Accordingly, LBE's legitimacy and ability to regulate participation in the RPE began to be undermined. Eventually, the local authority was forced to abandon its policy, not so much because of CRC or EMG anti-bussing public campaigns, but because of the mounting threat of its "colourblind" strategy losing all credibility in the RPE.

Recent race policy initiatives

The formalised incorporation - even legitimation - of race and ethnic minority issues into the town hall's policy process is now mostly associated with the urban Labour Left (Prashar and Nicholas, 1986; Saggar, 1987b; Lansley, 1989; Solomos, 1989b). These initiatives have emerged for a number of reasons, of which the agitiation and radicalisation of EMGs has been only one factor (Jacobs, 1982; FitzGerald, 1984; Ben-Tovim *et al.*, 1986). Whatever else, these high profile town hall "race equality" policies of the 1980s have not been the product of any central government initiative.

To digress from the immediate terms of this study for moment, the recent adoption of a new high profile on racial equality by the Labour administration in Ealing between 1986-90 has not necessarily meant that institutional initiatives have been always or easily transmitted into mainstream local service delivery (FitzGerald, 1986a; LBE, 1988). A major reform of the new administration was the creation of a large (30 member), high profile officer unit to co-ordinate and publicise its race policy strategy.[1] It is hard to accurately characterise this strategy other than to emphasise its obvious differences with that of previous LBE administrations. If "colourblindness" was the general strategy prior to 1986, then "race-specificity" seems an appropriate label for the new strategy between 1986-90. In other words, great emphasis was placed on setting up programmes and procedures to not only ensure formal equality but also to remedy the under-representation of ethnic minorities in LBE's workforce and service take-up. To that end, ethnic monitoring and positive action recruitment became familiar policy instruments in the armoury of the new strategy.

However, by the admission of a number of political supporters of the strategy over the four years of its life in Ealing Borough, these developments alone have not been able to bring about all the racial equality-oriented goals of the Labour administration (Interview: Labour councillor, LBE, 1986a; Interview: IWA leader, 1985). The officer unit found itself constrained not just by the reluctance and suspicions of major service delivery departments, but also by the lack of an adequate organisational machinery within local government to deal with multi-faceted race issues. Disappointment and frustration - among both the political and EMG supporters of the strategy - became increasingly commonplace, particularly between 1988-90. That said, following the defeat of Ealing's controversial Labour administration in the spring 1990 local elections, it is perhaps still too early to evaluate the full long-term legacy of its high profile reforms.

Conclusion

The story of the application of the liberal policy framework has been one of general failure accompanied by limited temporary successes. The successes centred mainly on the removal of race-specific policy debate from the RPE for a long period until the mid- to late-1970s. In addition, although the national cross-party consensus on race gradually broke down from the late-1960s onwards, the local RPE continued to be broadly consensual throughout most of the 1970s. Most significantly from the perspective of "colourblind"-oriented local authorities, a 'culture of inexplicitness' had been engendered in the local RPE (Young, 1985b: 286). Radical, race-specific policy proposals were not heard largely because they were perceived as illegitimate threats to the established policy framework.

However, there were a number of failures. The liberal settlement itself often led to a number of un-anticipated RPE conflicts which, ironically, it had originally set out to try to defuse. If race has been de-politicised as Messina (1989) and others suggest, then it has been at a superficial party political level, and at the risk of simmering unresolved tensions spilling over into dramatic conflict.

Three major failures of the liberal policy framework are closely associated with the options facing policy-makers in the 1980s. Firstly, the liberal framework emphasised the organisational suitablity of local authorities to co-ordinate local race-related public policy. Town halls found themselves ever more firmly in the driving seat of local RPEs, culminating in the S.71 legislation (1976). However, their role emerged against the backdrop of the availability of few reliable alternatives. The subsequent shortcomings in the suitability and performance of local authorities has been a major hurdle in the formulation of coherent, sustainable race policy. Despite the poor performance of town halls over the period studied, they continue to occupy *the* central role in the RPE. Consequently, many of the radical race policy initiatives witnessed in recent years have been forced to work through, rather than around, town halls (Solomos, 1989a: 87-90). The organisational mismatch between single function local authority responsibilities and the cross-functional requirements of race, will presumably continue to dog these recent developments.

Secondly, the theme of "community relationsism" appeared to have taken a tremendous and irreversible battering. The empirical evidence shows quite clearly that the poorly-defined role of the community relations movement acted as a major obstacle to establishing a coherent, sustainable RPE. In a number of ways, the role of the movement is not any clearer today than it was twenty-five years ago (Gay and Young, 1988). Moreover, the pace of radical left-wing race initiatives in recent years has further added to the sense of marginalisation of CRCs (see also Chapter 4 above). The funding of CRCs has been gradually shifted towards town hall sources and the phased severing of the financial link with their umbrella body, the Commission for Racial Equality, now seems to be on the cards (Messina, 1987). Whatever else, race policy has become firmly institutionalised and bureaucratised. The role available to voluntary organisations (including CRCs) appears minimal, and even then heavily dependent on the orientation of their local authority administrations.

Finally, the most significant - and unanticipated - failure of the liberal framework lay in the way in which its values and assumptions precipitated a whole host of new and largely unmanageable conflicts. The local RPE often became an *ad hoc* arena for conflict over broader concerns such as the alleged biases of the liberal policy framework. Detailed discussion over specific policies would often mask underlying tensions over the framework. The sense of failure of the framework can be seen in the way which these conflicts and tensions were perceived as illegitimate by dominant policy actors. The groups that had mobilised support around these conflicts were similarly ruled off-limits. The result was the planting of new grievances around which many CRC and EMG activists rallied in the late-1970s. The frustrations that these grievances yielded signalled a deeper crisis for the liberal policy framework. The crisis was only defused through the selective and limited incorporation of race-specific demands into legitimate RPE debate, thereby transforming the recognisable character of the RPE. Therefore, perhaps the ultimate irony of the liberal framework arises from its *de facto* racialisation of politics as the price for its attempts to obviate the politicisation of race.

Notes

1. In May 1986 a radically-led Labour administration was elected in Ealing. One of its major electoral platforms was a radical profile on race issues, promising to set up a major new race bureaucracy in LBE. The Race Equality Committee (members) and Unit (officers) - emerged from this process during 1986-87. However, it is *not* the purpose of this study to examine or evaluate developments in Ealing - or elsewhere - beyond 1986. The Labour administration and its Race Equality Committee and Unit were, nonetheless, major changes in the authority's approach to race relations. The Labour administration suffered a heavy defeat in the subsequent and most recent local elections of May 1990. A new Conservative administration, strongly committed to dismantling much of the race bureaucracy established during the period 1986-90, was returned with a decisive 10 seat majority. Fuller discussion of the experiences and record of the 1986-90 Labour administration must, however, be deferred to further research, either by the present writer or by others.

9 Discussion

The politics of race policy

The single most significant contribution of this study has been the highlighting of the deep-seated system of values and assumptions that prevents race from occupying a legitimate place in the policy agenda. Of course, no-where has this lesson been felt more surely than in the world of local politics and government. This study has been based on a detailed examination of the local context and it has shown how the politics of race policy has been heavily influenced by the liberal framework. The study has also demonstrated that many of the disputes over race policy witnessed over the past twenty-five years were in fact a reflection of underlying conflict over the framework within which such policy was approached, debated and implemented. Therefore, it is worth stressing that the identification and analysis of race-related public policy is far from being a straight-forward task. Indeed, it would appear that the question of just what is racial - and what is not - has been a major bone of contention between policy-makers and actors both locally as well as nationally. On the one hand, there has been the familiar "colourblind" policy stance of public agencies including many town halls, whilst on the other hand there has been a great outpouring of racial explicitness by several radical, urban Left administrations in recent years. As already noted at the outset of this study, the contrast in their respective approaches, language and activities could not be starker. However, this study has sought to argue that the contrast does not end there, but reflects the fact that there exists in contemporary British politics an important and hitherto sidelined debate as to whether the so-called "race dimension" *can* and/or *should* occupy a legitimate place on the agenda of public policy. The evidence has shown time and time again either that the dimension was not part of the policy agenda, or, as was more routinely the case, that the debate never really saw the light of day. Either way, the result has been much the same: namely, that conflicts of race have effectively disappeared into the cracks of the policy process.

One notable illustration of the real conflict over the policy framework can be seen in the various goals that are said to be ascribed to race policy. As Young (1985b: 286) reports, these goals may range from racial harmony through to ill-defined conceptions of multi-culturalism, equality of opportunity and racial equality. Moreover, he notes, the compatability of these goals is often the subject of fierce political debate. Evidence from the local context suggests that policy-makers and actors are either confused or at odds with one another over the goals of public policy (or both), and that the role played by central government has done little to sharpen the aims of an otherwise incomplete policy sector. For the most part, the dominant theme of British race policy (such that exists) has been the pursuit of some form of soothing harmony in local race relations. The activities of the centre beginning more than twenty-five years ago, have steadily emphasised the need to ensure that tensions and strains in local public service delivery (eg. in areas such as education and housing) did not spark off direct racial conflicts. In other words, the familiar de-politicisation of race hypothesis of several writers (Hill and Issacharoff, 1971; Katznelson, 1973; Messina, 1989) seems to have been partially confirmed by this study. However, the contribution made in these pages has deliberately sought to explore beyond the familiar conclusions of the established literature, and has involved two key aims: firstly, to ask *why* and *how* race has been rendered politically- invisible; and secondly, to shift the spotlight of specialist research on race and politics towards the underlying *causes* and *effects* of the endemic "colourblindness" that shrouds British politics and policy-making.

A great many of the developments in British race relations over the past twenty-five years appear to stem from the influence of the liberal framework and may be interpretted in these terms. As I have argued in this study, the liberal paradigm did not merely characterise the reforming efforts of central government a generation ago, but also set the markers by which the local politics of race has subsequently evolved. Explanation based on the liberal framework has not been intended to paint a tight, deterministic picture of local experience, but rather to put forward a new and challenging perspective. The policy framework has also been utilised in this study in order to inject some new blood into an otherwise unsatisfactory literature on race and local politics. In my view, this literature has simply failed to explain the common, unifying roots of the different experiences of the local politics of race . The contention of this study has been that the politics of race - both at the centre and at the local level - cannot be fully understood without reference to the policy framework within which conflicts of race have been defined, shaped, and, to a large degree, constrained. At a general level, British race relations can be described and explained in terms of the impact of the liberal framework, and I would argue that the apparent reluctance of the overwhelming majority of writers to cast their analytical nets beyond the safe waters of behaviourialism, has been one of the most disappointing features of the literature.

Any discussion of this study's general implications for the political analysis of race and racism would not be complete without reference to current developments and future trends. This point is particularly pertinent in relation to the analysis of recent controversial episodes in the local politics of race, with the events in Brent, Bradford and Dewsbury perhaps the best-known. These pages are not a suitable arena for a general rehearsal of the various arguments involved in these recent cases, but it is nevertheless worth commenting upon aspects of the underlying debate they seemed to uncover. As the evidence from the two London boroughs featured in this study have demonstrated, the local politics of race can vary enormously from one geographic area to another. However, such variance has occured against the backdrop of a unifying framework. The evidence has indicated that the sharply contrasting climates that have arisen in recent years in different boroughs - say between paternalism and radicalism - have been the result of the differential application of a common policy framework. Further, the study has argued that recent conflicts over race can be explained in terms of the pressures placed on the liberal framework to keep race off the political agenda. Such pressures, most usually from those committed to undermining the liberal paternalism of existing race policy, have resulted in a strong challenge being launched against the dominant liberal framework.

A similar process seems to be taking place in the education policy-related conflicts that have recently arisen in London and West Yorkshire (the McGoldrick, Honeyford and Dewsbury affairs respectively). In each of these episodes, it is undoubtedly the case that sharp controversy and dissensus have shot to national prominence largely because of the absence of local consensus concerning the future shape and direction of race policy. In the West Yorkshire cases, the crucial source of the conflict stemmed from the apparent unwillingness - nay, refusal - of white parents (Dewsbury) and an educationalist (Bradford) to continue to go along with a policy framework that no longer delivered the anticipated racial inexplicitness in local education policy. In the eyes of a group of white parents and an individual headteacher, the time-worn melting-pot principle - that was supposed to keep the "race dimension" off the political agenda and was said to have been the traditional basis of education policy - no longer appeared to square with the reality of the classroom. In other words, it was the apparent break-down of the liberal framework that lay behind the protests of white parents and the headteacher, though, of course, their critics charged that the causal direction was the other way around. In the London case, a putatively unimpeachable headteacher appeared to come into conflict with her political masters in an affair that symbolised the sharply polarised debate that now exists between radical and liberal interpretations of race policy. The headteacher may well have been unfortunate in being hurled into the eye of a storm which to many observers seemed a long distance from the world of a suburban classroom. However, the affair served as a interesting microcosm of wider disputes over the degree to which the racial explicitness of an individual's comments would be tolerated by a radical town hall administration closely associated with a rather different form of race policy explicitness. In these circumstances, the lines separating conservatives, liberals and radicals in the contemporary world of British race policy must seem terribly confusing to heirs of Roy Jenkins' liberal settlement of a generation ago.

Race, power and politics in Britain

As previously noted, the claim that race was effectively de-politicised in the British political system has become a familiar - though unsatisfactory - one in the established literature. To take a recent example, Messina (1989) has argued that the two major parties tacitly agreed to keep race off the political agenda in the era since 1958. As the title of his book implies,[1] the theme of his argument is very firmly centred on the sphere of party competition, and is therefore rooted in the familiar institutional and behavioural approach of much political analysis. As our earlier survey of the literature showed, such studies have become a regular feature of the landscape of the political analysis of race in Britain and other developed liberal democracies. As I have argued elsewhere (Saggar, 1991c), the dominant approach of the discipline has been both theoretically lacking and more than a little intellectually sterile. Moreover, as Parekh notes (1990: 257), the narrow party competition-oriented focus of research such as Messina's 'will not...interest those looking for a specifically British political theory of race relations'. The point being made is that the literature has long needed to dramatically broaden its approach to the politics of race and ethnicity. One such source of a broader, more theoretically-rigorous approach has been the contribution made by students of the policy process, and it has been an implicit aim of this study to shift attention in that direction.

Another important aspect of this study has been a return to the themes and debates of urban political analysis. In doing so, the study has sought to place research questions regarding black political participation into the context of competition for scarce public and other resources. But, as I have emphasised, such competition has taken place in an environment that has been far from ideologically neutral, let alone open and accessible to new groups and demands. Indeed, the introduction of race-related demands and issues in urban politics has been fraught with difficulties and biases. For most of the period analysed, it was clear that the ideological and historical impact of the liberal framework served to remove race from the political agenda. This pertinent feature of the framework of race policy has led to the question: *how* has race been kept off the agenda? Moreover, the experience of the liberal framework has also resulted in a curious over-reaction to the rediscovery of race on the edges of the political agenda. To be sure, the effective demise of the race issue in British politics has been prematurely predicted (Rose *et al.*, 1969) or announced (Banton, 1987) on several occasions. The implications of these claims for the local context of race have been enormous since they would suggest that the absence of overt political activity around race conflicts reflected a consensus on the issue (Gaventa, 1980). However, as this study has stressed, the general absence of sharp conflict on the issue over the past twenty-five years has largely been the product of a policy framework that placed a premium upon racial inexplicitness - in other words, the doctrine of "colourblindness". It has only been comparatively recently that the terms of this framework have been subjected to sustained criticisms from those committed to broaden the conceptualisation of race in public policy. Even then, the framework has managed to resist many of these pressures by a familiar process involving the mobilisation of bias against those calling for the rapid introduction of the so-called "race dimension" into public policy.

In answer to the question raised previously regarding *how* race has been kept off the political agenda, this study has advocated an approach centred on the analysis of the construction, maintenance and reform of policy agendas. Students of the policy process will recognise the importance of studies of agenda-setting and their close relationship with studies of political power. In this study I have advanced two simple yet critical points: firstly, that examination of the policy framework reveals a great deal about what is kept on and what is kept off the policy agenda; and secondly, that such an examination provides us with important insights into the nature of political power in the sphere of race policy. These contributions should hopefully serve to provide a long-overdue breath of fresh air into an established specialist literature on race and politics which, with a few exceptions, has sadly become isolated and divorced from more mainstream themes and debates in the discipline.

If, as this study has argued, the politics of race in Britain can be more fully understood through the analytical spectacles of the liberal policy framework, then the implications for future research are likely to be exciting. For one thing, researchers in this field must surely begin to look beyond - and hopefully seek to complement - the narrow behavioural and institutional approaches of the existing volume of research (Saggar, 1991c). This is not to say that the important behaviourally-oriented work of writers such as Katznelson (1973) and Messina (1989) does not have an important role to play in our understanding of the politics of race in Britain.[2] But, due credit having been granted, suspicion grows that the theoretical penetration of much of the work in this field has sadly failed to keep pace with the rather more imaginative and incisive developments elsewhere in the discipline. Shifting the research spotlight into the shadows of policy studies and debates on political power, must be one of the most exciting directions for future research. If this study has helped to raise theoretically challenging questions about the complex relationship between race and politics, and if it has served to stimulate new interest in the re-ordering of priorities for future research, then it will have achieved its aims.

Notes

1. *Race and Party Competition in Britain.*

2. Several commentators have remarked on the curious fact that many writers in the field of race and politics in Britain have been Americans; see for example Solomos, 1989: 16. Whether this reflects the strong behavioural roots and tradition of political science in the US, or is little more than superficially interesting coincidence, is not at all clear.

Appendix A: Selected background statistics on Ealing and Barnet

Table A.1

Background details, Ealing and Barnet, 1981 and 1985

	Total [a] population	Con. rule [b] (years)	Lab. rule [c] (years)	Per cent non- [d] manual workers
Ealing	292,400	11	10	35.9
Barnet	301,200	21	0	48.9
Outer-London average	223,900	—	—	40.9
Greater London average	205,100	—	—	37.4

[a] Registrar General's estimates of the resident population, mid-1985.
[b] Conservative LBE administrations: 1968-71, 1978-82 and 1982-86.
[c] Labour LBE administrations: 1965-68, 1971-74 and 1974-78.
[d] General Census showing percentage of population living in households headed by someone in occupational groups A-C1 (ie. non-manual), 1981.

Source: adapted from OPCS, 1984a and 1986

Table A.2

Country of birth of population, Ealing and Barnet, 1981 Census

Percentage of population born in:-

	All countries outside UK	Irish Republic	NCWP	Other countries outside UK
Ealing	28.2	4.5	17.0	6.8
Barnet	22.4	2.9	9.2	10.2
Outer-London	14.6	2.5	8.0	4.2
Greater London	18.2	3.0	9.5	5.6

Source: adapted from OPCS, 1984a: 30

Table A.3

NCWP-origin, Ealing and Barnet, 1981 Census

	Percentage of population in households with NCWP-born head
Ealing	25.4
Barnet	12.8

Source: adapted from OPCS, 1984a: 30

Table A.4

Live births by birthplace of mother, Ealing and Barnet, 1983

	NCWP:-		All outside UK:-	
	Number	Per cent of total births	Number	Per cent of total births
Ealing	1,594	37	2,146	50
Barnet	711	19	1,393	38
Outer-London	10,277	19	15,079	28
Greater London	19,945	22	29,947	33

Source: adapted from OPCS, 1984b: 5

Appendix B: A note on methodology

Race policy research: some notes on fieldwork

In recent years, London local politics have been increasingly focused on race issues and conflicts. Controversy and fierce debate over the race issue has become a familiar characteristic of the local political systems of a large number of boroughs, with Ealing in particular featuring regularly in such conflict. Against this backdrop, researching an issue as alive and potentially volatile as race presents a whole series of problems in itself and, for some of the reasons outlined below, pursuing such research through to publication can be a difficult test of nerve. This appendix describes the methodological approach and content of the study. The following pages also presents some brief notes on the methodological difficulties and dilemmas that arose during the study's fieldwork stage. These notes are designed to provide the reader with an accurate account of the methods and sources that lie behind this study and to place on record a few of the author's own reflections on the experience of carrying out research in this area.

The research project was begun in October 1984 and completed in October 1988. A large amount of the material used in the study was collected through primary sources during fieldwork research carried out over a 16 month period. Fieldwork was carried out in the boroughs of Ealing and Barnet from September 1985 to December 1986; this was done on a full-time basis until September 1986 whilst resident in Barnet, and thereafter on a part-time basis due to teaching commitments. This stage of research was mainly devoted to carrying out interviews in London.

The material collected through fieldwork research fall into four chief categories: a survey of the local press in both boroughs; a survey of the agendas and minutes of council meetings and meetings of major committees; a series of interviews with individuals and representatives of groups involved in local politics and race relations; and evidence gathered through attendance of public meetings of councils, council committees, and community organisations. Each of these components of fieldwork research are described below.

A comprehensive survey of the local press in both boroughs was carried out for the years covered by the study. The main aim was to compile a chronological account of race and race-related issues in local politics in the boroughs studied. In addition, detailed notes were taken on aspects of local politics in general, in order to map out the political context in which race issues were debated.

In the case of Ealing, the relevant local newspaper used for the survey changed both its title and format midway through the period examined. The *Middlesex County Times and West Middlesex Gazette* (Southall edition) was consulted for the period 1957-77; thereafter, the *Southall Gazette* (Southall and Ealing editions) was consulted for the period 1977-86. Both of these titles are referred to as the "Gazette Series" in the study and were read at the British Newspaper Library at Colindale. In the case of Barnet, the *Hendon and Finchley Times* (Finchley edition) was consulted for the period 1964-86. In addition, secondary notes were compiled from the *Barnet Borough Times* (Finchley edition). Both of these titles are referred to as the "Times Series" in the study and were read in the reference section of Hendon Library.

The identification of a significant local issue was followed up by an attempt to make contact with and/or interview prominent figures associated with these issues and debates. In many cases contact was established and short interviews followed. These cases rarely extended beyond a fifteen year historical time limit. Many once-prominent figures in the period before 1970 were difficult to trace. Quite often, the received views of these individuals were paraphrased by other interviewees who had either served with or been active alongside these individuals. However, it was generally difficult to contact or interview many of these important local figures, and therefore the weight attached to the press survey in the research methodology for the period before 1970 is conditional on this fact.

Finally, the the tail-end of period covered by the press survey overlapped with the period in which the survey was carried out. A number of current local issues were not only surveyed in the local press but were also described in detail by many of the interviewees (as well as debated in various public forums). However, the ability to gain interview evidence on such current issues was occasionally tempered by interviewees' (understandable) reluctance to speak candidly about current, rather than more historic, matters.

Council and committee records

A comprehensive survey was carried out of the agendas and minutes of full council meetings as well as a selection of major committees. This survey fell into three phases. Firstly, the official record of Southall Borough Council, Southall Divisional Education Executive, and the Education Committee of Middlesex County Council for the period 1957-65, was examined for the purposes of the case study on dispersal. Minutes relating to the *ad hoc* "immigrant affairs" committees of the former two bodies were also examined. These records were examined at Southall Library, though a number of Middlesex County Council items had to be accessed from Ealing Library. Secondly, the official record of the London Borough of Ealing for the period 1965-86 was examined. Minutes relating to the authority's Immigrants Committee were surveyed, in addition to the records of the full council and its major service delivery committees. These records were read at Ealing Library, with occasional assistance from staff in the Town Clerk's Office of the local authority. Thirdly, the official record of the London Borough of Barnet for the period 1965-86 was examined. No further records - ie. of "immigrant affairs"-type committees - beyond those of the full council and major committees existed in this case. These records were read at the Barnet Local History Library and Hendon Library.

In addition, with the assistance of supporting correspondence from my temporary supervisor (1985-86), a number of background papers were made available to me by senior officers in both authorities. Access to these papers proved to be very helpful in filling some of the gaps left in the research based on the local press survey alone.

Interviews

A series of élite interviews were caried out with prominent local figures in each of the boroughs. Interviews were normally arranged through prior correspondence, though on a handful of occasions, they were the result of chance meetings with individuals. The length of the interview varied enormously, from 20 minutes up to 3 hours. The majority however lasted for approximately 90 minutes. No attempt was made to adhere to a tight timetable and interviewees were encouraged to elaborate on whichever points they thought to be significant. Locations for interviews also varied a great deal, including council offices, council committee rooms, council members' rooms, community groups' offices, private homes, restaurants, etc.

Interviews were conducted on the basis of an interview schedule prepared in advance. The purpose of the schedule was to try to keep interviews on a roughly common track. The same topics and themes would then be covered in all the interviews, though a slightly revised schedule was used for each of the main interview category-types (see Table B.1 below). Using the schedule as a guide, interviews were structured as loosely as possible. The rationale was that interviewees who were encouraged to discuss matters in an informal, relaxed manner, were more likely to speak candidly and to elaborate their views without fear of having to stick to a pre-determined agenda. The results obtained from the majority of interviews suggests that this rationale was correct.

The interview schedule contained six principal topics or themes to be explored. Additional, supplementary topics were inserted according to the category of respondent. The topics covered were: firstly, respondents' level of background knowledge of ethnic minority communities in the borough, as well as any special interest in, or relationship with, local race relations; secondly, respondents' appreciation of the local authority's main policies and programmes in the field of race (including funding of EMGs); thirdly, respondents' perceptions of party political differences and agreement on race issues; fourthly, respondents' views on the role played by ethnic organisations in local decision-making; fifthly, respondents' views on the role of community relations councils; and sixthly, respondents' general opinions on the impact of race issues on the local political system. Specific examples were inserted wherever suitable for respondents to comment upon, though, in the main, most respondents required little prompting to illustrate their views. Each topic was raised as an open-ended question in the first instance. The aim was to get respondents to describe events, processes, impressions, opinions, etc. in their own terms, and not to give the impression that their responses were in any way a test of where they stood (ie. "for" or "against") on specific issues. Respondents' positions on specific issues were usually made adequately clear in their responses and only occasionally required a follow-up closed-type question.

All interviews were conducted on a confidential, non-attributable basis. Respondents were assured of this undertaking both when originally approached as well as at the start of the interview. The undertaking meant that their comments, if used in the final study, could not be attributed to them, either directly or indirectly. Moreover, their co-operation and comments would not be known, either to other interviewees in particular, or to other local figures in general. In all but one case the undertaking was accepted without significant need for clarification; in this particular case, an exchange of correspondence between my temporary supervisor and the potential respondent eventually clarified the matter and secured the respondent's co-operation. Wherever interview data was considered for inclusion in the study, respondents were sent transcripts of interviews to check for accuracy and to invite further comments. Finally, relevant first draft chapters were sent to a small number of respondents seeking their comments. This group was selected on the basis of their particular usefulness as interviewees and/or their interest shown in the findings of the research project. A tiny number used this opportunity to offer further comments on topics raised in their interviews.

Most interviewees were prepared to discuss a wide variety of issues relating to race relations; many were also prepared to go into them in great depth. The schedule also served as a handy guide to either restart interviews that had dried up, or to prompt respondents to remark on related questions. On the latter, discussion was generally moved on to related matters of interest with little difficulty. In many cases the interview proceeded very smoothly and the existence of a schedule often faded into the background. Doubtless, a number of respondents treated the exercise less as a formal interview and more as a detailed discussion.

The precise number of interviews to be conducted during fieldwork research was not specified in advance. Table B.1 below shows the number of interviews that were carried out in each borough according to interviewee category. Only a fraction of these interviews are cited as evidence in the study.

Table B.1
Interviews by interviewee category, fieldwork research, 1985-86

		Ealing		Barnet
Councillors		8		8
[Labour	5		4]	
[Conservative	3		4]	
EMG/community group leaders		11		9
CRC leaders/activists		4		3
Total		23		20

Source: author's fieldwork records

Interview candidates were selected on the basis of three criteria. Firstly, local politicians and leaders of community groups were targetted on the basis of their *significance* in local race relations. Since many councillors were, in general, not active on race issues, it was relatively easy to identify those who were active. All relevant councillors were written to on the basis of their interest in race relations issues. Identifying relevant community groups was also a relatively straight-forward task. The real choice lay in deciding which groups to approach and which to leave to one side. Again, all of the well-known groups were targetted together with a small selection of more minor groups. The number of relevant groups in Ealing for example extended to more than fifty (at the last count), and therefore a large number of minor groups were bound to be overlooked.

Secondly, majority and minority party leaders were targetted together with the chairs of major council committees. These councillors were selected on the basis of their roles as frontbench *leaders* or spokesmen and spokeswomen of the party groups, and not solely because of their interest in race issues. Interviews were granted by three out of four majority and minority party leaders. The chairs or vice-chairs of each borough's General Purposes/Policy, Education, Social Services, and Housing committees, were also approached; interviews were obtained from five out of eight.

Thirdly, interview subjects for academic research - particularly on a sensitive issue such as race relations - will often emerge through a process of *self-selection*. That is to say, some individuals approached on the basis of the above two criteria may still remain elusive. In their place, numerous other, less highly-prioritised individuals may be keen to offer themselves for interview. For example, four senior councillors proved impossible to track down, including a former majority party leader. There was, however, usually little shortage of community group leaders available and willing to grant interviews. Many of these interviewees proved to be interesting and worthwhile subjects, but nonetheless they were poor substitutes for those individuals originally, though unsuccessfully, approached. The scholarly interest shown by academic researchers can all-too-often be perceived as a handy platform for many local political figures and community leaders to rehearse their arguments, with the council chamber or other forum in mind.

Meetings

A number of meetings of statutory and voluntary bodies were routinely attended in both boroughs during fieldwork research. These included meetings of the full council and major council committees and sub-committees, relevant EMGs and community groups, and CRCs. In addition, occasional *ad hoc* meetings called by community groups and CRCs on single issues of concern were also attended. For example, ECRC and BCRC both held a series of public consultation meetings during the fieldwork period to discuss *inter alia* "Multi-cultural Education", "Religious Faith in the School Curriculum", "The Response to Swann", and "The Abolition of the GLC".

One of the main reasons for attending these various meetings was in order to confirm impressions of local race relations garnered from other sources. Race relations appears to be one of those issues which lends itself to a degree of stage-managed theatrics; that is to say, whenever the issue was openly debated at meetings such as these, there was rarely any lack of interested individuals eager to have their say. A large proportion of local figures connected with local politics and race relations clearly had their own opinions on the issue, and were not reluctant to use these meetings as platforms to air them. This observation even applied to a number of local politicians who were not normally known to have an interest in the subject. The result was that these meetings proved to be a very interesting and informative background source of information for the research project.

A number of these meetings proved to be useful in terms of establishing and/or renewing contact with local figures. Whilst councillors were normally contacted through their group leaders or party whips, it was sometimes necessary to chase after some of them at these meetings. Leaders and activists of community groups and CRCs were usually approached informally at various meetings they attended and/or participated in. The use of direct, face-to-face meetings with these individuals proved to be the most reliable way of soliciting their views, both informally as well as through formal interviews.

Finally, attendance at these meetings was useful in order to guage current issues and policy debates. (Current in this context would refer to the period of fieldwork during the mid-1980s.) Whilst much of the research project was concerned with composing an historical account of local race relations, the current picture could not afford to be ignored. Moreover, in order to gain a handle on the historical data, it was necessary to place it in the context of the current picture: if crucial changes in the policy debate have occured, against what is such change to be measured? These meetings helped to characterise the current policy debate which would act as a measure of the scale and nature of historical change.

Bibliography

Books, chapters and articles

Alavi, H. 1965: *The White Paper: A Spur to Racialism*, Campaign Against Racial Discrimination, London

Alderman, G. 1983: *The Jewish Community in British Politics*, Clarendon Press, Oxford

Bachrach, P. and Baratz, P.S. 1970: *Power and Poverty: Theory and Practice*, Oxford University Press, London

Bagley, C. 1970: *Social Structure and Prejudice in Five English Boroughs*, Institute of Race Relations, London

Banton, M. 1984: 'Transatlantic Perspectives on Public Policy concerning Racial Disadvantage', *New Community*, 6, 280-87

Banton, M. 1985: *Promoting Racial Harmony*, Cambridge University Press, Cambridge

Banton, M. 1987: 'The Beginning and the End of the Racial Issue in British Politics', *Policy and Politics*, 15, 39-47

Barker, A. 1975: *Strategy and Style in Local Community Relations Councils*, Runnymede Trust, London

Bartholomew, D.J. *et al.* 1961: *Backbench Opinion in the House of Commons 1955-59*, Pergamon, London

Beetham, D. 1970: *Transport and Turbans: A Comparative Study of Local Politics*, Oxford University Press for the Institute of Race Relations, London

Behrens, R. and Edmonds, J. 1981: 'Kippers, Kittens and Kipper Boxes: Conservative Populists and Race Relations', *Political Quarterly*, 52, 342-47

Ben-Tovim, G. and Gabriel, J. 1982: 'The Politics of Race in Britain, 1962-79: A Review of the Major Trends and of Recent Debates', in Husband C. ed., *Race in Britain: Continuity and Change*, Hutchinson, London

Ben-Tovim, G. *et al.* 1986: *The Local Politics of Race*, Macmillan, London

Benyon, J. ed. 1984: *Scarman and After: Essays Reflecting on Lord Scarman's Report, the Riots and their Aftermath*, Pergamon, London

Bhachu, P. 1985: *Twice Migrants: East African Sikh Settlers in Britain*, Tavistock, London

Bonham-Carter, M. 1987: 'The Liberal Hour and Race Relations Law', *New Community*, 14, 1-8

Bulpitt, J. 1983: *Territory and Power in the United Kingdom*, Manchester University Press, Manchester

Bulpitt, J. 1985 'The Autonomy of the Centre's Race Statescraft in England', *Environment and Planning C*, 3, 129-47

Bulpitt, J. 1986: 'Continuity, autonomy and peripheralisation: the anatomy of the centre's race statecraft in England', in Layton-Henry, Z. and Rich, P. eds, *Race, Government and Politics in Britain*, Macmillan, London

Butterworth, E. 1972: 'Dilemmas of Community Relations, Part 1', *New Community*, 1, 205-8

Cable, V. 1969: *Whither Kenyan Emigrants?*, Young Fabian Pamphlet 18, Fabian Society, London

Calvocoressi, P. 1968: 'The Official Structure of Conciliation', *Political Quarterly*, 39, 46-53

Clarke, S. and Ginsburg, N. 1977: 'The Political Economy of Housing', in *Political Economy of Housing Workshop*, Conference of Socialist Economists, London

Cockburn, C. 1977: *The Local State*, Pluto Press, London

Connelly, N. 1985: *Social Services Departments and Race: A Discussion Paper*, Policy Studies Institute, London

CRC 1975: *Participation of Ethnic Minorities in the General Election of October 1974*, Community Relations Commission, London

CRE 1980: *Votes and Policies: Ethnic Minorities and the General Election 1979*, Commission for Racial Equality, London

CRE 1983: *Local Authorities and Section 71 of the Race Relations Act 1976*, Commission for Racial Equality, London

CRE 1984: *Ethnic Minorities and the 1983 General Election: A Research Report*, Commission for Racial Equality, London

CRE 1989: *A New Partnership for Racial Equality*, Commission for Racial Equality, London

Crewe, I. 1979: 'The Black, Brown and Green Votes', *New Society*, 12 April 1979

Crewe, I. 1983: 'Representation and Ethnic Minorities in Britain', in Glazer, N. and Young, K. eds, *Ethnic Pluralism and Public Policy: Achieving Equality in the United States and Britain*, Heinemann, London

Crosland, C.A.R. 1956: *The Future of Socialism*, Cape, London

Daniel, W.W. 1968: *Racial Discrimination in England*, Penguin, Harmondsworth

Deakin, N. 1965: *Colour and the British Electorate*, Pall Mall, London

Deakin, N. 1970: *Colour, Citizenship and British Society*, updated and abridged version of Rose 1969, Panther, London

Deakin, N. and Lester, A. eds 1967: *Policies for Racial Equality*, Fabian Research Series 262, Fabian Society, London

Dearlove, J. 1973: *The Politics of Policy in Local Government*, Cambridge University Press, London

Dummet, A. and Dummet, M. 1982: 'The Role of Government in Britain's Racial Crisis', in Husband, C. ed., *Race in Britain: Continuity and Change*, Hutchinson, London

Dunleavy, P. 1980: *Urban Political Analysis: The Politics of Collective Consumption*, Macmillan, London

Edwards, J. and Batley, R. 1978: *The Politics of Positive Discrimination: An Evaluation of the Urban Programme, 1967-77*, Tavistock, London

EHAS 1980: *Southall Ignored: A Report on Housing Conditions in Southall*, Ealing Housing Aid Service, London

Ennals, M. 1968: *U.K. Citizens of Asian Origin in Kenya: An Independent Survey*, Committee on U.K. Citizenship, London

FitzGerald, M. 1983: 'Are Blacks an Electoral Liability?', *New Society*, 8 December 1983

FitzGerald, M. 1984: *Political Parties and Black People: Representation, Participation and Exploitation*, Runnymede Trust, London

FitzGerald, M. 1986a: *Section 71 of the Race Relations Act: A Case Study*, Commission for Racial Equality and Ealing Community Relations Council, London

Flett, H. 1981: *The Politics of Dispersal in Birmingham*, SSRC Research Unit on Ethnic Relations, Birmingham

Foot, P. 1965: *Race and Immigration in British Politics*, Penguin, London

Gaventa, J. 1980: *Power and Powerlessness*, Clarendon Press, Oxford

Gay, P. and Young, K. 1988: *Community Relations Councils*, Commission for Racial Equality, London

Gilroy, P. 1987: *There Ain't No Black in the Union Jack: The Cultural Politics of Race and Nation*, Hutchinson, London

Glazer, N. and Young, K. eds 1983: *Ethnic Pluralism and Public Policy: Achieving Equality in the United States and Britain*, Heinemann, London

GLC 1985: *London's Ethnic Minorities: Census Statistics from the 1981 Census*, Statistical Series Report No.44, Greater London Council Intelligence Unit, London

Gordon-Walker, P. 1962: *The Commonwealth*, Secker and Warburg, London

Heclo, H. 1978: 'Issue Networks and the Executive Establishment', in King, A. ed., *The New American Political System*, American Enterprise Institute, Washington D.C.

Heinemann, B. 1972: *The Politics of the Powerless: A Study of the Campaign Against Racial Discrimination*, Oxford University Press for the Institute of Race Relations, London

Hill, M. and Issacharoff, R. 1971: *Community Action and Race Relations: A Study of Community Relations Councils in Britain*, Oxford University Press for the Institute of Race Relations, London

Hindell, K. 1965: 'The Genesis of the Race Relations Bill', *Political Quarterly*, 36, 390-406

Hiro, D. 1971: *Black British, White British*, Eyre and Spottiswoode, London

Horowitz, D. 1970: 'The British Conservatives and the Racial Issue in the Debate on Decolonisation', *Race*, 12, 169-88

Husbands, C. 1983: *Racial Exclusionism and the City: The Urban Support of the National Front*, Allen and Unwin, London

Jacobs, B. 1982: 'Black Minority Participation in the USA and Britain', *Journal of Public Policy*, 2, 237-62

Jacobs, B. 1986: *Black Politics and Urban Crisis*, Cambridge University Press, London

Jenkins, R. 1959: *The Labour Case*, Penguin, Harmondsworth

Jenkins, R. 1966: Transcript of speech to the National Committee for Commonwealth Immigrants, 23 May 1966, National Committee for Commonwealth Immigrants, London

Jenkins, R. 1967: *Racial Equality in Employment*, National Committee for Commonwealth Immigrants, London

Jenkins, R. and Solomos, J. eds 1987: *Racism and Equal Opportunity Policies in the 1980s*, Cambridge University Press, Cambridge

Jenkins, S. 1971: *Here to Live: A Study of Race Relations in an English Town*, Runnymede Trust, London

John, D. 1969: *Indian Workers Associations in Great Britain*, Oxford University Press for the Institute of Race Relations, London

Jordan, A. and Richardson, J. 1987: *Government and Pressure Groups in Britain*, Clarendon Press, Oxford

Katznelson, I. 1970: 'The Politics of Racial Buffering in Nottingham, 1954-68', *Race*, 11, 431-41

Katznelson, I. 1973: *Black Men, White Cities: Race Relations and Migration in the United States 1900-30 and Britain 1948-68*, Oxford University Press for the Institute of Race Relations, London

Kaufman, G. 1965: 'Dutch Auction on Immigrants', *New Statesman*, 35, July 1965

Kirp, D. 1979: *Doing Good by Doing Little*, University of California Press, London

Kogan, M. 1975: *Dispersal in the Ealing Education Schools System*, Race Relations Board, London

Kramer, D. 1969: 'White Versus Coloured in Britain: An Explosive Confrontation?', *Social Research*, 36

Labour Party, 1958: *Racial Discrimination: Statement by the Labour Party*, The Labour Party, London

Labour Party, 1962: *Report of Annual Conference 1962*, The Labour Party, London

Lansley, S. *et al.* 1989: *Councils in Conflict: The Rise and Fall of the Municipal Left*, Macmillan, London

Layton-Henry, Z. 1978: 'Race, Electoral Strategy and the Major Parties', *Parliamentary Affairs*, 31, 268-81

Layton-Henry, Z. ed. 1980: *Conservative Party Politics*, Macmillan, London

Layton-Henry, Z. 1984: *The Politics of Race in Britain*, Allen and Unwin, London

Layton-Henry, Z. 1988: 'Black Electoral Participation: An Analysis of Recent Trends', unpublished paper presented to the annual conference of the Political Studies Association of the United Kingdom, Plymouth Polytechnic, April 1988

Layton-Henry, Z. and Rich, P. eds 1986: *Race, Government and Politics in Britain*, Macmillan, London

Layton-Henry, Z. and Studlar, D. 1984: 'The Political Participation of Black and Asian Britons', unpublished paper presented to the Council of European Studies, Washington DC, USA, October 1984

Lawrence, D. 1974: *Black Migrants, White Natives: A Study of Race Relations in Nottingham*, Cambridge University Press, Cambridge

LBE 1988: *Ealing's Dilemma: Implementing Race Equality in Education*, report of the independent inquiry into the recruitment and promotion of ethnic minority teachers in the London Borough of Ealing, London Borough of Ealing, London

Le Lohé, M. 1983: 'Voter Discrimination against Asian and Black Candidates in the 1983 General Election', *New Community*, 11, 101-8

Little, A. and Robbins, D. 1983: *Loading the Law: A Study of Transmitted Deprivation, Ethnic Minorities and Affirmative Action*, Commission for Racial Equality, London

Marris, P. 1968: 'The British Asians in Kenya', *Venture*, 20, 15-17

McAllister, I. and Studlar, D. 1984: 'The Electoral Geography of Immigrant Groups in Britain', *Electoral Studies*, 3, 139-50

McKay, D. and Cox, A. 1979: *The Politics of Urban Change*, Croom Helm, London

Messina, A. 1984: 'The Impact of Race on British Politics: Policy Consensus and Party Decline in the Post-War Period', unpublished Ph.D. dissertation, Massachusetts Institute of Technology, USA

Messina, A. 1985a: 'Race and Party Competition in Britain', *Parliamentary Affairs*, 38, 423-36

Messina, A. 1985b: 'Race and Local Politics in Britain: A Study of Ealing Borough', unpublished paper presented to the Carolinas Symposium on British Studies, East Tennessee State University, USA, October 1985

Messina, A. 1987: 'Mediating Race Relations: British Community Relations Councils Revisited', *Ethnic and Racial Studies*, 10, 186-202

Messina, A. 1989: *Race and Party Competition in Britain*, Clarendon Press, Oxford

Miles, R. 1982: *Racism and Migrant Labour*, Routledge and Kegan Paul, London

Miles, R. and Phizacklea, A. 1984: *White Man's Country: Racism in British Politics*, Pluto Press, London

Morrison, L. 1976: *As They See It: A Race Relations Study of Three Areas from a Black Viewpoint*, Community Relations Commission, London

Mukherjee, T. 1982: 'Sri Guru Singh Sabha: Southall', in Ohri, A. ed., *Community Work and Racism*, Routledge and Kegan Paul for the Association of Community Workers, London

Myrdal, G. 1944: *An American Dilemma: The Negro Problem and Modern Democracy*, Harper, New York

Nairn, T. 1974: 'English Nationalism: The Case of Enoch Powell', in Nairn, T. ed., *The Break-up of Modern Britain*, New Left Books, London

Nandy, D. 1967a: 'An Illusion of Competence', in Deakin, N. and Lester, A. eds, *Policies for Racial Equality*, Fabian Research Series 262, Fabian Society, London

Nandy, D. 1967b: 'The NCCI: An Assessment', unpublished paper presented by Dipak Nandy to the Executive Committee of the Campaign Against Racial Discrimination, June 1967

NCCI 1967: *Report for 1966*, National Committee for Commonwealth Immigrants, London

NCCI 1968: *Report for 1967*, National Committee for Commonwealth Immigrants, London

NCCL 1980: *23rd April 1979*, National Council for Civil Liberties, London

Newton, K. 1976: *Second City Politics: Democratic Processes and Decision-Making in Birmingham*, Oxford University Press, Oxford

Olsen, J. 1976: 'Organisation Participation in Government', unpublished paper, University of Bergen, Norway

OPCS 1973: *General Census 1971*, Office for Population Censuses and Surveys, London

OPCS 1984a: *Census 1981: Key Statistics for Local Authorities - Great Britain*, London, HMSO, 1984

OPCS 1984b: 'Births by Birthplace of Mothers, 1983: Local Authority Areas', *OPCS Monitor*, Ref. FM1 84/10, Office of Population Censuses and Surveys, London

OPCS 1986, 'Mid-1985 population estimates for local government and health authority areas of England and Wales', *OPCS Monitor*, Ref. PP1 86/2, Office of Population Censuses and Surveys, London

OPCS 1987: 'Births by Birthplace of Mother, 1986: Local Authority Areas', *OPCS Monitor*, Ref. FM1 87/3, Office for Population Censuses and Surveys, London

Ouseley, H. 1981: *The System*, Runnymede Trust, London

Ouseley, H. 1984: 'Local authority Race Initiatives', in Boddy, M. and Fudge, C. eds, *Local Socialism*, Macmillan, London

Parekh, B. 1990: 'The Politicisation of Race Relations', review of Messina 1989, *Government and Opposition*, 25, 256-60

PEP 1967: *Racial Discrimination*, Political and Economic Planning, London

Powell, J.E. 1969: *Freedom and Reality*, Elliot Right Way Books, Kingswood

Prashar, U. and Nicloas, S. 1986: *Routes or Roadblocks?: Consulting Minority Communities in London*, Runnymede Trust, London

Prashar, U. 1985: review of Glazer and Young 1983, *Public Administration*, 63, 122

Profitt, R. 1986: 'The Role of the Race Adviser', in Coombe, V. and Little, A. eds, *Race and Social Work: A Guide to Training*, Tavistock, London

Pullé, S. 1973: *Police-Immigrant Relations in Ealing*, Runnymede Trust and Ealing Community Relations Council, London

Ratcliffe, P. 1981: *Racism and Reaction: A Profile of Handsworth*, Routledge and Kegan Paul, London

Rath, J. and Saggar, S. 1990, 'Ethnicity as a Political Tool in Britain and the Netherlands', in Messina, A. *et al.* eds, *Ethnic and Racial Minorities in Advanced Industrial Societies*, Greenwood Press, New York

Rex, J. and Moore, R. 1967: *Race, Community and Conflict: A Study of Sparkbrook*, Oxford University Press for the Institute of Race Relations, London

Rex, J. and Tomlinson, S. 1979: *Colonial Immigrants in a British City: A Class Analysis*, Routledge and Kegan Paul, London

Rhodes, R.A.W. 1981: *Control and Power in Central-Local Government Relations*, Gower, Farnborough

Rhodes, R.A.W. 1985: 'Policy Networks', unpublished paper presented to the Ph.D. Colloquium, Department of Government, University of Essex, March 1985

Rhodes, R.A.W. 1986: *The National World of Local Government*, Allen and Unwin, London

Rhodes, R.A.W. 1988: *Beyond Westminster and Whitehall*, Unwin Hyman, London

Richardson, J. and Jordan, A. 1979: *Governing Under Pressure*, Martin Robertson, London

Richmond, A. 1973: *Migration and Race Relations in an English City: A Study in Bristol*, Oxford University Press for the Institute of Race Relations, London

RIPA 1983: *Racial Equality in Public Sector Employment*, Royal Institute of Public Administration Report 4.3, Royal Institute of Public Administration, London

Rose, E. *et al.* 1969: *Colour and Citizenship: A Report on British Race Relations*, Oxford University Press for the Institute of Race Relations, London

Rose, E. 1987: 'A Myrdal for Britain: A Personal Memoir', *New Community*, 14, 83-88

Runnymede Trust/NCVO 1980: *Inner Cities and Black Minorities*, Runnymede Trust and National Council for Voluntary Organisations, London

Saggar, S. 1984: 'Britain's Ethnic Minorities and the 1983 General Election: An Analysis', unpublished dissertation, Department of Government, University of Essex

Saggar, S. 1987a: 'The 1984 Labour Force Survey and Britain's "Asian" Population', *New Community*, 13, 395-411

Saggar, S. 1987b: 'The Rediscovery of Race in London: Developments in Local Government in the 1980s', unpublished paper presented to the annual conference of the Political Studies Association of the United Kingdom, University of Aberdeen, April 1987

Saggar, S. 1990a: 'Discovering and Rediscovering Race', *Parliamentary Affairs*, 43, 392-94

Saggar, S. 1990b: 'The Multi-racial City: London', in Parsons, D.W. and Cope, D. eds, *World Cities: London*, National Institute for Research Advancement, Tokyo

Saggar, S. 1991a: 'The Changing Agenda of Race Issues in Local Government: The Case of a London Borough', *Political Studies*, forthcoming

Saggar, S. 1991b: *Race and Politics in Britain*, Philip Allan, Hemel Hempstead, forthcoming

Saggar, S. 1991c: 'Race and Politics', in Hawkesworth, M. and Kogan, M. eds, *Routledge Encyclopaedia of Government and Politics*, Routledge, London, forthcoming

Saunders, P. 1975: 'They Make the Rules: Political Routines and the Generation of Political Bias', *Policy and Politics*, 4, 31-58

Saunders, P. 1979: *Urban Politics: A Sociological Analysis*, Hutchinson, London

Sivanandan, A. 1976: 'Race, Class and the State: The Black Experience in Britain', *Race*, 1, 347-68

Sivanandan, A. 1982: *A Different Hunger: Writings on Black Resistance*, Pluto Press, London

Solomos, J. 1989a: 'Equal Opportunities Policies and Racial Inequality: The Role of Public Policy', *Public Administration*, 76, 79-93

Solomos, J. 1989b: *Race and Racism in Contemporary Britain*, Macmillan, London

Southall Rights/CARF 1981: *Southall: Birth of a Black Community*, Southall Rights and Campaign Against Racism and Fascism, London

Steel, D. 1969: *No Entry*, Hurst, London

Stewart, M. and Whiting, G. 1982: *Ethnic Minorities and the Urban Programme*, University of Bristol School for Advanced Urban Studies, Bristol

Street, H. *et al.* 1967: *Anti-Discrimination Legislation: The Street Report*, Political and Economic Planning, London

Studlar, D. 1986: 'Non-White Policy Preferences, Political Participation and the Political Agenda in Britain', in Layton-Henry, Z. and Rich, P. eds, *Race, Government and Politics in Britain*, Macmillan, London

Wallman, S. *et al.* 1982: *Living in South London*, Gower, Aldershot

Wilson, H. 1968: Transcript of speech by Prime Minister, Birmingham, 5 May 1968, The Labour Party, London

Young, K. 1982: 'An Agenda for Sir George: Local Authorities and the Promotion of Racial Equality', *Policy Studies*, 3, 54-70

Young, K. 1983: 'Ethnic Pluralism and the Policy Agenda in Britain', in Young, K. and Glazer, N. eds, *Ethnic Pluralism and Public Policy: Achieving Equality in the United States and Britain*, Heinemann, London

Young, K. 1984: 'The Challenge to Local Government', in Benyon, J. ed., *Scarman and After: Essays Reflecting on Lord Scarman's Report, the Riots and their Aftermath*, Pergamon, London

Young, K. 1985a: *After the Act: Policy Review for Local Authorities in Multi-Racial Areas*, Policy Studies Institute, London

Young, K. 1985b: 'Racial Disadvantage', in Jones, G. *et al.* eds, *Between Centre and Locality*, Gower, London

Young, K. and Connelly, N. 1981: *Policy and Practice in the Multi-Racial City*, Policy Studies Institute, London

Zubaida, S. ed. 1970: *Race and Racialism*, Tavistock, London

Parliamentary debates and papers

H.C. Deb. 685: *Commons Debates*, 27 November 1963, vol. 685, cols. 438-44

H.C. Deb. 702: *Commons Debates*, 27 November 1964, vol. 702, col. 1254

H.C. Deb. 708: *Commons Debates*, 9 March 1965, vol. 708, cols. 248-50

H.C. Deb. 709: *Commons Debates*, 23 March 1965, vol. 709, cols. 378-79 and 443

H.C. Deb. 729: *Commons Debates*, 14 April 1966, vol. 729, cols. 1333-37

H.C. Deb. 735: *Commons Debates*, 8 November 1966, vol. 735, col. 1252

H.C. Deb. 754: *Commons Debates*, 15 November 1967, vol. 754, cols. 453-73

H.C. Deb. 763: *Commons Debates*, 23 April 1968, vol. 763, cols. 67-81

H.C. 405-I: *Education*, Report of the House of Commons Select Committee on Race Relations and Immigration, session 1972-73, vol. I - Report

H.C. 405-III: *Education*, Report of the House of Commons Select Committee on Race Relations and Immigration, session 1972-73, vol. III - Evidence and Appendices, cols. 620-718 and 1243-57

H.C. 413-I: *The Problems of Coloured School-Leavers*, Report of the House of Commons Select Committee on Race Relations and Immigration, session 1968-69, vol. I - Report

H.C. 413-II: *The Problems of Coloured School-Leavers*, Report of the House of Commons Select Committee on Race Relations and Immigration, session 1968-69, vol. II - Evidence

H.C. 448-III: *The Organisation of Race Relations Administration*, Report of the House of Commons Select Committee on Race Relations and Immigration, session 1974-75, vol. III - Appendix, cols. 234-42

H.C. Standing Committee B: *Parliamentary Debates*, 24 June 1965, Session 1964-65, vol. 1, cols. 318-44

Government publications

Cmnd. 2119: *First Report by the Commonwealth Immigrants Advisory Council*, July 1963, HMSO, London

Cmnd. 2266: *Second Report by the Commonwealth Immigrants Advisory Council*, February 1964, HMSO, London

Cmnd. 2458: *Third Report by the Commonwealth Immigrants Advisory Council*, September 1964, HMSO, London

Cmnd. 2739: *Immigration from the Commonwealth*, White Paper, Prime Minister's Office, August 1965, HMSO, London

DES 1965: *The Education of Immigrant Children*, Department of Education and Science Circular 7/65, July 1965, HMSO, London

Home Office 1982: *Section 11: Revised Guidelines*, Home Office Circular 97/82, February 1982, HMSO, London

Home Office 1983: *Section 11 of the Local Government Act 1966: Review of Posts*, Home Office Circular 94/83, March 1983, HMSO, London

RRB 1967: *Report of the Race Relations Board 1966-67*, HMSO, London

Newspapers and periodicals

Gazette Series: *Middlesex County Times and West Middlesex Gazette*, Southall edition, 1957-77, and *Southall Gazette*, various editions, 1977-86

Times Series: *Hendon and Finchley Times* and *Barnet Borough Times*, Finchley editions, 1964-86

Ealing News: 'The "People's" View?', signed article by Sir George Young, Conservative MP for Ealing Acton, January-February 1980

Focus: 2 April 1968

New Statesman: 21 April 1967

New Society: 21 April 1967

The Daily Telegraph: 25 July 1967

The Economist: 21 April 1967

The Financial Times: 'Integrating Immigrants: The Problems that Southall Faces', unsigned article, 8 March 1968

The Guardian: 13 January 1967; 4 December 1967

The Observer: 23 April 1967

Shakti: 'Ealing's Questionable Employment Policies', signed article by Christine Aziz, December 1983

The Spectator: 21 April 1967

The Sunday Times: 8 January 1967; 23 January 1967

The Times: 18 April 1967; 'In a Strange Land', signed article by Philip Mason, Director of the Institute of Race Relations, 26 January 1968

Radio and television broadcasts

ITV 1965: 'Dateline', Independent Television, first broadcast 8 November 1965

LWT 1980: 'Skin', London Weekend Television, first broadcast 9 November 1980

Primary documents

Ealing Borough

ECRC 1972: Minutes of ECRC Emergency General Meeting, 22 August 1972

ECRC 1979: Minutes of ECRC Annual General Meeting, 26 June 1979

ECRC 1982: Minutes of meeting between ECRC and LBE, agenda item 1: Police Liaison Committee, 16 March 1982

ECRC 1983a: 'Section 11 Funding', ECRC Briefing Paper, issued 4 February 1983

ECRC 1983b: 'Response to the London Borough of Ealing's Consultative Document Regarding Section 11 Finance', LBE document dated July 1983, November 1983

EFRA 1965: 'The Effects of Immigration on Residential Areas', report and questionnaire prepared by Ealing Federation of Ratepayers' Associations for a special meeting with representatives of political parties serving on LBE Council, 29 September 1965

EFRA 1968: 'A Report on Immigration, 1967-68', February 1968

EIFC 1966: 'List of Participating and Affiliated Organisations', July 1966

EIFC 1967: 'Annual Report, 1966-67', June 1967

EIFC 1968a: Minutes of EIFC General Council Meeting, 28 January 1968

EIFC 1968b: 'The Education of the Immigrant Child', report prepared by EIFC, September 1968

EIFC 1969: Community Relations Officer's Annual Report, delivered to EIFC Annual General Meeting, 12 June 1969

LBE 1965a: Minutes of Education Committee, June 1965

LBE 1965b: Minutes of Staff Conference, agenda item 'Immigrants', LBE Health Department, 9 July 1965

LBE 1965c: 'Effects of Immigration on Residential Areas', reply by LBE Public Relations Office of Town Clerk's Department to questionnaire prepared by Ealing Federation of Ratepayers' Associations, 29 September 1965

LBE 1965d: Minutes of the Immigration Section meeting, 13 October 1965

LBE 1965e: Letter from LBE Town Clerk to Chairman and Members of Immigrants Committee, 1965 - exact date not given

LBE 1967: 'A Report on the Health and Circumstances of Asian Immigrants in the London Borough of Ealing', report of the LBE Medical Officer of Health, November 1967

LBE 1968a: Minutes of the Education Committee meeting, March 1968

LBE 1968b: 'Report for 1966', report of Immigrant Education sub-committee, March 1968

LBE 1968c: Draft brief for deputation to meet David Ennals, Parliamentary Under-Secretary of State at the Home Office, 10 May 1968

LBE 1970a: Minutes of Council meeting, 20 January 1970

LBE 1970b: Minutes of General Purposes Committee meeting, 16 February 1972

LBE 1970c: Minutes of Council meeting, 5 March 1970

LBE 1971a: Minutes of General Purposes and Establishment Committee meeting, 4 January 1971

LBE 1971b: Minutes of Council meeting, 19 January 1971

LBE 1971c: 'Lord Windlesham Makes Race Relations Fact Finding Visit to Ealing', LBE Press Release, 9 March 1971

LBE 1971d: Report of survey by LBE Education Department on dispersal numbers, May 1971

LBE 1971e: 'Projected Growth in Immigrant Schoolchildren in Ealing Schools', report by LBE Chief Education Officer, October 1971

LBE 1972a: 'Ealing Council Warns Minister Over New Immigrants', LBE Press Release, 14 August 1972

LBE 1972b: Notes for Leader of the Council for the visit to Ealing by the Secretary of State for Social Services, 2 October 1972

LBE 1972c: Letter from LBE Town Clerk to the Secretary of State for Social Services, 24 October 1972

LBE 1973a: Memorandum from the LBE Director of Social Services to a Conservative councillor, 26 April 1973

LBE 1973b: 'Race Relations: Questions for Discussion', notes prepared for visit to Ealing by the Central Policy Review Staff, 13 June 1973

LBE 1979a: Minutes of Education Committee meeting, April 1979

LBE 1979b: Minutes of Council meeting, 14 May 1979

LBE 1980a: Minutes of Policy and Resources Committee meeting, 8 January 1980

LBE 1980b: Minutes of meeting between representatives of LBE Council and ECRC, agenda items 1 and 2, 30 January 1980

LBE 1980c: 'CRE Questionnaire', memorandum from LBE Town Clerk to LBE Director of Social Services, 10 September 1980

LBE 1983: 'Code of Practice for Race Relations', draft copy of report by LBE Town Clerk to the Establishment Board, 1 December 1983

MCC 1963: Minutes of Middlesex County Council Education Committee meeting, February 1963

MCC 1965: Middlesex Schools Medical Officer's Report for 1963, January 1965

SBC 1963: Minutes of Council meeting, July 1963

SDEE 1957a: Minutes of SDEE meeting, January 1957

SDEE 1957b: Minutes of SDEE meeting, March 1957

SDEE 1963: Minutes of SDEE meeting, July 1963

SDEE 1964a: Minutes of SDEE meeting, January 1964

SDEE 1964b: Minutes of SDEE meeting, April 1964

SDEE 1964c: Minutes of SDEE meeting, July 1964

SDEE 1965: 'The Education of Immigrant Children', report of SDEE Immigrant Education sub-committee, March 1965

Barnet Borough

BCRC 1982a: Letter from BCRC senior officer to LBB Chief Executive applying for LBB grant-aid, December 1982

BCRC 1982b: Letter from BCRC senior officer requesting BCRC representation on LBB Council committees, 1982 - exact date not given

GGCRC 1972: 'Ugandan Asians', press statement issued by Golders Green Community Relations Council, October 1972

HCS 1980: Letter from Honorary Secretary and Trustee of Hindu Cultural Society to LBB Chief Executive applying for Urban Aid funding, 25 July 1980

IANL 1984: Letter from Honorary Secretary of Islamic Association of North London to LBB Chief Executive applying for land or buildings suitable for community centre, 22 March 1984

LBB 1972a: Minutes of General Purposes Committee meeting, 6 September 1972

LBB 1972b: Agenda of Council meeting, 4 September 1972

LBB 1972c: Minutes of Council meeting, 6 October 1972

LBB 1972d: Minutes of Council meeting, 8 November 1972

LBB 1978: Agenda of Council meeting, agenda item 2.1, 19 December 1978

LBB 1980a: Minutes of General Purposes Committee meeting, 24 November 1980

LBB 1980b: Agenda of Council meeting, agenda item 2.5, 16 December 1980

LBB 1982a: Agenda of Council meeting, agenda item 1, 20 April 1982

LBB 1982b: Minutes of Annual General Meeting of LBB Council, report of General Purposes Committee, agenda item 2, 8 May 1982

LBB 1982c: Agenda of General Purposes Committee meeting, agenda items 16 and 17, 11 October 1982

LBB 1983a: Minutes of General Purposes Committee meeting, agenda item 7, 10 January 1983

LBB 1983b: Agenda of General Purposes Committee meeting, agenda item 3, 17 October 1983

LBB 1984a: Agenda of Building Resources Committee meeting, agenda item 3.2, 12 April 1984

LBB 1984b: Agenda of Building Resources Committee meeting, agenda item 3.3, 12 April 1984

LBB 1984c: Agenda of General Purposes Committee meeting, agenda item 9, 14 May 1984

LBB 1984d: Agenda of Development and Estates Committee meeting, agenda item 5.2, 3 September 1984

LBB 1984e: Agenda of Development and Estates Committee meeting, agenda item 3.6, 8 October 1984

LBB 1984f: Agenda of Development and Estates Committee meeting, agenda item 3.3, 12 November 1984

LBB 1985a: Minutes of Development and Estates Committee meeting, agenda item 3.11, 7 January 1985

LBB 1985b: Minutes of Council meeting, 21 February 1985

LBB 1985c: Agenda of General Purposes Committee meeting, agenda item 4d, 20 May 1985

LBB 1986a: Agenda of General Purposes Committee meeting, agenda item 4e, 13 January 1986

LBB 1986b: Agenda of Development and Estates Committee meeting, agenda item 5.2, 17 March 1986

Interviews

Only interviews cited in the text are listed below (24 cited out of a total of 43 interviews). For further details see Table B.1, p.176 above.

Serving and former councillors

Conservative Councillor, LBB, 1986a

Conservative Councillor, LBB, 1986b

Former Conservative Councillor, LBB, 1985

Former Conservative Councillor, LBB, 1986a

Former Conservative Councillor, LBB, 1986b

Labour Councillor, LBB, 1986a

Labour Councillor, LBB, 1986b

Conservative Councillor, LBE, 1986a

Conservative Councillor, LBE, 1986b

Conservative Councillor, LBE, 1986c

Labour Councillor, LBE, 1986a

Labour Councillor, LBE, 1986b

Labour Councillor, LBE, 1986c

CRC, EMG and other activists

Asian Youth Group Leader, 1986

BCRC Leader, 1985

BCRC Leader, 1986

BCRC Executive Member, 1985

IWA Activist 1985

IWA Leader, 1985

Former IWA President, 1985

ECRC Leader, 1986

ECRC Executive Member 1986

ECRC Officer, 1985

Southall UCA Leader, 1986

Other

FitzGerald, M. 1986b: correspondence with author, November 1986

Name index

References from Notes indicated by 'n' after page reference.

194

197

198